P9-DVF-542

ANCIENT MYSTERIES

Ancient Mysteries

Rupert Furneaux

001.93
F1

McGraw-Hill Book Company
New York   St. Louis   San Francisco   Düsseldorf
Mexico   Toronto

ACKNOWLEDGEMENTS

Plate 1 Copyright © ENA Popperfoto
Plate 2 Copyright © Donald McLeish Collection Popperfoto
Plate 3 (a) Copyright © ENA Popperfoto, (b) Copyright
© Popperfoto
Plate 4, 5 Copyright © Popperfoto
Plate 6 Copyright © the Redemptorist Fathers of New York
1963
Plate 7, 8 Copyright © Francis Sandwith ARPS Popperfoto
Plate 9, 10 Copyright © Popperfoto
Plate 11 Copyright © G. F. Allen Popperfoto
Plate 12 Copyright © Popperfoto
Plate 13, 14, 15 Copyright © Phaiden Press

2 3 4 5 6 7 8 9   M U B P   7 9 8 7

Library of Congress Cataloging in Publication Data

Furneaux, Rupert.
Ancient mysteries.

Bibliography: p.
1. Man, Prehistoric.   2.   History, Ancient.
3.   Interplanetary voyages.   4.   Curiosities and wonders.
I.   Title.
GN741.F87   001.9′3   76-50671
ISBN 0-07-022630-X

CONTENTS

Mythical Continent

HAS FABLED ATLANTIS BEEN LOCATED?

Submerged in a single day and a night! A mighty continent sunk beneath the sea! Its population wiped out in an instant! What a stimulus to imagination, even to sheer lunacy. No wonder the famous legend of Atlantis has created a mystery which countless people have sought to solve.

The Greek philosopher, Plato, who told the story, said that Atlantis lay outside the Mediterranean, beyond the Pillars of Hercules, as the gateway to the Atlantic was called in 345 B.C., about the time he wrote. But modern geological research has shown that no great continent could have existed and become submerged in mid-Atlantic within human memory.

So was Plato romancing? Or did he, as he emphatically stated, record history, confused and only half-remembered as it may have been? He gave as the source of his information his ancestor, Solon, who had visited Egypt in 590 B.C. The priests instructed him in ancient history. After Plato's death the editor of his works, Crantor, sent inquiries to Egypt to which the priests replied that the records of the lost continent were still extant 'on pillars'. Using Solon's notes, Plato composed two dialogues.

In his shorter *Timaeus*, Plato described the island, or islands, of Atlantis as being as large as Libya (meaning North Africa, west of Egypt) and Asia Minor combined. Its king had founded a wonderful empire, extending into the western Mediterranean. Then came frightful earthquakes and inundations. Atlantis sank beneath the sea. That had happened 9,000 years before Solon's time.

Plato supplied greater detail in his *Critias*. The metropolis of the empire had been built on a small, round island, its coastline steep and precipitous. The royal palace, built on a second and much larger island, was a 'marvel to behold for size and beauty'. It was furnished with hot and cold baths. The temple, sacred to Poseidon, was resplendent with silver and gold. Every four or five years the kings gathered to administer the laws and hunt and sacrifice bulls. In course of time they became greedy and domineering, whereupon Zeus planned their destruction. Before this occurred an Athenian army which had gone out to fight the Atlanteans had been destroyed by a natural calamity. The Atlanteans had been contemplating war against Athens and Egypt.

Atlantis was a highly organized state, a land of conscious amenity, leisure, fine architecture, resplendent art, abundant public services, a Bronze Age society, literate, war-like, contemplating the conquest of Egypt and Athens. No such state existed 9,000 years before Solon's time. Either his priestly informants or Solon himself had confused the date, making the disaster occur millennia rather than centuries before 590 B.C. 900 years is a far more realistic estimate. That would date the destruction of Atlantis in about 1500 B.C. Although not yet a Greek city, Athens then existed, and Egypt was at the height of her power.

Where, then, was Atlantis? It was not far from Greece and Athens, for the Atlanteans contemplated their conquest and an Athenian army set out to foil their designs.

Atlantis has been located in many places – in Mexico, Central Asia, the Sahara, Spain, Greenland, Newfoundland and even in Britain.

Geoffrey Ashe in *Camelot and The Vision of Albion** has presented the case for Britain, the land of the 'Hyperboreans' to the Greeks of Plato's time. It contained, according to the fifth-century B.C. writer, Hecataeus of Abdera, a unique shrine, the magnificent precinct of Apollo – possibly Stonehenge – and was inhabited by the 'fairest and noblest race of men that ever lived'. Britain was an Atlantic island, one of the several from which it was possible to pass to the opposite continent encircling the ocean, as Plato had described Atlantis. His topographical details seemed to fit the northern sea route to America via Iceland, Greenland and Newfoundland. Mr Ashe does not suggest that Britain became submerged, but rather that following considerable contact with the Aegean at about

* Heinemann, 1971.

the time the building of Stonehenge was in progress, Britain became lost to view, swallowed up in the northern mists and forgotten. Plato adopted the romantic story of Britain's lost glory to portray his ideal state. However Ashe admits that the Cretan theories are more prevalent.

And possibly more persuasive. Can Minoan Crete be recognized as the seat of the Atlantean empire, the volcano Thera the cause of its decline? That possibility was first suggested in 1907 by the British scholar, K. T. Frost. Sir Arthur Evans's excavations at Knossos in the 1920s, and the decipherment of the Linear B script by Michael Ventris and J. Chadwick in 1960 have shown that the Minoan civilization of Crete collapsed suddenly at the height of its power and for no apparent reason in about 1500 B.C. Significantly the volcanic Thera, sixty-five miles to the north of Crete, erupted catastrophically at that time.

Professor Spyridon Marinatos, the chief of the Greek Archaeological Service, began his search to link the eruption of Thera and the end of Atlantis in 1939. Other scientists have contributed to the discussion, notably the American geologists Dr Ninkovitch and B. C. Heenen, who have dredged up cores of sediment containing volcanic ash from the sea bed of the eastern Mediterranean, and Professor A. G. Galanopoulos, director of the Seismological Institute of the University of Athens. Their contributions have been summarized by Professor J. V. Luce, a specialist in Plato and classical studies.*

The theory assumes that Crete was swamped by the tidal wave set up by Thera's catastrophic eruption, the fertility of its soil ruined by heavy deposits of ash and pumice. The story of the disaster was carried by refugees to Egypt where, 900 years later, it was repeated in garbled form to Solon. He translated the Egyptian name of Keftui for Crete as Atlantis, derived from the description of that mountainous island as the 'land of the pillar', held up in the sky by the giant Titan, Atlas. Unaware that the story related to Crete, Plato located Atlantis outside the Mediterranean in the ocean also named after Atlas, in the belief that no Mediterranean power had been strong enough to have threatened both Athens and Egypt.

* *The End of Atlantis*, Thames and Hudson, 1969

9

To prove this theory, three questions require answers. What was the intensity of Thera's eruption? What evidence is there that Crete suffered from a volcanic disaster? What parallels exist between the civilizations of Minoan Crete and Plato's Atlantis?

Before the catastrophic eruption in the fifteenth century B.C. which wrecked the island, Thera, or Santorin as it is now called, was one island, 10 miles (16 kilometres) in diameter, with a volcanic cone 5,250 feet (1,600 metres) in height. Its eruption may have been the greatest and most destructive of historic times, surpassing even Krakatoa's famous outburst in 1883. Whereas the island of Krakatoa, in the Sunda strait between Sumatra and Java, lost 8 square miles (22 square kilometres) as is shown by the size of its caldera, Thera must have lost four times as much material, for its caldera comprises 32 square miles (83 square kilometres). A caldera is the 'cauldron' formed by the collapse of the magma chamber when it has become exhausted by eruption. The collapse forms a huge cavity into which the sea pours and is ejected with explosive violence.

In Krakatoa's case, the wave set up by the explosion swept across the strait, rising to the height of 120 feet (36 metres), submerging towns and villages and drowning many of the 36,000 victims of the disaster. It roared on round the world, raising the level of the English channel by 2 inches (5 centimetres). The ejected pumice, the characteristic product of explosive magma, smothered Sumatra and Java and built floating islands in the sea. The ash formed a dust cloud which plunged the straits in darkness for three days and swept round the earth, lingering in the atmosphere for two years and causing climatic changes. Krakatoa's 'big bang' was heard 3,000 miles (4,800 kilometres) away across the Indian Ocean. Another Javanese volcano, Tambora, in 1815 deposited pumice and ash which destroyed the fertility of the land, causing the deaths of 80,000 people by starvation and disease.

Thera's collapse may have been even more prodigious, its effects far greater and more widespread.

Excavations on Thera suggest that the island suffered disaster in two stages. First it was submerged beneath enormous quantities of pumice and volcanic ash. The volcano's debris destroyed the inhabitants' houses which conformed to Minoan architecture and contained similar pots and frescoes. The removal of 65 feet (20 metres) of pumice has disclosed a Bronze Age Pompeii, a civilization similarly frozen in time, but without the bodies. No skeletons or personal treasures have been found at the lowest levels. Their absence suggests the people of Thera, warned by the volcano's activity, had time to flee. They probably sought shelter in Crete, of which Thera was an outpost or colony.

Thera reached its peak some time between 1500 and 1470 B.C., the period indicated by the pottery and the carbon dating of timber recovered from the ruined buildings. The ancient volcano, its magma exhausted, blew its top. It exploded in violent paroxysm, plunging the eastern Mediterranean in darkness, its 'big bang' being heard probably from one end of that sea to the other. It set up a seismic wave, a giant *tsunami* as such waves are now called. Rising to prodigious height, perhaps hundreds of feet, it raced across the intervening sea, striking and inundating the coast of Crete.

Archaeological investigation has shown that every harbour, and every town and palace in eastern Crete was suddenly destroyed, and never rebuilt. Only Knossos, the capital, escaped, owing to its location some 3 miles (5 kilometres) inland where it was sheltered by a range of low hills. Pumice and ash engulfed the fields, destroying their fertility.

At Amnisos, the port of Knossos on the north coast, Professor Marinatos found evidence of the tidal wave. Buildings had been reduced to their foundations, sea-borne pumice had been forced into their crevices. The walls of the so-called Villa of Frescoes had collapsed inwards, sucked in by huge masses of receding water. The other harbours and towns so far excavated yield the same evidence of sudden destruction by water and falls of ash. The limestone gorge besides the naval base of Kato Zakro has retained its ancient name of the Valley of the Dead.

Before 1500 B.C., Minoan Crete had dominated the eastern Mediterranean. So powerful was her navy that no land defences had been built. No state was capable of challenging her sea supremacy. Then, almost overnight, Crete collapsed. Shorn of her naval protection, her fertile soil rendered suddenly unproductive, she fell easy victim to the Mycenaean invaders from Greece.

The once powerful Minoans had succumbed to a natural calamity. No other conclusion seems possible.

Professor Luce has culled evidence from ancient myths and legends to show how widespread was the disaster caused by Thera. Greek poems mention the sudden depopulation of Crete. Herodotus stated that Crete had disappeared some time before the Trojan War, that is before 1400 B.C. The legend of Deucalion's flood, dated in the Parian Marble at about 1529 B.C., suggests that the mainland of Greece was also inundated, as were many Aegean islands. Plutarch records that on the island of Lycia Poseidon sent 'a wave which reared up and flooded the land'. Rhodes suffered a severe flood which caused heavy loss of life. Centuries later the Samothracians were still sacrificing on altars which had been set up in a circle round the island to mark the floodline of a great inundation from the sea. Even the famous Argonauts were caught in the aftermath of the disaster. Sailing past Crete, Jason and his crew were engulfed in awful darkness and bombarded by fragments of stone.

Egyptian texts supply no concrete information, probably because of the Egyptians' distaste for solid history. The Ipuwer Papyrus, however, indicates that trade with Crete was cut off suddenly about the time of Thera's eruption. This Egyptian silence seems strange, for Thera's eruptive violence should have been felt even at the distance of 650 miles (1,000 kilometres). Volcanic dust has been found in cores raised from the sea bed close to Egypt. Several investigators have attributed the ten plagues of Egypt, the Israelites' crossing of the Sea of Passage, and the pillar of fire by night and the pillar of cloud by day to Thera's eruption. But a date around 1470 B.C. seems far too early for the Exodus.

The vital question remains to be answered. Was Atlantis Crete? The parallels are remarkable. Both island civilizations disappeared suddenly as the result of a natural calamity.

Atlantis, according to Plato, was ruled by a monarchical

and class system. Its women held high status, its people were literate, leisured, skilled in engineering, enjoying the comforts of hot and cold baths, regularly hunting bulls which ranged over a temple precinct. The islands were protected by precipitous cliffs, one island small and round, the other large and rectangular in shape.

Before Thera erupted, its island was small and round, possibly the legendary metropolis. Crete is long and thin, mountainous, with a large central plain in which was set Knossos, the royal palace. King Minos ruled over a hundred towns. Every five years, as in Atlantis, their governors assembled to administer the laws and hunt the bulls which roamed the temple precinct. Legend tells that the Athenian Theseus came to Knossos to free his people from the tribute levied by Crete. He was forced to fight the legendary Minotaur, half man, half bull, and frescoes depict him dragging the slain bull from the labyrinth.

Sir Arthur Evans's excavations at Knossos disclosed a sophisticated culture, the most highly developed civilization of the ancient world, splendid in architecture, rich in artistry, elegant, leisured, yet centrally organized under a monarchy, with a code of laws giving equal status to women and dividing the classes. Springs provided hot water for baths, cold water for lavatories set in the palace walls. An extensive irrigation system ensured the soil's fertility. The Minoans' pottery, jars, weapons and frescoes are exhibited in the Herakleion museum.

Of the parallels between Crete and Atlantis, K. T. Frost had this to say in 1913, long before the two civilizations were compared. 'The whole description of Atlantis which is given in the *Timaeus* and *Critias* has features so thoroughly Minoan that even Plato could not have invented so many unsuspected facts.' Plato's account of the island which ruled over a great and wonderful empire precisely described the 'political status of Knossos'.

The great harbour, for example, with its shipping and its merchants coming from all parts; the elaborate bath rooms, the stadium and the solemn sacrifice of the bull are all thoroughly, though not exclusively, Minoan: but when we read how the bull is hunted 'in the temple of Poseidon without weapons but

13

with staves and nooses', we have an unmistakable description of the bull ring at Knossos, the very thing which struck foreigners most, and which gave rise to the legend of the Minotaur. Plato's words exactly describe the scenes on the famous Vapheio cups which certainly represent catching wild bulls for the Minoan bull fight, which, as we know from the palace itself, differed from all others which the world has seen in exactly the point which Plato emphasises – namely that no weapons were used.*

Young Frost did not live to see his theory vindicated. He was killed in World War I.

Plato, it seems, has also been vindicated. He had no idea that he was accurately describing the civilization of Minoan Crete, for his day, Crete had become a backwater, its glories forgotten. But they might never have been fully appreciated had not Plato written history.

* K. T. Frost, 'The *Critias* and Minoan Crete', *Journal of Hellenic Studies* 33, 1913, pp. 189–206.

Megalithic Mysteries

THE GREAT PYRAMID. ITS PURPOSE?

Should you visit Egypt, and proceed 8 miles (13 kilometres) south-west of Cairo to Giza to inspect the world's most famous stone structure, you are likely to be told, as I was, that the Great Pyramid was built as a fortress-tomb to protect the body of Pharaoh Khufu. The Greeks called him Cheops. 100,000 men, according to Herodotus, laboured for twenty years to ensure Khufu's physical resurrection, his certainty of life after death. The ancient tomb-robbers rifled his tomb and despoiled his mummy, as they desecrated those of the other pharoahs, save Tutankhamen.

These are fundamental truths of Egyptology, its accepted credo. They are as valid as the dogmas of religion or belief in extra-terrestrial life. There is no proof that the pyramid was designed as a tomb, rather evidence to the contrary.

No Egyptian texts describe the pyramid's building or refer to it. Herodotus is our earliest source of information. On his visit to Egypt in 440 B.C. he was told that the pyramids north face was reputed to contain a secret hinged door and its interior an underground chamber. A later visitor, the Roman geographer Strabo, who travelled up the Nile in 24 B.C., says that the entrance gave on to a narrow passage, leading to a damp, vermin-infested pit. Apparently the door was found and the pit inspected in Roman times for its walls were later noticed to be marked with torch burns. The site of the secret door became lost.

The pyramid was first entered in A.D. 820. The young Caliph Abdullah Al Mamun, an enthusiast for the mathematical and navigational sciences, believed that it contained a secret chamber within which had been stored astronomical maps and tables and other vast treasures. Collecting a band of engineers, architects and masons and a gang of workmen, he searched the northern face for the secret door. Unable to find it he set his men to burrow into the limestone in hope of striking the internal passage. The workmen excavated a narrow tunnel to the depth of 100 feet (30 metres). They were at the point of despair when they heard a heavy thud within the pyramid.

Digging on they broke into a narrow passage which sloped downwards. On its floor lay the heavy stone which had fallen from the roof. Climbing back up the passage the Arabs found the hinged door in the north face, 49 feet (15 metres) above the pyramid's base and ten blocks higher than they had calculated. They had broken into the Descending Passage. Creeping downwards they reached a rough-hewn pit, deep within the natural rock. A horizontal passage ran for a further 50 feet (15 metres) ending in a blank wall, and a narrow shaft led downwards for 30 feet (9 metres). The pit and its extensions were empty.

Returning to the point where they had burrowed into the Descending Passage, the Arabs noticed that the fallen stone had concealed the tip of what appeared to be a block of granite. Did this plug conceal the entrance to another passage, one leading upwards into the heart of the pyramid? The plug, which appeared to weigh several tons, was tightly wedged against the surrounding limestone blocks. Despairing of chipping it away, Mamun ordered his masons to cut a way round it.

This tedious excavation revealed that the granite plug was 6 feet (1.8 metres) in length, and was the first of several of equal length, all tightly wedged within the narrow Ascending Passage. Chopping their way past these obstructions, the masons found themselves in a low, horizontal passage. It led to a small, square, empty room, which became called the Queen's Chamber.

Returning to the junction with the Ascending Passage the workmen noticed a void above. Climbing on each other's shoulders they entered a gallery (the Grand Gallery), 28 feet (8.5 metres) high and leading upwards. Climbing its 150 foot (45 metre) slope they reached another horizontal passage, partly blocked by a stone which reduced its height to 41 inches (81 centimetres). Stooping low they penetrated into another chamber, larger than the first, its walls and roof formed of squared and tightly jointed blocks. (This 'Kings Chamber' is 34 feet long, 17 feet wide and 19 feet high, or about 10.5 by 5 by 6 metres). In its centre stood a huge granite sarcophagus. It had no lid and was empty.

The story of the first entrance, which is told by several Arab historians, establishes facts of fundamental importance. The Ascending Passage was completely sealed and the granite plugs had not been tampered with. Yet the chambers were empty. How had the pall-bearers who had carried the dead pharoah to his last resting place escaped? Some would have had to remain behind to release the plugs. What had happened to the pharaoh's body? Tomb-robbers had not by-passed the granite plugs. No early European investigators asked these questions. They accepted that the pyramid had been built as a tomb.

Disappointed in their efforts to disclose the secrets of the pyramid, the Arabs stripped the exterior of its limestone casing, using it to build Cairo's mosques and palaces, and leaving piles of rubble around the base of the pyramid which now appeared as a series of ascending stone courses, reaching the height of 480 feet (145 metres). The pyramid's base covers 13 acres (about 5 hectares). It was examined by a succession of curious European visitors. The granite plugs blocking the Ascending Passage were removed in 1817.

John Greaves came to Egypt in 1638. An Oxford mathematician, he hoped to find within the structure data which might help to establish the earth's dimensions and provide an imperishable standard of linear measurement. He sought the basic unit of measurement employed in the pyramid's construction. He was foiled by the masses of debris surrounding the pyramid's base, which prevented its measurement. He made one remarkable discovery. In the wall at the start of the Grand Gallery, where it met the Ascending Passage, he noticed a block of mortared stone which seemed to have been slightly misplaced. Forcing it aside, he found a narrow shaft leading downwards. He followed it to the depth of 60 feet (18 metres). It continued into the murky darkness. This 'well shaft' was fully investigated in 1840, when its last 50 feet (15 metres) were found to be blocked by rubble and sand, and its exit carefully camouflaged. It reaches into the Descending Passage.

From the measurements obtained by Greaves within the pyramid, Sir Isaac Newton deduced that it had been built to two different units of measure, the longer 'sacred cubit, as he named it, of approximately 25 British inches, and the shorter 'profane cubit' of 20.63 British inches (or approximately 63 and 52 centimetres respectively). Thereby the discoverer of gravity created a phantom which developed in time into the theory that the pyramid had been built to represent a prophecy in stone.

A succession of scholars followed Greaves in search of eternal truth. Their discoveries, assumptions and frustrations can be briefly summarized. David Davison in 1765 found three small rooms above the King's Chamber, the walls of one inscribed with the cartouche of the Pharaoh Khufu. It was later realized that these chambers had been constructed to relieve pressure from the flat ceiling of the King's Chamber. Davison also found air ducts leading into the chamber from the pyramid's exterior, 200 feet (60 metres) distant.

The French mathematician, Edme-François Jomard (one of the savants brought to Egypt by Napoleon in 1798) concluded from his careful investigation that the pyramid was accurately oriented to the four points of the compass, and had been built on the meridian which exactly bisected Egypt's delta, thus forming a perfect geodesic landmark. Standing at the base of the Descending Passage, he deduced that an ancient astronomer, by looking up the narrow passage through the entrance, could have observed the transit of some circumpolar star.

Jomard rejected the theory that the pyramid had been built as a tomb. He believed it had been constructed to perpetuate an ancient system of measures, and he concluded that its designers had possessed an advanced knowledge of geometry and geodosy. Jomard's deduction became overshadowed by the theories which sprang from the Victorians' fear that the advancement of science was endangering belief in religion.

John Taylor was a mathematician and a keen amateur astronomer. He was also deeply religious. He accepted the Bible as being literally true, not a difficult feat in the 1860s. He deduced from the measurements that had been made that the pyramid had been built to record the dimensions of the earth and the length of the solar year. The pyramid's proportions had been intended to express certain geometric and astronomical laws, to preserve and pass them on to future generations. He called this a 'stunning discovery'. It placed him in a terrible quandary.

Taylor believed that his calculations showed that the pyramid had been constructed in 2100 B.C. That was a mere 300 years after the Flood which the Bible appeared to date in 2400 B.C. It was impossible to believe that man had progressed sufficiently in that short time to have designed such a mathematically perfect structure. Seeking a solution to this paradox, Taylor saw the light. The pyramid's designers had been influenced by divine revelation. That identified them as members of the chosen Adamic race. Taylor also noticed the similarity of the pyramid's unit of measure to the British inch. He died in 1864, leaving it to his disciples to conclude that the inheritors of the divine dispensation must therefore be the British race, the descendants of the Lost Tribes of Israel. Taking up the torch, the Scotsman Robert Menzies declared that the pyramid's passage system was nothing less than a chronological representation of prophecy, corroborating the Bible and on a scale of one pyramid inch to one year of time. We need to digress from the story of the evolution of rational thinking to follow the development of this startling theory.

According to a small group of fervent believers, who were particularly active between 1890 and 1935, the Great Pyramid demonstrated the divine plan for the Adamic race. By the translation of the lengths of the pyramid's corridors and chambers into years, months and days, it was possible to foretell the future of that chosen section of the human race from the Creation in 4000 B.C. to A.D. 2045$\frac{1}{2}$, the date of the final tribulation. David Davidson, an engineer from Leeds in England, became the leading interpreter of this revelation. He spent months diligently measuring the pyramid's passages and chambers, publishing his findings in two pamphlets in 1924 and 1934, *The Great Pyramid, Its Divine Message* and *The Hidden Truth in Myth and Ritual*. Davidson claimed that the structural symbolism of the pyramid had been incorporated under 'the Divinely inspired intuitive supervision of proto-Hebrew master builders'. He accepted that the unit of measure employed had been the sacred cubit, representing 25.02 British inches (about 63 centimetres). He evolved what he called the 'pyramid inch'.

Davidson adopted as his time-space starting point an imaginary mark deep in the ground outside the pyramid on the line projecting downwards from the slope of the Ascending Passage. He designated his adjustable starting place as the year 4000 B.C. Progressing upwards, measuring one inch for each year, he arrived at the junction of the Ascending and Descending Passages in the year 1486 B.C. which he declared represented the year of the Exodus of the Israelites from Egypt, a date which is considered far too early for that famous event. He named that spot the Gate of Ascent. The length of the Ascending Passage represented the years between the Exodus and the birth of Jesus Christ in 4 B.C., another disputed date. The short horizontal passage leading to the foot of the Grand Gallery represented the Passage of the Messiah, marked by the crucifixion.

Reaching the top of the Grand Gallery, Davidson measured the length of the passage leading to the King's Chamber. Calculated by the pyramid inch it exactly fitted the period 4 August 1914 to 11 November 1918, the duration of World War I. Spurred on by this stupendous discovery, Davidson proceeded to name the King's Chamber as the Chamber of the Open Tomb, and to define other prophetic dates. One of Taylor's disciples, Colonel Garnier, had already indicated 1882 as the year of the Second Advent. Davidson adjusted this to 1913, to give it a better chance to happen. He utilized the length of the King's Chamber to symbolize the years 1936 to 20 August 1953. As far as we know, nothing of great importance occurred on that day. According to Davidson the days of final tribulation would begin in $2001\frac{3}{4}$ and end in $2045\frac{1}{2}$. But Davidson's theory that the pyramid had been built as a time capsule had been demolished by Sir Flinders Petrie's discovery in 1880 that its builders had worked not to a sacred cubit but to the royal cubit, representing 20.63 British inches (about 52 centimetres).

Returning to more sober argument, we need to notice the visit to Egypt in 1864 of Charles Piazzi Smyth, the Astronomer Royal of Scotland, who, like John Taylor, sought to reconcile science and religion. In Smyth's case science triumphed. His careful measurements disclosed that the pyramid's builders had known the relationship of the radius of a circle to its circumference, knowledge hitherto believed to have been the exclusive prerogative of the Greek sages. The area of the pyramid's base divided by twice its height does give the famous figure $\pi = 3.14159$.

On his return to Scotland Smyth stated his emphatic opinion that the pyramid revealed most surprisingly accurate knowledge of high astronomical and geographical physics nearly 1,500 years earlier than the infantile beginnings of such things amongst the ancient Greeks. Thereby he deeply offended scholarly opinion which attributed to the Greeks the discovery of all mathematical knowledge. Smyth was derided and called a 'pyramidiot'.

Petrie's, and later J. H. Cole's, accurate measurements enabled the rational-thinking theorists to express more revolutionary ideas. Moses Cotesworth concluded that the pyramid had been devised as an accurate calendar to record the movement of the stars round the heavens. Richard Proctor made a remarkable discovery. A scholar as well as an astronomer, he noticed the statement of the Roman author Proclus to the effect that the pyramid had been used as an observatory *before* its completion. From this clue Proctor evolved a theory so shockingly simple that it was ignored by the academic establishment.

The Great Pyramid had been designed as an astronomical observatory, the most advanced and perfect instrument short of the modern telescope. Its designers had incorporated in its heart a huge graduated slot, perfectly aligned on the meridian across the heavenly vault. Looking up through the Descending Passage, the ancient astronomers had been able to observe the panoply of stars, noting their transits. Seen from the end of the passage, the star Alpha Draconis in 2160 or 3440 B.C. had been 3°.43′ from the North Pole. For it to be observed, the passage would have needed to be inclined at an angle of 26°.17′, exactly the slope achieved by the ancient astronomers.

Having constructed his giant slot, this ancient telescope, why did the designers build further? They needed to secure additional information, believed Proctor. As the pyramid grew, they created the Ascending Passage, also at the angle of 26°.17′, to check the meridian alignment, adopting the ingenious device of filling the space at the junction with the Descending Passage with a pool of water to reflect upwards the light of the chosen star. Why, Proctor asked himself, had the Grand Gallery been required? Analysing the problem from the viewpoint of the astronomer, rather than the architect, he realized that the ancient astronomer had required a very high slit with vertical walls by which to map the sky. It enabled him to note the exact second of a star's transit. Thereby he could have established its declination, its angular distance north or south of the celestial equator. At this stage the Grand Gallery was open to the sky.

Thus far, Proctor estimated, the pyramid had been built up to its fiftieth stone course, precisely the level of the Grand Gallery. The pyramid stood in truncated form, its square top serving as a plan for mapping the heavens, exactly as Kepler and Galileo had used squared charts. From their plan the ancient Egyptians had been able to divide the earth into zones by degrees. Proclus had stated correctly that the pyramid had been used as an astronomical observatory before it had been completed.

The Egyptian astronomers' amazing sophistication has been further disclosed by examination of the temples at Karnak and Luxor, and from the study of ancient texts. From them Professor Livio Stecchini (Professor of Ancient History at William Paterson College, New Jersey), who has devoted his career to the study of ancient measures, deduced that the ancient Egyptians had determined the shape of the earth which they knew to be a true circle, its size (only rediscovered in the eighteenth century of our era), its precise circumference, the geographical distance from equator to poles, the fact that the earth is flattened at the poles, degrees of latitude and longitude to within a few hundred feet and the fact that they were shorter at the equator and longer at the poles, and the exact dimensions of ancient Egypt. They could measure the length of the year precisely. They understood the system of map projection whereby spherical surfaces are reduced to flatness. They had designed the pyramid's base to correspond to the distance the earth rotates in half a second. They had been 2,000 years in advance of the Greek sages who had derived their knowledge from them.

Amongst their many mathematical achievements, the Egyptians had computed what is known as the Fibonacci series (in which each new number is the sum of the preceding two) whereby, had they so wished, they could have accurately foretold the number of rabbits which could be born in a year from one pair, which is 377 pairs.

Yet within two millennia nearly all this carefully compiled knowledge had been lost. The Greeks learned it only in garbled form. How did the ancient Egyptians acquire their knowledge? They may have evolved it over several centuries, or it may have been discovered by a single genius, an ancient Einstein. Andrew Tomas would have us believe that it was brought to Egypt by the survivors of lost Atlantis.*

The Great Pyramid is believed to have been built in about 2500 B.C. during the reign of Khufu, a pharaoh of the fourth dynasty. At the start of the operation engineers cleared and levelled the plateau and affixed the corner blocks to delineate the pyramid's base. By Sir Flinders Petrie's calculations, it comprises 2,300,000 stones, weighing $2\frac{1}{2}$ tons each and measuring 50 by 50 by 28 inches (127 by 127 by 71 centimetres) in size. How these stones were raised has vexed many investigators. Some think that the pyramid was encircled by an earthen ramp up which the stones were hauled. Others believe they were raised on balancing machines. Herodotus was told that twenty years were required, the 100,000 workmen labouring for three months each year during the period of the inundation of the Nile. The pyramid may have been a public works'

* *Atlantis: From Legend to Discovery*, Hale, 1972.

project to provide the people with food during the period of enforced idleness.

The priestly astronomers may have also persuaded Pharaoh Khufu that the building would serve as his tomb, a promise they may have had no intention of keeping.

Peter Tompkins* suggests that the pyramid's designers, having learned all they wanted to know from their astronomical observatory, having created their entire science of astronomy, geography and geodesy by stellar observation, walled up their instrument to prevent disclosure of their secrets.

To Tompkins the most puzzling riddle was the granite plugs which had been used to block the Ascending Passage. They made re-entrance to the chambers impossible. Khufu's tomb was empty, yet it could not have been plundered. Tomb-robbers could not have reached it, the pall-bearers could not have escaped from it.

The theory that the tomb-robbers climbed up the well shaft and the pall-bearers escaped down it, seems to be contradicted by the facts. When found, the stone concealing its top was tightly sealed, its bottom exit was carefully camouflaged, its lower part filled with debris. One man from either party would have had to remain in the gallery to re-seal the stone after the others had descended. His skeleton would have been found by the Arab explorers. This well shaft is thought to have been an airduct, to ventilate the Descending Passage.

How, then, had the plugs been lowered into the Descending Passage? This seems to be the crux of the question, the possible answer to the mystery of the Great Pyramid.

Those egyptologists who believe that it was built as a tomb assume that after the pharaoh's mummy had been carried into the chamber, the pall-bearers slid the three huge granite plugs into position from above. They escaped down the well shaft, carrying with them the massive lid of the sarcophagus. The unlikelihood of this procedure led to the suggestion that the plugs had been released by remote control with engineers triggering their descent from the bottom. Neither theory seems feasible. David Davidson made one

* *Secrets of the Great Pyramid*, Allen Lane, 1971.

contribution to science. He pointed out as an engineer that the half-inch clearance at the top of the Ascending Passage would have been insufficient to allow the plugs to be slid downwards without jamming. It would have required walls as smooth as glass, whereas the walls of the Ascending Passage had been left very rough.

Could the plugs have been placed in position early during the course of the pyramid's construction, by the time it had served its purpose as an observatory? The priestly architects completed the structure to provide an apex, with the adjacent smaller pyramids, to serve as a landmark for their triangulation surveys and possibly to satisfy the pharaoh that they were still building his tomb.

Has the pyramid other secrets to disclose? Some egyptologists believe that it contains undiscovered secret rooms possibly containing the pharaoh's funeral equipment, his necessities for the after-life. In the 1960s Luis Alvarez, the 1968 Nobel prize winner for physics, devised a machine for scanning the passage of cosmic rays which he hoped would reveal the hidden chamber. He tested it in the pyramid of Kephren, Khufu's son. The tapes he obtained have been run through the computer at Berkeley, California, so far without noticeable result (Alvarez, L. W., 'Search for Hidden Chambers in the Pyramids', *Science* 167, 1970, pp. 832–9).

In 1974 the Danish Professor Hubert Paulsen, a retired architect, announced, following extensive research within the Pyramid, his theory that an undiscovered chamber exists probably beneath its foundations. He bases his theory on the geometric principles on which the Pyramid was built. This chamber may have been the pharoah's tomb and may contain treasures even more remarkable than those found in Tutankamen's tomb.

Kurt Mendelssohn has suggested another explanation for the pyramids, both those of Egypt and those constructed by the Mayas and Aztecs. They were vast community jobs devised to weld separate tribes into one society by means of a huge common task. Thereby their builders created the national state.*

The pyramid may have disclosed another secret. The French

* *The Riddle of the Pyramids*, Praeger, 1974.

scientist, Bovis, noticed something odd. Garbage cans in the King's Chamber contained the bodies of several small animals which had crept in and died there. They were dehydrated and mummified. Reading Bovis's report, the Czech engineer, Karen Drbal, experimented with pyramid-shaped models. Milk and yoghurt placed therein remained fresh and did not deteriorate. A razor blade stayed sharp after 200 shaves. Does a pyramid-shaped container accumulate electromagnetic waves or cosmic rays? No one knows the answer, but several manufacturers have adopted pyramids as containers for perishable goods. That may be the only secret the ancient priests failed to discover.

THE TEMPLE BUILDERS OF MALTA

In 1902 a workman, digging a trench for the foundations of a house at the village of Hal Saflieni on the island of Malta, broke into a subterranean cavern. He accidentally disclosed the huge underground temple and cemetery, hewn from the solid rock and called the hypogeum from the Greek word meaning a subterranean vault. In 1914 a farmer tilling his fields at Tarxien found his tools striking huge blocks of stone concealed beneath the surface of the soil. He revealed a magnificent megalithic monument, a complex of temples. These and many others on the islands of Malta and Gozo have been called 'the world's most impressive prehistoric monuments'. Their gradual excavation and investigation roused considerable archaeological curiosity, speculation and controversy.

These massive megalithic structures seemed alien to tiny Malta. The combined areas of the two islands, 119 square miles, could not have supported sufficient population to transport and erect such huge stones. The impetus and technical expertise must have come from the eastern Mediterranean, brought by Cretan, Greek or Phoenician architects.

As excavation progressed nothing resembling these Aegean cultures was found. Rather, the mounds of rubble revealed strange, new and unfamiliar objects, pottery and tools which had been fashioned by a remote, nameless and gifted race, a people hitherto unknown to history.

Malta's temples and tombs are now dated before 3,000 B.C., 1,000 years earlier than the rise of the civilizations from which they were once thought to have derived their impetus. How this considerably revised dating came about requires explanation.

Before World War II the dating of prehistoric remains, where there were no written records, was achieved by the technique of cross-dating, by matching pottery items to those of other cultures of known date, and by counting tree-rings (trees conveniently grow rings of varying density and thickness depending upon climatic factors at the rate of one ring each year). By these aids a firm chronology was created. Then, in 1949, Professor Willard F. Libby discovered the radio-carbon dating system, made possible by the development of atomic physics.

Its basic principles are simple. The earth is continually bombarded by cosmic radiation, by small sub-atomic high energy particles. They produce small quantities of radio-carbon in the atmosphere, including Carbon-14, a rare isotope. This is absorbed by plants and by the animals which eat the plants. The plants and animals retain their Carbon-14 in the same proportions as it exists in the atmosphere. When the plant or animal dies and ceases to absorb carbon, the carbon decays spontaneously and slowly, at a constant and known rate. What remains in the sample can be exactly measured and dated. This system rested on the assumption that the con-centration of Carbon-14 in the atmosphere had remained constant throughout all time.

The new dates produced by this system did not tally with the firm chronologies accepted by archaeologists. In some cases there seemed to be 'yawning millennia'. This applied particularly to Western European cultures where no historical records existed. These discrepancies led to the reassessment of the Carbon-14 dating system. Some unrecognized factor must be operating. It was discovered in 1967 from the examination of the tree-rings of the long-lived bristlecone pine which grows in California. It has a life of more than 5,000 years. The number of tree-rings did not match the time schedules produced by the carbon dating of wood samples taken from the fallen pines. The assumption that the concentration of carbon had been constant was untrue. About 6,000 years ago it had been far higher than in the twentieth century. As a result samples had given readings which were misleadingly young. Chronologies before 2000 B.C. required up-dating by 500 years, those before 3000 B.C. by as much as 800 years. This revolution in carbon dating gave Malta's megaliths new significance.

The buildings at Mgarr are thought to be the most ancient. Professor J. D. Evans calls one 'this tatty little structure',* but of the greatest importance for the elucidation of the origin and meaning of the temples. This building, which measures 35 by 25 feet (10.5 by 7.5 metres) overall 'contains in embryo most of the main features of what was to become the architectural unit' of the other temple complexes, 'the groups of chambers centreing round a central spine composed of courts and corridors'. This plan, seemingly odd and arbitrary, had obviously been deliberately chosen in preference to a simpler shape. Evans gained the irresistible impression that a clumsy attempt had been made to reproduce something from another medium. Other discoveries strongly suggested a fairly satisfactory origin for these temples. They were based on the shape of the rock-tombs, several of which had been excavated. They proved to be the key to the whole development, both of the rock-cut and the built monuments. The basic form of these tombs is more or less a kidney-shaped chamber, entered through a small circular port-hole at the bottom of a cylindrical pit. At Xemxija, for example, two chambers are joined by a corridor, though each has its separate entrance, and are partitioned, showing remarkable resemblance to the kidney-shaped plan of the temple at Mgarr.

Professor Evans could only guess at what prompted the builders to reproduce their rock-cut monuments above ground. Those below ground housed collective burials, but no trace of human remains were found at Mgarr or the other temples. Why should a building, designed to be a shrine or temple, imitate the form of a tomb? To Evans the answer was clear, 'only if

* *Malta*, Thames and Hudson, 1963.

the rites to be celebrated there have to do with the dead'. That was confirmed by everything the archaeologists learned about the religion of the ancient Maltese. Possibly the temples were first used as tombs, but ceased to be and became appropriated to the religion which grew from the cult of the dead.

It seems certain that these rock-tombs were hewn from the rock before the temples were built. Collective burials may have begun in natural caves. That gave rise to the idea of scooping out chambers from the rock, as was done with the hypogeum and the Cavern of Darkness at Ghar Dalam.

The vast hypogeum at Hal Saflieni has a complex ground plan, representing the final stage of development of these rock-tombs. A number of small chambers are linked to a labyrinth of halls, passages and stairways, work which must have taken centuries to execute. They extend over an area of 1,600 square feet (148 square metres) and descend in three levels, the lowest 30 feet (9 metres) beneath the surface. As they descend the halls become larger, the chambers are better finished and decorative features appear. The succession of rooms appear to lead to a Holy of Holies, possibly the seat of an oracle. Words spoken there echo and re-echo from wall to wall and from chamber to chamber, evoking fear of the mystery and power of unseen spirits. 7,000 skeletons were found packed in earth within the hypogeum. The cave of Ghar Dalam yielded the bones of an extinct species of dwarf rhinoceros and eight human teeth. These teeth may have sunk to a lower level giving the impression that they are older than they may be, even Neanderthal.

The hypogeum's labyrinth of chambers and passages must have been excavated by means of stone wedges and tools of antler horn, for the marks they made can still be seen. Even so, the herculean task of excavation must have been dwarfed by the labour required in temple building above ground. The two enormous temples at Ggantija on the island of Gozo contain stone uprights 16 feet (4.8 metres) high. One is 26 feet long and 13 feet wide (about 8 by 4 metres) requiring a colossal engineering feat in transportation and erection. The temples are fronted by a spacious terrace 40 feet (12 metres) wide, supported by a great retaining wall. Its imposing façade has been described as the earliest architectural concept existing in the world. Within lie broad courtyards with curved ends. A doorway leads to another huge trefoil-shaped court. No wonder the modern Maltese call one temple the Tower of the Giants. It measures 100 feet (30 metres) in length and breadth, and its largest chamber is 35 feet long and 30 feet wide (10.5 by 9 metres).

Of the other temples so far identified, Tarxien is thought to have been built last. Its three chief buildings were constructed at different times, but on the same basic plan as the earlier complexes. It has several interesting features, including spiral relief carvings and friezes of animals. Within one of its chambers stands a rectangular block of stone, 12 feet (about 3.5 metres) square, partly sunk beneath the ground. Three of its sides are surrounded by walls, the fourth is bordered by a stone step. Holes had been bored in it, and near these strange cavities were found over a hundred stone balls of various sizes. Was this device an oracle? The suppliant threw the balls, learning his fate from the particular hole in which they landed. Tarxien has also yielded the lower part of a female statue, over life size and seated on a block of stone. This and other representations of the female form, always of grotesque fatness, suggests that the temple builders worshipped a female deity.

All the temples have one feature in common, a broad central corridor leading to a small apse at the rear where are found niches, stone tables and storage pits containing the bones of domestic animals. How the huge stones were transported from the quarries poses a conundrum which may be partly answered by the deep 'cart tracks' cut into the limestone rock, which have been noticed throughout the island and appear to run in every direction. They have been investigated by a succession of British Royal Navy officers who were stationed in Malta. The tracks give the impression of a railway network, with junctions and marshalling yards. At some places they cross and at others run in parallel lines. Each pair is spaced about 55 inches (139 centimetres) apart. Captain H. S. Gracie has argued they could not have been made by any wheeled vehicle. They are V-shaped in section, quite deep and slightly rounded at the bottom, whereas cart tracks are broad, shallow and flat-bottomed. They often curve suddenly and in such a manner that wheeled vehicles would have stuck. Gracie suggests that the vehicle must have been a slide-car, an ancient and still used form of transport, consisting of two wooden shafts supported by a draught animal, while the rear ends trail along the ground. His theory was tested in 1955 during the production of a television film about Malta's prehistory. A wheeled vehicle jammed in these tracks, whereas the slide-car ran easily along them. Centuries of use must have been required to cut the tracks so deeply. They formed an elaborate communication system, over plain and hill, providing an easy form of transport from settlement to settlement and from the quarries to the temples.

Malta's temples and tombs are unique in their massive piling of stone upon stone and their deep excavation. They represent a remarkable engineering feat, the single great achievement of the society which concentrated on one task to the exclusion of all else, save subsistence. The ancient temple builders neither built houses of stone nor evolved a system of writing. We know them only from their monuments. They evolved all the techniques of an advanced civilization, devoted to the service of one simple, unquestioned cult.

Who these temple builders were is a mystery. Possibly migrants from the north, they may have crossed to Malta by the land bridge which once existed, linking Italy and Sicily to North Africa. On its disappearance they dwelt in sea-girt isolation, requiring no weapons, remote from the mainstream of culture, wrapped up in their own peculiar and bizarre cult. They became the greatest megalith builders of antiquity.

How this mysterious people created a society capable and willing to labour incessantly in order to tunnel and build has puzzled archaeologists and ethnologists. Their numbers can never have been great. Their meagre land, lacking great rivers, could not have supported more than 11,000 people. That estimate is based on population density of similar areas today. They perfected a simple agricultural economy based on tools of stone and bone.

The distribution of their temples may provide a clue to the

evolution of their social organization. Plotted on the map in relation to arable land, these complexes fall into clusters, each commanding a major area of territory and making it appear that the islands were divided into six separate settlements. But no one community, numbering about 2,000 people, could have mobilized the labour required to excavate caverns and raise temples. Professor Colin Renfrew has evolved a theory to account for the erection of these impressive monuments.*

Primitive societies, he points out, developed one of two types of social organization, the egalitarian (where everyone is his own boss) and the state, the hierarchical structure of bureaucracy and specialization. In Malta, he thinks, the original simple farming community evolved into a highly complex organization, dominated by a single chief, the ancestral founder of a stratified social hierarchy. This big chief and his many successors gained their power from enormous prestige. His sons may have become sub-chiefs, each ruling a separate territory.

The big chiefs instituted a revolutionary economic system, the creation of surplus by the collection of tribute. Farmers were forced to grow more food than they required, fishermen to catch a superabundance of fish. Thereby the chief built up the resources to encourage and pay for craft specialization, the skilled men who made pottery, built boats, constructed slide-cars and hewed stone.

To achieve this greater productivity, he needed to inspire his people, to edify and encourage them to work for the well-being of the community, to create organic solidarity. That required government by consent, group approval of the great enterprise. That was satisfied by the people's superstition, their hope for an after-life and their fear of eternal punishment. Under this compelling influence, the small population undertook public works, the construction of tombs and temples which normally would have required far greater numbers of people. By this craft specialization and centralized organization they built temples every bit as impressive as the ziggurats of Sumer, the pyramids of Egypt and the statues of Easter Island.

* *Before Civilization*, Jonathan Cape, 1973.

Then, in about 2550 B.C., the temple-builders vanished as mysteriously as they had come. There was no gradual decline, no sudden deviation from their cult, no falling off of devotion to their religion. They disappeared without trace. They may have been overwhelmed by the sudden influx of new people, migrants from the north, fierce invaders wielding copper daggers and axes. Wrapped up in their religion, unaccustomed to war, over-centrally organized, they succumbed to aggression as easily and as quickly as did the Aztecs and Incas. They left behind temples of a peculiar kind not found elsewhere. They had no imitators. They gained no disciples, acknowledged no masters. They perfected their culture possibly a thousand years before other peoples equalled their strange civilization. We know them only as the temple builders.

GREAT ZIMBABWE

The dense complex of huge stone buildings, massive towers and rambling walls, scattered over sixty acres of hill and valley at Zimbabwe, Rhodesia, have provided a fertile field for romance and exotic interpretation since their discovery by Europeans in the sixteenth century.

The famous ruins comprise two major complexes: the Hill Ruin, perched 350 feet (106 metres) above the plain, and the Elliptical Ruin in the valley. The one is assumed to have been a fortress, the other a temple. The Hill Ruin is the earlier. It is thought to have been built by an unknown people whose building techniques were surpassed by the more skilful craftsmen who constructed the temple. Like their predecessors, they piled stone upon stone without mortar. They stepped back their stones, as the walls rose, to give a cumulative effect of sloping upwards. The temple's outer walls are 30 feet (9 metres) high. Within they built thinner and unroofed partition walls, which subdivided the interior, and the Conical Tower which is 32 feet (9.7 metres) high and 50 feet (15 metres) in circumference. Both generations of builders quarried their stone from the granite slabs which outcrop from the near-by hills. The smaller buildings in the valley meander over the slopes without obvious plan. Often they fill in spaces between huge boulders.

The Portuguese, when they reached the coast of East Africa, heard from Arab traders rumours of gold mines and huge stone buildings in the interior. The first explorer to reach the area, Antonio Fernandes, found a 'fortress of stone . . . without mortar'. Taking up the story in 1552, the historian João de Barros hinted at similarities with the palaces of the Queen of Sheba described in the Bible. The missionary João dos Santos identified Zimbabwe as the place from which the fabulous queen had derived her gold. Zimbabwe was the Biblical Ophir, the source of King Solomon's wealth. It was not difficult to reach such conclusions at a time when the Bible was accepted as a precise record of historical fact.

These conjectures created a chain of imaginative reasoning. Solomon's ally was Hiram, King of Tyre, a Phoenician. According to Herodotus, the Phoenicians had circumnavigated Africa between 609 and 593 B.C. at the bidding of the Pharaoh Necho. Zimbabwe was therefore the land of Punt, depicted on the walls of the tomb of Queen Hatshepsut. It was probably a Phoenician foundation.

From these speculations arose the great myth, potent with romance, of ruined cities full of gold, deep in unexplored Africa, ruled once and possibly still by white queens, held in superstitious awe by their black subjects.

The certainty that Zimbabwe had been built by outsiders, aliens from the north, became an entrenched myth, one which received further impetus from the visit in 1872 of the young German geologist, Carl Mauch. He came in search of the large stone ruins which, he was told, 'could not have been built by blacks'. He thought they were a complete riddle. He guessed that one building was a copy of Solomon's temple at Jerusalem. Another was similar to the palace built by Solomon to house the Queen of Sheba. These assumptions placed the origin of the ruins in the tenth century B.C.

Cecil Rhodes, on his occupation of Mashonaland in 1890, blindly accepted the Ophir theory. On his visit to Zimbabwe, the local tribesmen were told that 'the Great Master' had come

34

'to see the ancient Temple which once belonged to white men'.

The first discordant note was struck in 1891. The Royal Geographical Society and the British Association for the Advancement of Science, sent the antiquarian Theodore Bent to inspect the ruins. Although he approached the problem in the belief that they were the work of an outside agency, he failed to detect any resemblance to Phoenician architecture. Privately he confessed little faith in the antiquity of the ruins which he thought were of native origin. The white settlers dismissed his opinion as absurd. The African natives were incapable of such work, a view which was reinforced by their own disclaimers. The local tribesmen had no traditions that the buildings had been erected by their ancestor. Phoenician origin was a convenient theory at a time when the British were emulating the enterprise of that small trading nation which, in the distant past, had established colonies in Africa as the British were doing in the nineteenth century.

Bent's privately expressed theory was attacked in 1905 by the journalist Richard Nicklin Hall who composed a massive volume entitled *The Ancient Ruins of Rhodesia*. His fervent advocacy of alien origin won him the appointment of curator of Zimbabwe, the by now famous ruins which had been accorded protection by the Rhodesian legislature. Hall, in the tradition established in 1892 by Sir John Willoughby, a soldier entirely lacking archaeological experience, gutted the ruins in search of clues to reveal the remains of the 'ancient builders'. His 'disastrous activities' and 'reckless blundering', as they were later described, all but obliterated the vestiges of the various cultures which had contributed to Zimbabwe's construction.

The publication of Hall's book and his lectures in England focused attention on the Zimbabwe ruins with the fortunate result that the British Association invited the archaeologist David Randall-MacIver, a pupil and colleague of Sir Flinders Petrie of Egyptian fame, to visit Rhodesia. MacIver rejected the uncritical credulity which the ruins had been accorded. He recognized that the problem of Zimbabwe could only be solved by using sound archaeological methods. He was handicapped by the devastation caused by the previous amateur excavators

35

and by the lack of any contemporary means to date the deposits he was able to unearth. He found no evidence of any alien influence, but rather that of gradual native evolution. His conclusion that the buildings had been raised by the indigenous people of the area was dismissed in Rhodesia with traditional contempt for the 'overseas expert'.

MacIver's findings forced a change of attitude. Zimbabwe had been built, no doubt, by Africans, but under the supervision of an alien architect, claimed the colonists. Called upon to rebutt MacIver, Hall conceived the theory of distinct cultural periods 'each more decadent than the last', followed by inevitable decline and decadence due to a 'sudden arrest of intelligence and mental development which befalls every member of the Bantu race at the age of puberty'. The racial theory had been explicitly stated. It has been used since to prejudice the question of Zimbabwe's origin.

The controversy simmered for twenty years until 1929 when the British Association sent another archaeologist, Gertrude Caton-Thompson, to investigate the famous site. She concentrated on 'the most fundamental question' – the date of construction. That required stripping an area from surface to bedrock. She selected the Maund Ruin, a small site which had suffered less damage from her predecessors than the larger buildings. She also ran trenches through the Elliptical Ruin.

She found a complete absence of objects attributable to exotic peoples, nothing resembling any pre-Roman Middle Eastern civilization, and 'not one single item that was not in accordance with the claim of Bantu origin and mediaeval date'. Her conclusions were distasteful to the white settlers. Clutching at a straw, her discovery of Chinese ware, they attributed the ruins to the work of traders from across the Indian Ocean. Anything was better than the local blacks.

With the tools available to archaeologists prior to World War II it was impossible to date the structure with any exactitude. Any theory, however improbable, remained feasible as long as the date of construction was still in doubt. The aftermath of the war supplied archaeologists with a new dimension, the radio-carbon method of dating, whereby the age of organic matter can be roughly determined.

Two pieces of wood, which had been used to support a drain within the walls of the Elliptical Ruin, were subjected to this test. One produced the date A.D. 590, plus or minus 120 years, the other A.D. 700, plus or minus 90 years. These dates were not, however, conclusive and were probably far too early, because the local tree from which the wood had been cut lives for 500 years. These tests indicate that the buildings were constructed about A.D. 1250.

This information, together with the reassessment of the finds previously made – iron tools and weapons, copper, bronze and gold ornaments – has enabled archaeologists and historians to create a rough picture of Zimbabwe's past.

The site appears to have been first occupied by Stone Age hunters who had moved away by A.D. 300. They were succeeded after an interval by cattle herders who began the mining of gold which became the source of Zimbabwe's later prosperity. It was easy at first with the ore outcropping from the hillsides. As time progressed the miners dug deep vertical shafts extending to 100 feet (30 metres). It was a rich lode yielding three ounces of gold to the ton. The miners were women and children. That is disclosed by the crushed skeletons of victims of cave-ins. These early people, whose origin is unknown apart from the fact that they belonged to the Negro race, built the Hill Ruin.

New immigrants arrived in about A.D. 1000. Their pottery and certain place names which have survived in the area identify them as Negroes who came possibly from the Congo. There may have been two tribes, the Rozwi and the Mwenye, the one the organizers, the other the craftsmen who created the Zimbabwe culture. Using the gold to expand their trade, these people extended their empire throughout the area of modern Rhodesia, creating other megalithic structures. Finds of Indian beads and Chinese porcelain in the area indicate that they traded, through the Arabs who inhabited the coast, across the Indian Ocean. No objects of Zimbabwe manufacture have been found in these countries. They paid for their imports in gold.

Zimbabwe's medieval residents built for ostentation as their wealth increased and they were visited by traders whom they wished to impress. The population may not have exceeded 2,000 adults, some 400 of whom were the craftsmen who hewed, carried and piled up the stones, creating buildings within which the rulers lived in huts.

The period of profound peace which allowed the culture to develop may have ended in the fourteenth century. For some unknown reason the period of stability, of expanding trade and religious ceremonial, ended in disruption. The soil may have become exhausted, or rainfall diminished. The Zimbabwe culture declined, the building stopped, but the kingdom survived. It maintained its local domination until 1825 when the Zimbabwe people were slain and dispersed by the Zulu invasion. The survivors became absorbed within the neighbouring Shona tribes, retaining and passing on vague memories of their ancestors' former greatness.

Much of Zimbabwe's history is hazy. The white Rhodesians prefer that it should so remain. Museums which exhibit artifacts labelled as of native origin have been threatened with closure. Archaeological interpretations are discouraged. Their findings have been attacked in the Rhodesian parliament.

Speaking in 1969, the Rhodesian Front member, G. H. Hartley, derided the 'notion' of Zimbabwe's indigenous origin as 'sheer conjecture'. He thought the trend of some people to portray the ruin in one light only should be corrected. The minister of the interior replied that he had so intimated to those concerned, meaning the staff of the National Historical Monuments Commission, 'as long as no irrefutable evidence is available as to the origin of the ruins'. It was wrong that visitors to the country should be influenced by one train of thought. A year later, the minister announced that a new guide book was in preparation in which 'all theories relating to Zimbabwe will be presented absolutely impartially'.

Fortunately, as far as the outside world is concerned, the known facts have been presented by Peter Garlake in his book *Great Zimbabwe*.* He served as senior inspector of monuments in Rhodesia between 1964 and 1970. He describes the Zimbabwe ruins as 'unmistakably African', the work of an indigenous people, owing nothing to outside influences.

* Thames and Hudson, 1973.

38

These 'buildings of stone', the meaning of the Shona word Zimbabwe, are a majestic and striking monument of ancient African capability. To modern Black Africans they are a symbol of coming renaissance.

EASTER ISLAND. WHO BUILT THE STATUES?

Thor Heyerdahl is an enthusiast. To back his belief that the islands of Polynesia had been peopled by American Indians sailing westward from Peru, rather than by Asiatics island-hopping eastwards, he and his Scandinavian friends embarked on the raft Kon-Tiki. In 1947, after a voyage of 4,000 miles from Peru and 102 days at sea, he landed in the Tuamotu archipelago. He had shown that ancient Peruvians could have made that voyage on balsa rafts by using the Humbolt current which sweeps across the Pacific. On several Polynesian islands Heyerdahl saw stone platforms reminiscent of the stonework of Peru and, like earlier visitors, he noticed that many Polynesians were remarkably white in colour.

Heyerdahl's adventurous voyage gave fresh topicality to the old theory. It had been advanced in 1803 by the Spanish missionary Zuniga and again in 1830 by the English missionary William Ellis. In 1926 it had been advocated by no less a person than Dr Paul Rivet, the director of the Musée de l'Homme, Paris. Heyerdahl's development of this theory outraged ethnologists and anthropologists. He claimed that the American sailors were white Caucasians, unidentified immigrants from the Mediterranean, the 'bearded white men' who had built the city of Tiahuanaco, 12,500 feet (3,800 metres) high in the Andes. They had left Peru and, sailing westwards for 2,000 miles (3,200 kilometres), had landed on tiny, uninhabited Easter Island, a mere dot in the ocean. They had cut and erected hundreds of gigantic stone statues depicting scornful, pitiless men alien to the Pacific, their Caucasian ancestors. Significantly, perhaps, they called their island the 'navel of the world', a name similar to a place near Tiahuanaco.

The famous Easter Island statues were certainly not sculptured by a forgotten race who inhabited a lost continent or archipelago which, according to imaginative and fanciful theory, became submerged thousands of years ago in a great cataclysm. No great geographical subsidence had occurred in that part of the Pacific within the period of human existence. Easter Island was born from volcanic eruptions, not unusual in the Pacific, and it is surrounded by an abyss 1,145 fathoms deep which extends for 10 miles (16 kilometres). No land could have disappeared and left such a depression. The island is bare, with scanty soil. It is incapable of supporting a population of any great density. It is 35 miles (56 kilometres) in circumference and comprises 48,000 acres. Yet, this small, rocky island, unfavoured by climate, developed a unique culture. Its inhabitants spent hundreds of years cutting the statues from the volcanic rock, transporting and erecting them on the Ahus, the stone burial platforms which line the coast.

Easter Island was discovered and named on Easter Sunday 1722 by the Dutch navigator Jacob Roggeveen. He inspected the ancient monuments, marvelling that they had been erected by naked savages, and noticed that many of the islanders had white complexions. Captain James Cook's visit fifty years later brought the island the celebrity it has never ceased to enjoy. He observed many white skins, and inspected the fallen statues on the Ahus. Something remarkable had occurred during these fifty years. In 1722 the statues were standing. By 1774 they had been overthrown.

The impoverished islanders, who numbered about 4,000 in Cook's day, were reduced to 111 in 1862 by the slave raid which carried off the able-bodied men to Peru. Only a few remained to pass down the ancient traditions, and knowledge of the island's pictorial script. It remains undeciphered. There are several versions of the islanders' folklore.

These racial memories have been interpreted to prove both the argument that the statue builders derived from Peru and that they were Polynesians who came from the west, probably from the islands of the Tahitian group. The evidence is confused and conflicting, partly because of the language difficulties between the recorders and the islanders. The famous statues are believed to portray men of Caucasoid type, possibly a dangerous conclusion to draw from stone images. Some reliance is placed on the prevalence amongst the islanders of blue eyes, red hair and white skins. In some cases these European characteristics may have been derived from the crews of the whaling and trading ships which visited the island in the nineteenth century.

The bulk of the population, which numbers about 2,000 people, shows the usual Polynesian characteristics, with the perceptible increase in the length of the cranium common to the periphery of Polynesian expansion. It is particularly marked on Easter Island which lies at the end of the chain. This feature is thought to reflect the ethnic layer which, in the islands of the South Seas, was replaced by shorter-skulled, darker invaders. The Easter Islanders speak a pure Polynesian dialect, free from borrowings from other language families, an indication of their early exodus from their homeland. These factors suggest that the migrants reached the islands and became isolated before the end of the vast Polynesian dispersion which culminated in the thirteenth century of our era.

Navigating by the stars, the Polynesians roamed the seas in their flimsy out-rigger canoes, reaching New Zealand, Hawaii and Easter Island. To discover remote Easter Island they would have needed to drift almost down to the Antarctic in order to catch the southern current and avoid the westward-flowing Humboldt current. This southerly and eastward drift current could also have taken them to the South American mainland where they could have acquired the sweet potato, the Peruvian plant which grows in abundance throughout Polynesia.

The islanders' folklore contains traditions of two migrations from Polynesia, the first of which was led by the Chief Hotu-Matua. He reached the island with 300 men after a voyage of 120 days, being immediately preceded by his brother with seven men. The second migration seems to have occurred some generations later. The islanders who claim to preserve the ancient stories speak of two waves of seafarers, one of which came without women, the Hanau-Momoko, meaning the wrecked or weakened men, and the Hanau-Eeepe, the long-eared or strong men.

It is difficult to determine whether both waves of migrants were Polynesian, or whether the Hanau-Eepe were another, earlier, unknown race. The tradition refers to 'the others' who are described as 'very big men, but not giants, who lived on the island well before the coming of Hotu-Matua'.

The term 'Eepe' may be confusing. Francis Mazière, of whom more later, believes that it meant not long-eared but strong men. One group of Easter Islanders were known as Short Ears, which suggests that another group were distinguished by having elongated ears. Ear elongation was practised throughout Polynesia and in Peru where the Inca rulers adopted the custom as a mark of class distinction.

Were these Long Ears and Short Ears two separate waves of Polynesian migrants? Or were the Long Ears an earlier race? The evidence is conflicting. It may be significant that the modern islanders who claim descent from this earlier race call themselves the Long Ears.

Heyerdahl relied on the version recorded between 1883 and 1889 by the American naval paymaster, W. J. Thompson, who was assisted by the resident missionary, Father Roussel. Thompson seems to have drawn upon the knowledge of two men, the islander Ure Vaeiko who claimed to know the oral traditions of his ancestors, and a Tahitian named Salmon who acted as cicerone to visitors, and who told different stories to suit his interrogators. Vaeiko could converse only in pidgin Spanish. More reliable versions may have been recorded by Francis Mazière who visited the island with his Tahitian wife in 1963. She was able to converse easily with the islanders in their own language, thereby gaining their confidence.

Thompson and the later missionary Father Sebastian Englert recorded 'king lists'. Thompson traced these fifty-seven names back to about A.D. 500. Englert, who spent many years studying the islanders' genealogies claimed that the first Polynesian colonists arrived in the sixteenth century, 1,000 years after Thompson's date.

By Heyerdahl's interpretation Hotu-Matua was not a Poly-

42

nesian. He came from Peru, accompanied by 300 men in two boats and reached the uninhabited island after a voyage of 120 days. The land from which he came was named Marae-toe-hau, meaning the 'burial place', a possible allusion to the Peruvian custom of mummification. The climate of the land was so hot that people sometimes died from the effects of the heat. At certain times of the year plants became scorched and shrivelled. This description is taken to refer to Peru, a hot and arid land. Hotu-Matua had been preceded by his brother who had sailed on the same course steering for the setting sun. Heyerdahl dated Hotu-Matua's arrival in A.D. 475, about the time when, according to Peruvian tradition, the 'white-bearded' culture bearers had sailed away to the west.

Mazière, who benefited by his wife's linguistic abilities, distinguishes between two waves of Polynesian immigration, by the Long Ears and Short Ears, separated by twenty generations. He accepts the possibility that 'the others' came first and commenced the building of statues. He recorded one version of the legend, which seems to have been coloured by later knowledge. An islander told him: 'The first men to live on the island were survivors of the world's first race. They were yellow, very big, with long arms, great stout chests, huge ears although the lobes were not stretched. They had pure yellow hair and their bodies were hairless and shining. They did not possess fire. This race once existed in two other Polynesian islands. They came from a land that lies behind America.'

Mazière believes that Easter Island was reached by two successive and overlapping Polynesian migrations towards the end of the thirteenth century. They found an established culture and a few survivors of an earlier race, their powers much diminished, people who came from the east and who provided the land with its astonishing legacy. He accepts that certain traces are apparent of an antediluvian people 'whose presence we are beginning to discover', and who 'possessed a superior knowledge of an entirely different world'. According to his native informers, this world existed amongst the stars.

Another controversial item of the island's history is the

legend of the massacre of the Long Ears by the Short Ears. According to the best respected versions, the Long Ears, who lived on the Poike promontory at the eastern end of the island, fearing rebellion by their slaves, fortified the promontory by digging a ditch from one coast to the other. They filled it with branches and grass intending to create a wall of fire. They planned to sally out and exterminate the Short Ears. They were betrayed by one of their Short Ear wives. She told her relatives. They crept round the cliffs and massacred the Long Ears, throwing their bodies into the trench they had fired. Two Long Ears were spared. They became the progenitors of the fair-skinned islanders. The Poike peninsula became 'the un-inhabited land'.

Heyerdahl excavated the ditch, finding reddened earth, clear evidence, he believed, of the legendary conflagration. Alfred Métraux, the French anthropologist who visited the island in 1934, claims that this ditch was a natural cleft formed by the meeting of two lava streams which coloured the earth red.

The massacre is dated about 1760, about the time when the statues on the Ahus, the funerary platforms, were thrown down. Statue building ceased abruptly. It may be significant that sculpturing was not resumed. The destruction and cessation suggests it had not been a Polynesian enterprise. Would they, asked Heyerdahl, have cast down the images of their own forefathers? Ancestors worship and tabu would have forbidden such a sacrilege. He believes that the Polynesians, who had been forced to labour building statues, rebelled and slew their masters – 'the others', the mysterious race who sculptured their statues in their own image.

Eighty statues were left half-finished in the quarry within the crater of the old volcano Rano Raraku, which rises close to the Poike promontory, the traditional home of 'the others'. 276 statues stand guard on the volcano's slopes. They are the subjects of the famous photographs. 300 more lie cast down on the Ahus, which encircle the island's tall cliffs. Still others line the island's ancient roadways.

These groups of statues are different. Those that once stood on the funerary platforms are enormous busts, monstrous, leg-

44

less cripples, with massive trunks. The largest is 33 feet (10 metres) high and 25 feet (7.6 metres) in circumference. It weighs twenty tons and, as did the others, once supported a cylinder, a red top-knot measuring 6 feet by 8 feet (1.8 by 2.4 metres). These 'hats' were carved from the crater of the Rano Roi volcano in the centre of the island. These statues are also distinguished from the others by having opened eyes. They stood with their backs to the sea gazing inland. They are believed to represent an early, somewhat cumbersome style of building.

The terrifying statues are the ones that stand on the slopes of Rano Raraku. Both Métraux and Mazière believed they belong to a different period and reflect a different spirit from those on the Ahus. Their noses turn up and their thin lips are thrust forward in a pout of scorn and derision. They lack eyes. Descending projections on either side of the head may represent protruding ears or a head-dress. Their bases were peg-shaped for planting in the earth. They were all carved to a single model, marking a change of style from the older statues on the funerary platforms. Their hands were finely sculptured with elongated fingers. The majority are between 17 and 26 feet (5 and 8 metres) in height. The largest is 72 feet (22 metres) and the smallest 10 feet (3 metres). Gazing on them, Métraux felt a sense of shock and uneasiness. He concluded that they were the work of a strange people.

Eighty statues remain unfinished in the quarry inside the volcano's crater, partly or nearly carved from the rock. Métraux thought that a few blows with the hammer would have been enough to sever the thin strips of stone holding the bodies to their matrix. He described them as an army about to be born, waiting to be taken down and raised on the volcano's slopes. It seemed to be a day of rest.

The workmen have gone home to their villages, but tomorrow they will be back and the mountainside will ring with the blows of their stone hammers; it will echo with laughter, discussions and the rhythmic chanting of the men hauling the statues. How could they fail to come back, these sculptors who have left their tools lying at the foot of the work, where one has only to bend down to pick them up?

To Mazière, the operations of this huge workshop seemed an open book. 'Under the leadership of the head stone-cutter the team, which must have numbered about fifteen men, set to work on the chosen rock-face.' Wielding their hard stone picks, they chipped away the stone along a line of holes, a hand's breadth apart. This line defined the statue's shape and size. Then began the critical work of shaping the head and cutting the back so as to be able to lift the whole statue from the rock. The sculptors gnawed away the giant's back until the figure was held by nothing more than a great spine. The stone masons required great judgement to crack this keel without breaking the statue. Many of these unfinished statues had been incised with lines and zigzags like a beautiful necklace. One set of carved lines suggested a rainbow, another formed a perfect circle, leading to an incised shape like a letter M. Mazière thought them to be 'nothing Polynesian'.

Mazière excavated two finished statues from the rubble which covered them. One was 33 feet (10 metres) long, the other 34 feet (10.3 metres). One represented a bearded giant, his trunk incised with patterns. Heyerdahl made a remarkable discovery. He dug from the soil a small, squat statue entirely different from all the others. It portrayed a bearded man, who could not have been either Polynesian or Peruvian. Heyerdahl also discovered a statue its chest incised with the outlines of a boat, with three masts and several sails.

All three investigators noticed distinctive styles of sculpture representing two periods of construction. The earlier sculptors may have worked alone for a long time. One Polynesian migration, or both of them, may have supplied them with workers, which enabled them to devote their leisure to devising better models.

How were the statues lining the funerary platforms, and those standing by the highways, transported and erected? This is a conundrum to which no satisfactory answer has been given. The islanders lacked wood for rollers and ropes for hauling. Using ropes and wooden levers and a team of 500 haulers

Heyerdahl transported and erected one small statue. His workers knew how to erect it by building a cairn of stones up which it was levered and allowed to drop into position on the other side. They said that the ancient tradition had been passed down. Even more obscure is the question of how the top-knots were raised onto the heads of the statues. Some of these cylinders were 23 feet long and 10 feet broad (7 by 3 metres). Mazière failed to find traces of earthen or stone ramps up which they might have been pushed or dragged. The modern islanders' explanation is that, like the transportation of statues, the work was done by magic, by spirit force.

The information gained from the islanders' traditions and from the study of the statues is insufficient to identify the statue builders. At the most it can be said that these statues bear some affinity to those of Peru, the land from which 'the others' may have come. The sculptors, whoever they were, indulged in a frenzy of statute building, possibly to portray themselves or their ancestors, men who appeared to be alien to the Pacific. The other evidence is equally inconclusive. The pictorial script of the Rongo-Rongo tablets is unique in Polynesia and for that matter in Peru where no system of writing was known before the Spanish conquest. The Easter Islanders made no pottery, which is found in profusion in Peru. The sweet potato could have been brought from Peru, its homeland, to Easter Island and to Polynesia, either by Peruvian seafarers or by Polynesian voyagers who may have reached the South American continent. Heyerdahl found reeds growing on Easter Island of similar species to those used on Lake Titicaca, near the city of Tiahuanaco to construct reed boats. The Easter Islanders also made reed boats. The blood group type B is equally lacking in Polynesia and Peru, but is dominant in South Eastern Asia, where, according to the orthodox view, the Polynesians originated.

Heyerdahl has failed to convince orthodox ethnologists with his theory of South American origin for the cultures of the Pacific. It is described as 'ingenious', a polite way of saying it is invalid or far fetched. On Easter Island he may be on surer ground. The crux of the problem may lie in the sudden cessation of statue building, following the massacre of the Long

Ears. It suggests a slave revolt rather than the abandonment of an ancient Polynesian practice. The statue building seems to have been begun by an unknown race, 'the others', who forced the Polynesian migrants to work on a useless task. We may never know who these sculptors were. They seem to have been hard, pitiless men, scornful, distasteful, alien both to the Pacific and to Peru. Perhaps, as Heyerdahl believes, they were Caucasians who somehow reached South America and who, on the revolt of their subjects, crossed the Pacific to be massacred by their even more unwilling slaves.

The true history of the island was probably lost in 1862 when the men who understood the Rongo-Rongo tablets and had memorized the oral traditions were carried off to Peru. Twenty-five years later the island passed into the possession of Chile. The island is now ruled by a Chilean governor and is used to graze 40,000 sheep. The islanders are kept within a village at the island's western end. They steal out at night to visit the family caves which honeycomb the island's cliffs. They say that stored therein are the proofs of the island's past history, the Rongo-Rongo books and stone and wooden emblems which portray its earliest inhabitants. The sites of many of these caves are lost. Visitors who have succeeded in persuading their owners to reveal their treasures may have been palmed off with modern fakes. The islanders are adept sculptors. So they should be.

Biblical Mysteries

IS THE ARK ON ARARAT?

The report made by the Russian aviator, Captain Roskovitsky, startled the world. Flying over Mount Ararat during World War I he spotted the shape of a huge ship's hull clearly defined and embedded in the heart of a glacier. Here was proof, greatly needed in the new age of scepticism, of the literal truth of the Bible. According to the Hebrew Book of Genesis the ark had come to rest on the submerged summit of Ararat, a mountain 17,000 feet (5,180 metres) high. The waters of the Great Flood must therefore have covered the earth. All humanity must have perished, except, of course, Noah and his sons and daughters. That conclusion seemed to be confirmed by the flood myths told by many primitive peoples. The ancient peoples of Mesopotamia, the land from which Abraham had migrated to Palestine in about 2150 B.C. had similar flood legends.

Like the creation myth, the Hebrew deluge story is a compound of two traditions, the earliest of which was brought to Palestine by Abraham. After a thousand years of verbal repetition it was written down in about the ninth century B.C. Following the return of the Jews from captivity in Babylon some centuries later, a priestly version of the flood legend was added, the two being merged into one contradictory story. The earlier tradition tells a simple, if exaggerated story, not far removed from the current Semitic myths. It is the later priestly writer who supplies the information that the ark grounded upon Ararat, thus implying that the flood was a universal one. He gives, too, the ark's dimensions and he states that the flood lasted for 364 days against the more feasible sixty days of the earlier version. That he makes its duration the solar year shows that his account was written after the Jews had learned to correct the errors of the lunar calendar by observation of the sun.

Despite his exaggerations, the priestly editor succeeds in

providing certain information omitted by the earlier writer. Borrowing from a Mesopotamian source he inserts the detail, which is found also in the earlier cuneiform inscriptions, that the ark was caulked with bitumen, the usual ship-building practice in Mesopotamia. By saying that Noah was the tenth descendant from Adam he indicates that the flood was believed to have occurred after a comparatively advanced state of civilization had been achieved. Man had already become, for example, a worker in iron and a maker of harps. He introduces, too, the placing of the bow in the sky, as a promise that the flood will not recur, a detail which is found in the earliest Mesopotamian flood legend. The priestly writer is, however, less concerned with the historical aspects of the deluge than he is with its religious significance. His purpose is to emphasize the ritualistic rather than the moral implications of the story and to reaffirm the legal and contractual relations between God and his chosen people, through whom the world is re-peopled.

That the authors of the two Hebrew versions of the flood story wrote centuries apart can be discerned from their treatment of religious matters. The priest omits Noah's sacrifice after his rescue because, in the eyes of a Jewish priest after the priesthood had become a sacerdotal caste, the offering of a sacrifice by a layman was an unheard-of impropriety and a dangerous encroachment. That the other author wrote many hundreds of years earlier can be observed from his ignorance of the law of the sanctuary which forbade the offering of sacrifice except at Jerusalem. Shorn of its latest priestly additions, the original Hebrew tradition, derived from the more ancient Mesopotamian legend, reads as follows: God decides to destroy man because of his wickedness. But Noah found grace in the eyes of Jehovah. He is instructed to build an ark.

And Jehovah said unto Noah, Come thou and all thy house into the Ark; for thee I have seen righteous before me in this generation. Of every clean beast thou shalt take to thee seven and seven, the male and his female; and of the beast that are not clean two, the male and his female; of the fowl of the air, seven and seven; to keep seed alive upon the face of all the earth. For yet seven days, and I will cause it to rain upon the earth forty days and forty nights; and every living thing that I have made will I destroy from the face of the ground. And Noah did according to all that Jehovah commanded him.

And Noah went in, and his sons, and his wife, and his sons' wives with him, into the Ark, because of the waters of the flood (and the animals too). And it came to pass after the seven days that the waters of the flood were upon the earth. And the rain was upon the earth forty days and forty nights. And Jehovah shut him in, and the waters increased, and bore up the Ark, and it was lift up above the earth. All in whose nostrils was the breath of the spirit of life, of all that was in the dry land, died. And every living thing was destroyed which was upon the face of the ground, both man, and cattle, and creeping things, and fowl of the heaven; and they were destroyed from the earth; and Noah only was left, and they that were with him in the Ark, and the rain from heaven was restrained; and the waters returned from off the earth continually.

And it came to pass at the end of forty days, that Noah opened the window of the Ark which he had made; and he sent forth a raven, and it went forth to and fro, until the waters were dried up from off the earth. And he sent forth a dove from him, to see if the waters were abated from off the face of the ground; but the dove found no rest for the sole of her foot, and she returned unto him to the Ark, for the waters were on the face of the whole earth; and he put forth his hand and took her, and brought her in unto him into the Ark. And he stayed yet other seven days; and again he sent forth the dove out of the Ark; and the dove came in to him at eventide; and, lo, in her mouth an olive leaf plucked off; so Noah knew that the waters were abated from off the earth. And he stayed yet other seven days, and he sent forth the dove, and she returned not again unto him any more.

And Noah removed the covering of the Ark, and looked, and behold, the face of the ground was dried. And Noah builded an altar unto Jehovah; and took of every clean beast, and of every clean fowl, and offered burnt offerings on the altar. And Jehovah smelled the sweet savour; and Jehovah said in his heart, I will not again curse the ground any more for man's sake, for that the imagination of man's heart is evil from his youth; neither will I again smite any more every thing living, as I have done. While the earth remaineth, seed time and harvest, and cold and heat, and summer and winter, and day and night shall not cease.

The Hebrew story, expunged of its later additions, describes a local inundation brought on by rain which endured for two months. Noah, having been warned, builds an ark and saves himself, his family and their animals. By observing the behaviour of birds he determines the state of the flood. There is nothing in the story to suggest that the flood was anything more than a local inundation in Mesopotamia, the home of the Hebrews until 2150 B.C.

The combined Hebrew story, with its later additions which gave the dimensions of the ark (approximately those of a ship of 17,000 tons), its grounding upon Ararat and the placing of the bow in the clouds, led to considerable speculation amongst the early Christians who had adopted the Hebrew books as their own sacred writings. Noah's problems in housing and feeding the animals were discussed for centuries. Many suggestions were put forward as to how he kept apart those which were natural enemies. The question whether the animal pairs had been allowed to mate led to considerable concern until it was pointed out that, 'It was not a time for leisurely love-making.'

While it was known that a similar story of a great flood in Mesopotamia had been told by a Babylonian priest named Berossos, who wrote in about 300 B.C., it was long thought that the Hebrew account was the oldest. According to the later authors who quoted him, for his *History* has not survived, Berossos related that Xisuthros the tenth king of Babylon was warned of the coming of a great flood and ordered to build a ship and embark upon it with his family and friends, taking with him food, drink and a number of animals. From the dimensions given his ship must have been as large as the Queen Mary. After the flood had been upon the earth and was in time abated, he sent out a succession of birds, the last of which did not return. Upon looking out he found that the ship was stranded upon the side of some mountain. He quit his ship, and, having offered sacrifice, disappeared. His friends learned that he was in Armenia.

During the early part of the nineteenth century the ruins of a number of ancient cities in Mesopotamia were excavated and the cuneiform writing of the early Mesopotamian peoples was deciphered. In 1845 over 20,000 cuneiform tablets, most of them in fragments, were found at Nineveh in what had once been the royal library of the Assyrian kings. George Smith, a draughtsman employed by the British Museum to copy them, became so intrigued that he learned to read cuneiform. On one tablet he noticed the words, 'The ship rested on the mountains of Nisir,' followed by the description of the sending-out of a dove. This brief reference convinced him that he had stumbled upon a flood myth dating at least from the last year of the reign of Assurbanipal, 626 B.C., the creator of the library. By 1872 the fragments had been partly pieced together and classified as twelve episodes in the life of a king named Izdubar, who is now known as Gilgamesh.

Although these fragments were written in the comparatively late script of the Assyrians it was clear that they had been copied from far more ancient texts written in the Sumerian cuneiform characters. Since then a complete copy of a Sumerian version of the flood story has been found, thus carrying the written record back to 2000 B.C. The original flood hero is named Ziusudra. Comparison of the various copies that have come to light shows that even at this early date a number of versions of the legend were current in both the Semitic and Sumerian languages. Thus, long before the Hebrews left Mesopotamia for Canaan, a tradition of a terrible disaster was current amongst both races which had inhabited the land of the two rivers for thousands of years. That such a flood had occurred is attested by the lists of early Mesopotamian kings who are stated to have reigned before or after the flood.

While the later versions of this legend state that it was told to Gilgamesh, King of Ereck, by the flood survivor Ut-napishtim, the earlier versions of the Epic of Gilgamesh omit it, which suggests that its later inclusion in the epic was an afterthought.

The story told by Ut-napishtim is as follows.

Ut-napishtim describes how he was living at Shuruppak, an old city on the banks of the Euphrates, when the gods decided to send a great flood. He was warned:

> Throw down the house, build a ship.
> Forsake wealth, seek after life,
> Hate possessions, save thy life,
> Bring all seed of life into the ship,
> The ship which thou shalt build,
> The dimensions thereof shall be measured,
> The breadth and the length thereof shall be the same,
> Then launch it upon the ocean.*

He asks what he shall tell the people of the town to account for his actions and he is told to disarm their suspicions by saying that he is leaving in order to escape the wrath of the god Bel who hates him; but on them Bel will reign riches. Utnapishtim builds his ship, and on the seventh day when it is finished he makes a feast for his work people. On the ship, which is caulked with bitumen, a deck house of six stories is constructed, and into it he loads all he possesses, silver, gold, seed, cattle and handicraftsmen. For its navigation he appoints a sailor.

> The sender of (the flood) made a hail to fall at eventide;
> I watched the aspect of the (approaching) storm,
> Terror possessed me to look upon it,
> I went into the ship and shut the door.

The storm is vividly described in symbolic terms:

> As soon as something of dawn shone in the sky
> A black cloud from the foundations of heaven came up.
> Inside it the god Adad thundered,
> The gods Nabu and Sharru (i.e. Marduk) went before,
> Marching as messengers over high land and plain,
> Irragal (Nergal) tore out the post of the ship,
> En-urta went on, he made the storm to descend.
> The Annunnaki (the storm gods of the southern sky)
>   brandished their torches,
> With their glare they lighted up the land.
> The whirlwind (or cyclone) of Adad swept up to heaven,
> Every gleam of light was turned into darkness
> ... the land ... as if ... had laid it waste.
> A whole day long (the flood descended) ...

* The Babylonian Story of the Deluge and the Epic of Gilgamesh, British Museum Publication.

> Swiftly it mounted up . . . (the water) reached to the
>   mountains.
> (The water) attacked the people like a battle.
> Brother saw not brother.
> Men could not be known (or, recognized) in heaven,
> The gods were terrified at the cyclone,
> They shrank back and went up to the heaven of Anu,
> The gods crouched like a dog and cowered by the wall.

Ut-napishtim tells how: the 'gods bowed themselves and sat weeping. Their lips were shut tight (in distress)' and 'for six days and nights . . . the wind, the storm raged, and the cyclone overwhelmed the land.' The storm abates:

> When the seventh day came the cyclone ceased, the
>   storm and battle.
> Which had fought like an army.
> The sea became quiet, the grievous wind died down,
> The cyclone ceased.
> I looked on the day and voices were stilled,
> And all mankind were turned into mud,
> The land had been laid flat like a terrace.

He opened the air hole and: 'The light fell upon my cheek. I bowed myself. I sat down. I cried, my tears poured down over my cheeks.' He looked everywhere: 'At twelve points islands appeared and the ship grounded on the mountain of Nisir.' After seven days, he sent out a dove, a swallow and a raven. The first two returned as they had no place to alight. The raven fed on the carrion on the waters and came not back.

On the peak of the mountain, Ut-napishtim made a sacrifice and: 'The gods smelt the sweet savour. The gods gathered together like flies over him that sacrificed.' The gods argue about the sending of the flood, and as a sign that it will not be repeated, the great bow of Anu is placed in the sky, and Ut-napishtim goes to dwell far off beyond the mouth of the rivers.

This flood legend vividly describes a local flood of unusual magnitude of which Ut-napishtim's story is obviously an eye-witness account. That the Hebrew copyist omits so much detail suggests that he drew upon some other version, one of the many which probably gave only a second-hand description of the awesome sight.

The truth of Ut-napishtim's story of a severe local flood disaster in lower Mesopotamia was confirmed in 1929. While excavating successive layers of the Sumerian civilization at Ur of the Chaldees, Sir Leonard Woolley came suddenly at 150 feet (45 metres) from the surface on a layer of solid clean clay, 8 feet (2.4 metres) thick. It ceased as suddenly as it had begun and marked a complete break in the continuity of habitation. Above it commenced a pure Sumerian civilization. Below it, to the depth of 10 feet (3 metres), were relics of a mixed culture, partly Sumerian and partly of another earlier race. The texture of the clay showed that it had been laid by fresh water. No ordinary rising of the river could have left that much sediment. The flood that caused it must have been unparalleled in local history. The extent of this sediment, even if no flood legends had survived, would have indicated that a great inundation had occurred within less than 1,000 years of the first occupation of the site.

Some miles away at Kish a similar layer of mud was found at the same depth. Above it were two thinner layers of sediment indicating that the great flood had been followed within the next 500 years by lesser ones. Their severity may have been lessened by the precautions taken to strengthen river banks and dams after the previous experience.

The great flood may have occurred in about 4250 B.C. This date is arrived at both by the depth of the mud deposits and from a calculation of the order of the various local dynasties which are recorded as having reigned after the flood.

The great Mesopotamian deluge may have been caused by a combination of circumstances. The spring flood may have been of unusual volume as a result of a heavy winter snowfall; it is possible that the winter climate of the area may have been more severe then than later; a dam may have burst; a hurricane from the south, from where the storm may have come, accompanied by torrential rain, may have piled up the flood waters. An unusually severe inundation resulted.

Geological knowledge disproves the belief that the flood was unique, as is implied by the stranding of the ark on the 17,000 foot (5,180 metres) high mountain. Many parts of the world have suffered local submergence, hence the multitude of legends similar to those of Mesopotamia.

Eager as travellers were to find the ark, fear of international incidents in a highly sensitive area, the Soviet-Turkish frontier, deterred exploration. An American expedition was allowed to ascend Ararat in 1948. It found nothing. By a remarkable coincidence the American 'archaeologists' visited the area at the time when the Russians were exploding their first atomic bomb in the near-by Caucasus.

A French expedition went in search of the ark in August 1952. The story has been told by its leader Fernand Navarra.* Climbing the mountain's western face, they reached the snow line at 12,500 feet (3,800 metres). Above Ararat was dominated by thirty square miles of ice cap, 100 to 130 feet (30 to 40 metres) thick. A huge lake was engulfed by a glacier. Navarra tells the story.

In front of us was always the deep, transparent ice. A few more paces and suddenly, as if there were an eclipse of the sun, the ice became strangely dark. Yet the sun was still there and above us the eagle still circled. We were surrounded by whiteness, stretching into the distance, yet beneath our eyes was this astonishing patch of blackness within the ice, its outlines sharply defined.

Fascinated and intrigued, we began straightway to trace out its shape, mapping out its limits foot by foot: two progressively incurving lines were revealed, which were clearly defined for a distance of three hundred cubits, before meeting in the heart of the glacier. The shape was unmistakably that of a ship's hull: on either side the edges of the patch curved like the gunwales of a great boat. As for the central part, it merged into a black mass the details of which were not discernible.

Alas, the ship was no more than a peculiar rock formation which, seen from above, would have looked like the outline of a vessel which had been preserved for centuries in ice.

* *The Forbidden Mountain*, Macdonald, 1956.

WHERE WAS GOLGOTHA?

The unification of Jerusalem since 1967 has led to considerable exploration by Israeli archaeologists to disclose the secrets
of the Old City from which their ancestors were expelled
1,900 years ago. They have done a great deal to reveal the
courses of the walls by which Jerusalem was surrounded before the city was razed to the ground in A.D. 70. Their investigations are significant for Christians because of the possibility
that the course of the Second Wall may one day be determined.
That would help to solve the mystery of the site of Golgotha,
the place of Christ's execution and burial.

When the writers of the Gospels named the scene of the
crucifixion Golgotha – 'the place of a skull' – they may have
thought that they were describing a place outside the walls of
Jerusalem which was so well known that it required no further
elucidation. It is more probable that they were referring to a
place of which the location had already been forgotten.

Mark, the earliest Gospel, describes the scene of the crucifixion as 'the place of Golgotha, which is, being interpreted,
the place of a skull'. Matthew writes 'a place called Golgotha,
that is to say, a place of a skull'. Luke refers to it only as 'the
place which is called a skull'. The fourth Gospel says 'a place
called the place of a skull, which is called in the Hebrew
Golgotha'.

The Gospels do not state where Golgotha was nor do they
say, as is frequently assumed, that it was so called because it
was a place which looked like a skull. The word used in the
Greek language in which all the Gospels were written is
kranion. When the Gospels were translated into Latin the
word *calvaria* was employed, thus leading to the expression
Calvary. The Gospels give no indication of the position of
Golgotha except that it was 'nigh unto the city', that it was
a place visible from afar, that it was close to a busy main road
and that near it was a garden containing rock tombs. The unknown author of the Epistle to the Hebrews says that it was

58

'without the gate', but it is nowhere stated which city gate is indicated.

Nor do the Gospels give any hint of how the name Golgotha was derived. About this there are three theories: firstly, that the skull of Adam was buried there; secondly, that it was the public place of execution where skulls were left lying around; thirdly, that it resembled a human skull. There was an ancient Jewish tradition that the skull of Adam had been buried in Jerusalem, but there is no tradition or record that any one spot was used as a place of execution either by the Romans or by the Jews. The Gospels refer to the place of a skull, not of skulls. The usual idea that Golgotha was on a mound or hill has no basis beyond the statement that it was visible from afar, which might have meant the floor of one of the valleys on which Jerusalem was built.

As a result, after nineteen centuries, no one knows where Golgotha stood or how the name was derived, although a particular site, marked by the Church of the Holy Sepulchre, has been identified with the scene of the crucifixion since A.D. 326.

Considerable doubt has been expressed by those who have been searching for biblical sites in Palestine as to the authenticity of these holy places in Jerusalem, but it is agreed that none of the other sites which have from time to time been indicated have any greater claim to recognition. While it has been said that 'all search can only be in vain', the present site may be the actual site. It was usual for the Romans to select a conspicuous place for the execution of felons. A site alongside the main thoroughfare to the north fulfils this condition.

The usual reason for casting doubt on the authenticity of this traditional site is actually the least valid. Many visitors to Palestine have been concerned to find that the Church of the Holy Sepulchre is *within* the city of Jerusalem, although the Gospels imply that the crucifixion occurred outside the walls, 'nigh unto the city'. The present position of these holy places within the city is due to the inevitable changes that have occurred in the layout and extent of Jerusalem in the course of 1,900 years. Within about a century of the crucifixion the Holy City was twice totally destroyed, and since then it has seen many conquerors and rulers of different faiths.

Doubts about the position of Golgotha have arisen for a number of reasons, not the least of which is the difficulty of determining the course of the Second Wall of ancient Jerusalem beyond which the crucifixion most probably took place. This Second Wall was in position at that time. The site marked by the Church of the Holy Sepulchre may have been within it or without it. To accord with the Gospel tradition it must have been without it as that wall was then the most northerly defence of the city.

There is good reason to think that the crucifixion took place to the north of the city; the other three sides of Jerusalem are so precipitous and broken by ravines that no one spot could have contained a concourse of people as is implied by Luke. A position north of the walls would have been equally applicable if Jesus had been led forth after the trial before Pilate from either the fortress of the Antonia by the Temple or from Herod's Palace, the Citadel, on the west of the city.

Gabbatha, or the pavement, as the place of judgement is called, was probably the guardroom in the basement of the Antonia, a large, pillared hall, its flagstones worn down by the legionaries' hobnailed boots. It exists still beneath the Convent of the Sisters of Zion.

No attempt was made in A.D. 326, when the site now marked by the Church of the Holy Sepulchre was located, to suggest that its recognition was due to the preservation of Christian tradition. It appears to have been identified as the site of a former Jewish cemetery.

There is no evidence that the early Christians venerated the place of the crucifixion. The Church historian, Eusebius, writing before the discovery of the site, says that pilgrims came 'to hear the story of Jerusalem' and 'to worship on the Mount of Olives'. None of the early Christian Fathers refers to the position of Golgotha. The manner in which the present site was chosen in 326 suggests that it was not previously known and that its identification was the result of a guess.

The search for the actual site was first instituted in A.D. 326 on the orders of the Emperor Constantine, the first Roman emperor to recognize the Christian Church. After the Council of Nicaea he declared that the place of the resurrection should be made 'conspicuous and an object of veneration'. A spot was in consequence selected by Bishop Macarius of Jerusalem, and on excavation a number of rock tombs were discovered and, some 280 feet (85 metres) to the east, a cistern containing three 'crosses'. One of these tombs was chosen, how we do not know, as the one in which Jesus had been lain and one of the crosses, or baulks of timber containing nails, was identified by its healing powers as the true cross.

While no eye-witness account of these discoveries has been preserved, our chief source of information is Eusebius, the Church historian who was at that time Bishop of Caesarea in Palestine. In his *Life of Constantine*, he says that on the excavation of the selected site 'immediately, and contrary to all expectations, the venerable and hallowed monument of Our Lord's Resurrection became visible', but he makes no mention of the finding of the crosses or of the identification of Golgotha itself.

According to another tradition, the Empress Helena, the mother of Constantine, came herself to Jerusalem to conduct the search and her identification of the site is said to have been accomplished with 'great difficulty'. According to one account, it was brought about by a miraculous revelation, and in another by the information supplied by a Jew who derived his information from family records. It is said that Helena, upon her arrival at Jerusalem, charged Macarius to search for the cross; at a loss to know what to do, he offered prayers and was answered by a miraculous revelation. In another account the place of the crucifixion was indicated to Helena by 'signs from heaven'. A pilgrim to Jerusalem in 754, named Wildebald, makes the remarkable statement that: 'Calvary was formerly outside the city but the Empress arranged that place so that it should be within the city.'

After the discovery of the sepulchre and the cistern containing the crosses, the rock in between was cut away to form a square mass of bare rock which was identified as Golgotha itself. No attempt was made to suggest that it looked like a skull, but beneath it a cave was found which was named as the burial place of the skull of Adam, suggesting that this is the most likely derivation of the word Golgotha.

The sepulchre itself fully conformed to a tomb of that period. It was a rock-tomb entered by a low doorway. The tomb chamber was 7 feet in length, 6 in breadth and 8 feet high (2.1 by 1.8 by 2.4 metres). On one side was an arched recess 6 feet (2.1 metres) long and 2 feet (.6 metre) from the floor. A semi-circular recess was cut around it and the other tombs which were also found; above was built the Church of the Resurrection and to the east the great Church of Constantine. The rock of Golgotha, marked by a cross, stood between the two buildings.

The churches built by Constantine were destroyed in 614 on the capture of Jerusalem by the Persians. The Persians were soon expelled by the Romans of the Eastern Empire who rebuilt the churches, but within a few years Jerusalem passed into Arab hands on the Mohammedan conquest of Palestine. The churches were again destroyed in 1010. They were rebuilt and enlarged by the Crusaders, and the Church of the Holy Sepulchre remained intact until 1808 when it was accidentally destroyed by fire. The present buildings date from 1810.

Since archaeologists have attempted to locate biblical sites in Palestine, a number of places around Jerusalem have been identified as 'the place of a skull'. On the presumption that Golgotha meant a place which looked like a skull, an outcrop of rock at Jeremiah's Grotto, some distance to the north of the ancient city, was picked upon in 1842. It was supported by General Gordon, of Khartoum fame, and became known as 'Gordon's Calvary', or the 'Gordon Tomb'.

While this little hill, which contains a rock-tomb, does now resemble a skull, it does not necessarily follow that it looked the same 2,000 years ago. Readers may recall that when the film *Cleopatra* was made, it was found necessary to take a sphinx to Egypt as the real one had become so weathered by time that it no longer looked as it had done 2,000 years before.

The reliability or otherwise of the identification of the site now marked by the Church of the Holy Sepulchre rests upon the determination of the course of the Second Wall, built by King Herod to enclose what was then the northern suburb. The earlier First Wall, on its north side, ran from the Citadel on the west to the Temple on the east.

The second Wall, according to the Jewish historian Josephus, who was born in Jerusalem and was an eye witness to the Roman siege, 'started (on the west) from the Gate in the First Wall, which is called Gennath, and encircled the slope towards the north and went up as far as the Antonia'. It was a short wall defended by only fourteen towers. Its western end is determined by the historian's reference to the gate to the gardens (Gennath). Portions of an early wall have been found on the north of David Street, on the line the wall may have taken. The predominance of Arab shops in that area makes it too sensitive for excavation.

It seems likely that the wall skirted the head of the central valley which in Herodian times ran north to south through the central part of the city. That may have caused its zigzag course. It appears to have jutted north, turned eastwards, reverted to the north and run eastwards again. The Church of the Holy Sepulchre stands at approximately the spot where the wall made its first, sudden eastward turn.

Did the site so identified lie inside or outside the wall? To fulfil the required conditions it must have been without the city's gate. A gate may have been placed at that spot to link up with the main road to the north. To have built it where the wall turned sharply could have had military advantages, providing an angle by which it could have been overlooked from two sides.

Jesus was crucified near an escarpment or cliff containing rock-tombs and enclosed within a garden, possibly part of the gardens to which the Gate Gennath led. Therein lies the paradox, the difficulty in identifying the site. The Jews would not have permitted burials within the city. That conclusion firmly positions the site outside the city's new wall. On the other hand, would the Jews have allowed their wall to be dominated by a cliff? Surely Herod would have enclosed it within the wall?

One final point seems to indicate that Golgotha must have been further to the north, or possibly elsewhere. The women who wished to anoint the body on the Sunday morning went by stealth, hoping not to be recognized as adherents of the crucified king. They would hardly have dared to approach a tomb close to the city's walls and overlooked by them.

The true site of Golgotha will probably always remain a mystery.

HOLY SHROUD OF CHRIST?

Jesus died quickly on the cross. Mark, the earliest Gospel, says that his body was wrapped in a linen cloth before burial in a rock-tomb. Its door was closed with a stone.

The possibility that this linen cloth may have survived (and may be preserved in Turin Cathedral) is derived from a number of ancient references. The Christian pilgrim, St Nino, an Armenian princess who died in A.D. 338, mentions 'shrouds of Christ' as existing in Jerusalem. Eusebius, the fourth-century Church historian, states that the Empress Helena, the mother of Constantine, the first emperor to recognize Christianity, who caused the Holy Sepulchre to be rediscovered, gathered certain holy relics and took them to Constantinople. Eusebius omits mention of a shroud. The fourth-century historian, Nicephorus Callistus, records that the Empress Pulcheria (A.D. 399–453) recovered certain sacred linen cloths from the Empress Eudokia and placed them in the new basilica of St Maria of the Blackernae in Constantinople. The French bishop, Aroulf, and St John Damascene, refer to linen shrouds called sudarium in Constantinople in the seventh and eight centuries.

Several equally uncertain references suggest the existence of a shroud or shrouds in Constantinople in the twelfth and thirteenth centuries. An English pilgrim says he saw such a cloth amongst the imperial treasures in 1150, and five years later its presence in the Cathedral of St Sophia is attested by the Benedictine Abbot Soermudarson. A more definite reference comes from William of Tyre, who states that he and King Amalric I of Jerusalem were shown, by the Emperor Manuel Commenus, the shroud of Jesus, preserved in the imperial treasury. Another visitor, Nicholas Mesarites, speaks of seeing, at a church in the city, 'the burial cloths of Christ; they are of linen and still fragrant of the ointments; they defied corruption, having clothed the naked, myrrh-strewn body.'

Robert of Clari, the chronicler of the Fourth Crusade, which captured Constantinople, states that in 1203 he saw the shroud in the Blackernae Church where it was exhibited every Friday. The figure of Christ was easily discernible. He says that the shroud disappeared from the church during the sack of the city by the Crusaders and nobody knew what had become of it.

Robert of Clari's statement that the 'figure of Christ was easily discernible' is the only link between the linen cloth which appears to have been exhibited in Constantinople prior to 1204, and the one bearing the image of Christ which seems to have made its appearance in France after the return of the Crusaders.

The Emperor Baldwin, writing to St Louis, king of France, in June 1247, refers to 'a portion of the burial cloth' as having come to France. Richard de Cluny states that the shroud was taken to Compiègne.

There are two versions of the shroud's arrival in France. In one, it fell as loot from Constantinople to Otto de la Roche, captain of the Marquis de Montferrat's soldiers. He sent it to his father. He gave it in 1206 to Amaedus, the bishop of Besançon, in whose cathedral it was exhibited every Sunday until 1349, when the cathedral was destroyed by fire. In the other version, the shroud was given to the Lords of Charny by Bishop Garnier. A document preserved in the Bibliothèque de Paris states: 'Geoffrey de Charny, Knight and Count de Charny, Lord of Lirey, obtained for his services from King Philip of Valois the Holy Shroud of Our Lord (and other relics) that they might be placed in a church he wished to build in honour of Mary Virgin.' This gift occurred probably in 1349, for Philip VI, to whom Geoffrey de Charny acted as standard bearer, died in 1350. Geoffrey himself was killed by the English at the Battle of Poitiers in 1356.

A shroud appears to have been in existence in the church at Lirey in Champagne in 1350. Some attempts have been made to link this Lirey shroud with the one supposed to have been in Besançon Cathedral prior to 1349. In the fire in the spring of that year, most of the cathedral's relics vanished, including the shroud. Three years later a painted copy was found in the rebuilt cathedral. This copy was preserved at Besançon until 1749 when it was burnt by order, but not before several copies had been made from it. The original shroud, it is claimed, was taken from the cathedral at the time of the fire by Geoffrey de Charny, who, in order to conceal his sacrilege, pretended that he had brought it himself from Constantinople.

The possibly true history of the shroud now preserved in Turin Cathedral commences in 1355. In that year Bishop Henri of Poitiers forbade the canons of Lirey to expose the shroud for public veneration. When the shroud was again exposed in 1389 it aroused the anger of Peter D'Arcis, the bishop of Troyes, in whose diocese Lirey lay. His intervention led to an unseemly row. It may have been caused by the bishop's indignation at the veneration of a spurious relic or perhaps by his jealousy of the canons' possession of such a lucrative asset. Geoffrey de Charny, it seems, in 1353 circumvented the bishop by dealing directly with the schismatic pope at Avignon, who gave his approbation for the building of the church at Lirey to house the shroud.

When in 1389 Peter D'Arcis threatened the canons of Lirey with excommunication if they did not withdraw the shroud from exposition, they and Geoffrey II of Charny implored the king of France and the papal legate, Peter of Thury, to intervene. Both men gave permission for exposition. When the bishop protested, the pope upheld the validity of the legate's approval and enjoined Peter D'Arcis to 'eternal silence' on the matter.

Peter then addressed a memorandum to the pope. He accused the canons of obtaining papal permission by underhand methods. He branded them as avaricious double-dealers and he declared that the shroud was a painting, a fraud exposed thirty-four years before by Henri of Poitiers who had conducted an investigation. The canons, he said, had kept the cloth in hiding when he had tried to secure it.

Peter D'Arcis's words about the alleged deception by the canons of Lirey are of considerable importance in respect to the history of the Turin shroud. He states: 'And lastly, after painstaking study and exploration of this matter, he [Henri

66

of Poiters] found the deception, and how the cloth had been artificially painted, a fact confirmed by the very man who had painted it; that it was the work of a human being and had not been miraculously made or bestowed.' There is some doubt of Peter's exact meaning here. The Latin verb *depingere* could have meant 'to paint' or 'to paint from', i.e. make a copy, and it is claimed that the words 'the man who painted it' could mean someone 'who had made a copy of it'. It is possible that the original shroud and the copy alleged to have been painted at Besançon may have become mixed up.

As a result of this objection, the king of France on 4 August 1389 withdrew his permission for the exposition of the shroud, but the canons continued to venerate it. They appealed to Pope Clement VII, who instructed them to state at every exposition that there was no question of the cloth being the true shroud, but only a copy. He extolled the canon's piety and refrained from branding them as charlatans. A few months later, in June 1390, Clement referred to the cloth in words of commendation in a bill of indulgencies, and he took the bishop of Troyes to task, requiring him to remove all obstacles to the exposition of the cloth under pain of excommunication. Once again the canons were ordered to state that the cloth was only a copy of the true shroud.

Thus it seems that in the opinion of its medieval owners and their jealous opponent, the image on the shroud was a painting, a *figure* as such works were then called, a picture 'not made with hands', the inspired work of an artist who had painted it either from the true shroud itself or who, by divine guidance, had faithfully portrayed Christ's passion on a linen sheet. Peter D'Arcis continued to claim that the image had been faked by a fourteenth-century artist. The shroud's supporters claim that the medieval owners and church dignitaries were wrong. The image on the shroud, only fully disclosed by photography in 1898 and 1931, is not a painting. It is the impression of the body of a man who had been crucified, a particular man.

The history of the shroud after 1390 is clearer. During the Hundred Years' War it was moved from one place of safety to another. The canons of Lirey gave it in 1418 to Count Humbert de Roche, whose widow refused to return it in 1443 with other relics. Some years later it was bequeathed by the last of the de Charny family to the wife of Louis I, Duke of Savoy, in whose family its ownership has since remained. Pope Sixtus IV authorized Louis to build a chapel at Chambéry to house it. In 1516 the shroud appears to have been at Lierre in Belgium, for the artist Albrecht Durer made a copy of it. His picture has some bearing on the question of the shroud's authenticity.

The shroud was returned to Chambéry where, on the night of 4 December 1532, it was damaged by the fire which swept the chapel. The historian Pingonius says that it was removed by four men who broke open the silver shrine containing it, but not before it had become marked by eight symmetrical burns from the molten silver and by the water used to cool the shrine. It was mended by nuns and was transferred in 1572 to Turin.

The confused history of this Turin shroud lacks corroboration. The early records indicate only that a number of sacred cloths were venerated in Constantinople, perhaps even in Jerusalem, as the Holy Shroud. The only link with the one which appears to have found its way to France in the thirteenth century is the early reference to a naked image, the peculiarity of the Turin shroud. The French shroud seems to have disappeared in 1349 and to have reappeared at Lirey, if the Besançon and Lirey shrouds are identical. The shroud's lack of definite history prior to 1355 is not surprising. It would be remarkable if such a relic had been documented and attested throughout its history.

According to its supporters, the authenticity of the Turin shroud does not, and indeed cannot, rely upon history; the circumstantial and scientific evidence is so strong, they say, that it overcomes the historical lapses. Until 1898 the shroud was accepted as a painting on linen, of ancient and miraculous origin, a likeness. Then a startling discovery put an entirely different complexion on the matter.

During an exposition of the shroud, an amateur photographer, Secunda Pia, was allowed to take a photograph in daylight. The result was almost unbelievable. To explain it we need to move ahead to 1931 when the shroud was photographed again, under far more favourable conditions, by the professional photographer Giuseppe Enrie. When the photographs were developed and printed, they disclosed the full figure of a man – in negative image. The photographic negative had all the characteristics of a positive, and the print of a negative. It showed that the image on the cloth had all the characteristics of a negative. The light values were reversed. The relieved areas, those most exposed to the light such as the forehead, nose and chest, were dark, while the depressed areas, such as the eye sockets and neck, were light. Only the bloodstains were natural; they were dark carmine on the cloth and came up light on the photographer's plate.

These photographs threw doubt on the long-accepted theory that the image had been painted. What ancient or medieval artist, it was asked, could have conceived and executed a negative image, a painting in reverse which conformed accurately to anatomical detail?

Taken by artificial light, Enrie's photographs show the tiniest details. They depict the image of a man of majestic mien, 5 foot 11 inches (1.8 metres) tall, long-haired, bearded, narrow-faced and completely naked. Marks on the body prove that the man had died by crucifixion, the Roman form of execution abolished in A.D. 337. The body is marked by lacerations, contusions, swellings, punctures, perforations, deep incisions, by bloodstains in which the blood has both run and coagulated, and by nails driven through the wrists and feet. Even more striking are the rivulets of coagulated blood on the forehead and the deep wound in the side, striking corroboration, it is claimed, that the body the shroud enclosed was that of Christ, the man who wore a crown of thorns and was pierced in the side by a spear.

The shroud, when extended to its full 14 foot 3 inches (4.3 metres), shows the front and back of a man, just as if he had been laid on one half with the other half drawn up over his head and extended to his feet. When the body was removed, the image remained impressed on the cloth.

The linen itself appears to be very ancient. It is of herringbone pattern similar to early Syrian fabrics which are characterized by the same diagonal method of weaving.

The scientists who have examined the enlarged photographs

say that there are no traces of pigment or brushmarks on the fabric, the threads of which would have adhered if the image had been painted. The likelihood that the linen is ancient does not, of course, provide proof of the authenticity of the image, for a medieval artist might have obtained an old piece of linen. But the objections to this theory are equally convincing. No medieval faker would have realized that his fraud required an ancient piece of linen, for no critic then would have questioned that detail. No medieval faker would have dared to paint Christ in the nude.

Tests made to explore death by crucifixion suggest that no artist could have so faithfully recorded the peculiar characteristics of that forgotten method of execution. It would have been equally impossible for an ancient or medieval artist to have created a body conforming to anatomical structure so faithfully. For example, the circulation of the blood was unknown until Harvey's discovery in 1628.

The body is lying on its back with its hands crossed in front, left hand over right wrist, and feet crossed, left over right. Rivulets of blood have trickled down the forehead as they might have done during life had it been punctured by thorns. There are bruises on the face and both back and front are heavily scarred by small dark clots, such as might have been inflicted by scourging with leather thongs tipped with metal. They appear to have been wielded by two scourgers striking upwards from the loins.

The wound in the hand is not in the palm. It is in the wrist through the exact spot where a nail driven from the inner side would emerge. The trickles of blood flow up the forearm as they would have done in the case of a man crucified with his arms stretched above his head at an angle of sixty-five degrees; they would have coagulated during life. The position of the wound in the wrist rather than in the palm is extraordinary, yet entirely realistic. It is the only spot where nails could have supported the body. The weight would have torn the hands away if the nails had been driven through the palms, the traditional and always depicted detail of the crucifixion.

No artist could have known, as the Romans knew, that the wrist was the correct place for the nail. Another strange feature emerges from examination of the hands. Neither thumb is visible. Experiments have shown that when a nail is driven through that particular spot it cuts the nerve, causing the thumb to flex inside the hand. It is another detail an artist could not have known. The wounds in the feet conform no less to reality. An experiment carried out on the foot of a corpse showed that the spike had been driven through the precise spot to give perfect support. The displacement of the thigh and knee show that the feet were nailed together.

The wound in the side conforms exactly, it is claimed, to the lance-thrust after death, described in John's Gospel. It appears on the image's left side which, as the image is reversed, indicates that it pierced the right side, as is always depicted in Christian art. There is an extensive flow of blood and serum which conforms with John's statement that from the wound came blood and water. Every detail conforms with the Gospel's statement; the lance struck slightly upwards, slipping over the sixth rib and fifth intercostal space behind which the heart line lies, and penetrating the heart at the right auricle which is almost always filled with blood after death, and the surrounding sac which is filled with pericardial fluid, thus giving forth the mixture of blood and water. They formed the characteristic stains on the linen. The side wound depicted on the linen conforms exactly, it is claimed, to the leaf-like shape of the *lancea* carried by the Roman auxiliaries.

The wounds, blood stains and trickles seem to conform to death by crucifixion and to the crucifixion of a particular person, the details of whose death are recorded in the Gospels. While most of the wounds are typical of anyone's death by crucifixion, one particular collection, the marks on the forehead caused by the crown of thorns, identify that person as Jesus, the shroud's supporters claim.

A great deal has been learned about crucifixion as a form of execution. There were two methods, the slow and the quick death.

The victim was secured to the cross-beam either by ropes or by nails. The cross-beam (the *patibulum*) was then pulled up and secured to the upright post (the *stipes*) fixed in the ground, the usual height of the cross-beam being about 10 feet

(3 metres), thus leaving the victim's feet raised 2 feet (.6 metres) above the ground. The feet were nailed to the upright post to give support to the body. Two extra methods of support were sometimes added, when it was desired to prolong the agony. With these in position the victim could linger for days. The *sedile* provided a seat and the *suppendaneum* or foot-rest gave additional support to the foot-spike. Without the *sedile* death resulted, as has been proved by the experiments carried out in the Nazi concentration camps, in between three to six hours.

Thus death could be lingering or swift, but in either case was accompanied by fearful agony. With the arms extended above the head, the cramping position resulted in acute shortness of breath and the victim struggled continually to raise and lower himself, his body see-sawing, sagging from the pierced wrists and rising on the transfixed feet. This continual pulling up and down led to extreme exhaustion and death. If it was desired to finish the victim off, the legs were shattered, thus removing support from the feet and increasing the weight on the arms with consequent contraction of the breathing and the prevention of the circulation of the blood. A lance thrust to the heart was given as a merciful *coup de grâce*. According to the Gospels, Jesus was accorded the quick death, for Pilate is recorded as marvelling that he had died after only three hours of torture.

There is considerable argument about the actual cause of death by crucifixion. There are two theories: asphyxia and circulatory failure. That has been tested by experiments wherein medical students were hung from the wrists and their breathing and circulation measured. Suspended without support, they lost consciousness in six to twelve minutes, owing to the sinking of the blood to the lower extremities. Death would have resulted from insufficient blood reaching the heart and brain. If they were allowed to rest their feet for twenty-second periods, the circulation returned to normal. The continued strain would eventually have led to complete exhaustion and death.

How could the image of the crucified body have been imparted to the linen cloth? According to one theory it was produced by ammoniac vapours coming in contact with the aloes of the linen shroud. It was found impossible to obtain a negative image by daubing a plastic bust with tincture of aloes and pressing it on linen.

Direct contact with a perspiring body is a more plausible theory. But it fails to account for the image's lack of distortion. That could have been achieved only if the shroud had been laid over the body, not wrapped around it, usual in burial. This lack of distortion is in favour of the shroud's authenticity. Jesus was accorded only temporary burial to conform with the Jewish ritual custom. The shroud may thus have been only laid on the body.

The image shows no signs of decomposition or corruption. That suggests that the body was removed from the linen before that stage had set in. Yet the impressed image bears all the signs of *rigor mortis* which had not passed before the body was freed from the cloth. If it had passed the image would have lost its clarity and precision, as the linen folds conformed to the shape of the body.

Objections to the shroud's authenticity include the claim that the negative character of the image, which appears to point so strongly in its favour, resulted from the nuns, who repaired the cloth after the fire of 1532, reversing it by mistake. But Durer's picture from the shroud's image, made sixteen years before the fire, also depicts it as a negative. Another objection suggests that a fourteenth-century artist bedaubed a statue of Christ with colouring matter and pressed it on to linen. This theory presumes the existence of a life-sized naked statue of Christ, unknown and inconceivable in the history of medieval art, when there was no realistic interpretation of the human form. The possibility that the faker used a human corpse is denied on the ground that such a deception was far too cunning for a fourteenth-century artist.

Another objection dismisses the negative character of the image as being the result of the changes in colour caused by time. This theory is supported by the picture painted from the image by Paleolto in 1598. It shows the image in two colours, pale yellow and red. People who were allowed to see the shroud in the fifteenth and sixteenth centuries speak of the image as being so vivid that the blood seemed freshly shed.

The image is now dark and not easily recognizable, except by photography. Why should the shroud have retained its brilliance for fifteen centuries and become almost invisible in four? That is exactly what we should expect from a fourteenth-century fabrication.

What is the answer to the problem posed by the shroud of Turin? Can it be the actual shroud of Christ miraculously preserved through nineteen centuries? The scientific evidence seems to rule out the theory that the image is a painting. It is too accurate, too exact a negative. No artist could have reproduced the human body with a fidelity to arouse the astonishment of modern doctors. The image appears to be impressed on linen by the body of a crucified man. But who? The circumstantial evidence points to the body of Christ. The Gospels say it was wrapped in a linen sheet and placed in a rock-tomb, from which Christ rose on the third day, presumably leaving the linen shroud behind him.

There is a fatal objection to the preservation and existence of a shroud of Christ. There was no empty tomb. The women on the third day went to the wrong tomb – one of many honey-combing a rocky cliff.

Mark, the earliest Gospel, tells the likely story. The others improved and added to his story to suit the development of the legend of the resurrection of Jesus. According to Mark, three women watch the burial. They return at dawn on the third day to anoint the body. They see a young man sitting by the door of a tomb. He may have been a grave-digger, excavating a new tomb. Recognizing them as followers of Jesus, he says, 'He is not here. See there his place,' pointing to another tomb. The women do not enter any tomb. Panic-stricken at being recognized as friends of a man who had been executed by the Romans for treason, for having set himself up as a usurper king, the women flee, trembling and astonished. They 'said nothing to any man because they feared'.

Would the women have kept silent if they believed that the tomb was empty, the body gone? When they told the disciples they were disbelieved. Eventually, after the disciples had come to believe that Jesus had appeared to some of them, the two stories merged to create the resurrection story.

In April 1973 it was announced that the piece of linen housed in Turin Cathedral would be subjected to scientific tests. Authorization for the testing of the fabric was given jointly by Pope Paul VI, Cardinal Pellegrino, and the ducal House of Savoy. These tests may establish whether or not the image is a painting, and the approximate date when the flax, woven into linen, grew. They cannot convince sceptics that it is the Holy Shroud of Christ. Between A.D. 6 and 70 the Romans crucified thousands of Jews, including several would-be Messiahs.

THE EDICT OF CAESAR

A Roman edict found in Palestine, and dated about A.D. 50, decreeing death for the violation of tombs, is a remarkable piece of evidence. Some twenty years earlier a Jewish sect had gained its impetus from the belief that its founder had risen from the dead. The Christians' sceptical opponents attributed the story to an act of tomb robbery.

The marble slab on which the edict was engraved in Greek was found near Nazareth in 1870. In 1878 it came into the possession of a scholar named Froehner. It remained unknown until 1930 when the Biblical scholar, Franz Cumont, drew attention to it. Its text was published by M. P. Charlesworth.* The English translation reads:

Ordinance of Caesar. It is my pleasure that graves and tombs remain undisturbed in perpetuity for those who have made them for the cult of their ancestors or children or members of their house. If however any man lay information that another has either demolished them or has in any way extracted the buried or has maliciously transferred them to other places in order to wrong them, or has displaced the sealing or other stones, against such a one I order that a trial be instituted, as in respect of the gods, so in regard to the cult of mortals. For it shall be much more obligatory to honour the buried. Let it be absolutely for-

* *Documents Illustrating the Reigns of Claudius and Nero*, Cambridge University Press, 1939.

bidden for anyone to destroy them. In case of contravention I desire that the offender be sentenced to capital punishment on charge of violation of sepulture.

Professor A. Momigliano (*L'Opera dell'Imperatore Claudio*, 1932) dates the edict by internal evidence to the reign of Claudius, the Roman emperor who reigned from A.D. 41 to 54. He detects increasing severity in the policy of Claudius towards the Jews, and believes that Christianity was the cause of the adoption of this harsher attitude. Detestation of the Christian Messianists is shown by historians who wrote after the Great Revolt of the Jews which broke out in A.D. 66 and took four years to suppress. Jerusalem was besieged and destroyed, its Temple burned to the ground. Huge numbers of Jews were killed or captured. Thousands were crucified. The pro-Roman Jewish historian Josephus blames the Zealots and the Messianists equally for causing the disastrous war.

Tacitus (*Annals* XX 44) records that by the death of Christus: 'the sect of which he was the founder received a blow, which for a time checked the growth of a dangerous superstition; but it broke out again and spread with increasing vigour, not only in Judaea, the soil that gave its birth, but even in the city of Rome.' He refers also to the persecution of 'those hated for their abominations, called Christians', during the reign of Claudius. Suetonius, the biographer of the Caesars, says that the Jews who 'made great tumult because of Christus' were expelled from Rome in A.D. 49. He adds that under Nero in A.D. 64: 'Punishment was also inflicted on the Christians, a class of men given to a new and mischievous superstition.'

Claudius, Dio Cassius records, closed the synagogues in Rome to prevent seditious discussion, and warned the Jews of Alexandria not to entertain Jews from Syria (of which Palestine was part), if they did not wish to be considered abettors of a 'pest which threatens the whole world'. He may have meant the Christians. The Apostle Paul, while in Thessalonica, and his companions were accused as men 'who have turned the world upside down, who did not obey the laws of Caesar, saying, There is another King, one Jesus'.

Yet another reference indicates Roman hostility to Christianity. Preparing the final assault on the Temple in

Jerusalem in A.D. 70, General Titus called a staff conference to debate its fate. According to the fifth-century Christian writer, Sulpicius Severus, while some officers argued that the reputation of Rome would suffer if so famous a sanctuary was destroyed, Titus voted for its destruction because it was a source of inspiration to both Judaism and Christianity. The credibility of his statement is enhanced by the fact that the pro-Roman Jewish historian Josephus, on the contrary, shows Titus as anxious to save the temple and shocked by its accidental destruction. Severus, it is thought, would not have dared to contradict Josephus, whose books were popular with the Christians, unless he felt he was drawing upon what he believed to be an impeccable authority, possibly the lost books of Tacitus.

By the time Severus wrote, Josephus had been conveniently turned, by the 'editing' of his works, into a favourable witness to Christianity.

Roman hostility to the Christians supports the view that the edict was intended to prevent the recurrence of an act which the Romans believed had resulted from tomb robbery and which had given the new sect its impetus. They had reason to be suspicious of the Christians. Jesus had been put to death for treason, for acclaiming himself in a Roman province as the king of the Jews. The *Lex Juliana Majestatis* of 48 B.C. made it an offence punishable by death to engage in any activity against the Roman emperor without whose consent no king could be proclaimed. Jesus's followers had campaigned throughout the empire, in Egypt, Asia Minor, Greece and in Rome itself, preaching the glorious return of their dead Messiah. The Romans were fully aware of the implications of the Jewish Messianic hope. The Messiah would be a king and a redeemer, who would overthrow the enemies of Israel and re-establish the Jewish kingdom, a political saviour. The disciples, we may recall, chose the dramatic moment of Jesus's apparent reappearance from the dead, to inquire whether it was his intention to 'restore the kingdom to Israel'. One of Jesus's intimate disciples, Simon, was a Zealot, a member of the extreme nationalist party.

Mark, who wrote the earliest Gospel, following the fall of

Jerusalem, was careful to disguise Simon's party affiliation, describing him as 'the canaanite', and omitting to add, as he usually does when using an Aramaic term, 'which is the Zealot'. It was not incompatible with Jesus's mission to have a Zealot as a friend. He is never shown castigating the Zealots, as he does the other politico-religious Jewish parties. Faced with the burning question, the Zealot test of loyalty to their cause, about the tribute money, Jesus is made to return what is thought to have been an equivocal answer. Asked whether or not it was lawful to pay tribute to Caesar, he replied emphatically in terms which to his interrogators were abundantly clear. He said, 'Render unto God' the things which were His – the produce of the Holy Land, and 'to Caesar' the things that were his – the coins that bore his image.

The late Professor S. G. F. Brandon found many affinities between the Christians and the Zealots.* The Jewish Christians, he believed, fought alongside the Zealots in their holy war against Rome and perished with them. The Acts of the Apostles, the story of the movement following the death of Jesus, singularly omits to mention the fate of the men who had walked and talked with him. Were their subsequent activities too embarrassing for Gentile Christians to record?

Had the Christians been the harmless religious fanatics the New Testament writers would have us believe, the Romans would not have persecuted them. They were tolerant of all religions. They allowed the Jews to opt out of the state cult, the worship of the divine emperor, permitting them to sacrifice 'for' rather than 'to' that symbol of political cohesion.

The Romans persecuted the Christian Messianists, as they did the Zealots and other Jewish extremists, fearing them as a disturbing influence in the tranquillity of Judaea, the link between the imperial provinces of Egypt and Syria.

The Emperor Claudius made a belated attempt to discourage tomb robbery. His edict came twenty years too late, after the birth of the religion which 300 years later overcame the Roman state and eventually overran the world.

The edict is a remarkable archaeological discovery corroborating Roman hostility to the Christians.

* Jesus and the Zealots, Manchester University Press, 1967.

THE BONES OF ST PETER

The tradition that the Apostle Peter was martyred in Rome during the Neronian persecution of A.D. 64 rests on the statement made about thirty years later to the Corinthians by St Clement of Rome. He says that Peter, 'having dwelt among us, having borne witness, departed to his appointed place of glory'. Peter's presence in Rome is inferred from the use of the name Babylon as a soubriquet for Rome, a usual Christian practice, in the First Epistle of St Peter, and by the unchallenged claim of the Roman pontiffs to primacy as Peter's successors. His death in Rome is supported by the early reference to a 'trophy' or memorial marking his place of martyrdom. As the centuries progressed it came to be believed that this spot on the Vatican hill marked his grave.

Search for Peter's grave was instituted in 1939 as a result of Pope Pius XI's desire to be buried amongst the popes and princes beneath the high altar of St Peter's. The investigation to find a suitable site for his tomb beneath the crypt revealed the pavement of Old St Peter's, the basilica built between A.D. 326 and 335 by Constantine, the first Roman emperor to recognize Christianity. Excavation disclosed a layer of ancient graves, the pagan cemetery of Roman times. In the foundations of an old wall, directly beneath the high altar, was found a heap of human bones, the headless skeleton of a person of advanced age, powerful build and undetermined sex. Belief that they may be the bones of St Peter rests on the contributions of archaeology and history.

In Roman times the Vatican hill lay beyond the city's limits, and across the Tiber. The southern slope of the hill, short of the public road, the Ostian Way, was used as a cemetery for the burial of rich and poor. The flat ground to the south east of the road became incorporated into the imperial gardens, which enclosed the Vatican circus. It was used by Nero for the torture and slaughter of the 'vast multitude' of Christians, as Tacitus describes them. The bodies of these felons, foreigners who had refused to honour the imperial cult, were probably thrown into the Tiber. Whether Peter's could have escaped that fate has been questioned. Its preservation requires the presence of a sympathizer possessing the influence or money to bribe the executioners. Such a man would have risked arrest as an adherent of an illegal organization.

It seems that some such person intervened because a century later, between A.D. 160 and 170, a shrine, the aedicula as it became called, was erected, not on the Vatican plain but on the slope of the hill, amongst the hundreds of sepulchral monuments covering the hillside. It may have replaced an earlier 'trophy'. It was seen by a priest named Gaius about A.D. 200 and was cited by him as a monument familiar to his fellow Christians, tangible evidence of Peter's martyrdom.

Confirmation for Gaius's statement comes from the sixth-century *Liber Pontificalis*, which attributes to Pope 'Anacletus' (which probably meant Anicetus, pontiff between A.D. 155 and 165) the building of 'a memorial shrine to the blessed Peter'.

To follow the argument we need to move ahead to the reign of the Emperor Constantine. Following his recognition of Christianity by the Edict of Milan in 315, he ordered the construction of a basilica to be named after St Peter, the founder of the Church of Rome.

Constantine deliberately chose for the site of the church and for the position of its altar the aedicula, Peter's monument. The shrine was given the place of honour, as the focal point of the church.

To build at that spot Constantine had to overcome extraordinary obstacles – the violation of hundreds of tombs and graves of people whose relatives were probably still living and construction on a shelving bank. That required the building of a huge projecting platform and the dumping of a million cubic feet of earth. Why did he not build his church on the level ground south of the road, the traditional site of Peter's martyrdom? At all costs the aedicula had to be incorporated in the building. Was that due to the belief that it marked the apostle's grave?

Constantine raised the aedicula 1 foot (30 centimetres) above the level of the pavement immediately in front of the apse, encasing it with marble. It may have served as the altar in the period before a separate altar was deemed necessary. The aedicula, it is believed, measured 9 feet by 5 feet 6 inches (2.70 by 1.70 metres). It covered a grating giving access to a vertical shaft which may have led to the grave. The shrine became an object of veneration. Pilgrims were allowed to lift the grating and lower objects to be sanctified by proximity to the holy relics below. Privileged visitors were permitted to thrust down their heads.

During the centuries following Constantine's death, for doctrinal reasons his basilica was subjected to countless additions and alterations. The old apse was demolished and the modern St Peter's was built in the sixteenth century. Its pavement was raised 30 feet (9.9 metres) above the mosaic floor of Constantine's basilica, which became in consequence the crypt of the new church. The aedicula, now below the new pavement, was set in the face of an old flanking wall, called the red wall, near the end of a sloping passage, named the clivus. The space below the aedicula may have been broached by the workmen as they sought to build foundations for the new church. At the depth of about 2 to $2\frac{1}{2}$ feet (60 to 80 centimetres), it is assumed, they came upon not the casket they expected to find but a heap of bones. They placed them in a niche beneath the foundations of the red wall, building a curved wall to keep out encroaching earth.

These assumptions are based on the discoveries made by the Vatican's archaeologists and engineers between 1945 and 1949. They overcame formidable difficulties, waging a constant battle with the Vatican's subterranean waters, ancient streams and leaking drains, and the danger of disturbing the church's foundations, which required under-pinning and buttressing with new walls and piers. They crawled through narrow spaces between the tightly packed ancient pagan tombs which hindered their work. Full understanding of their achievements and discoveries requires the examination of the many diagrams printed in the report of the excavations. It needs to be simplified here.

Working directly beneath the high altar named after Pope

Calixtus II (1119–24), in the heart of the old aedicula, the archaeologists came upon a recess in the foundations of the old red wall, within which was the enigmatic heap of bones. It is reasonable to assume that they are the bones of St Peter, for they were found at the spot where tradition recorded his grave.

But why were they in confusion, unceremoniously thrust beneath the foundations of an ancient wall, and lacking a head? The grave must have been rifled and ransacked. Thieves had disturbed the holy relics. The Goths who sacked Rome in A.D. 410 and the Vandals who did the same in 455 have been absolved from the charge of sacrilege, for both races were Christian. The Saracens are more likely culprits. They sacked Rome and plundered St Peter's in 846. The reigning pope, Sergius II, said that they 'invaded and occupied the Church of the Blessed Peter, Prince of the Apostles, committing unspeakable iniquities'. Prudentius of Troyes states in his *Annals* that they 'bore off all the ornaments and treasures, together with the very altar which had been placed over the tomb of the said Prince of the Apostles'. The pope, it seems, had disregarded the advice of Count Adalbert, the governor of Tuscany and Corsica, who had written warning of the approach of the Saracen fleet, advising the removal of the church's treasures and if possible the body of the apostle.

The Saracens presumably broke into the grave, disturbing the apostle's bones, casting them aside in their search for treasures. The Vatican authorities may not have discovered the loss of the sacred relics, housed in the inaccessible depths beneath the rifled shrine. They repaired the hole in the pavement and said nothing about it. It would have been gravely impolitic to have admitted that the bones of the apostle, the martyr from whose death in Rome their church gained its immense prestige, had been ransacked by infidels.

The modern visitor can descend behind the high altar to the *'tomba di San Pietro'*. As I did, he or she will find a stylized, marble monument, masking the niche where the famous bones were found.

Mysterious Peoples

DILMUN. THE FORGOTTEN KINGDOM

Sorting the Assyrian cuneiform tablets which had been found by 1880, Sir Henry Rawlinson, the decipherer of the wedge-like script, noticed frequent references to an island named Dilmun. It appeared to have been a little kingdom somewhere on the periphery of the Assyrian empire. The eighth century B.C. Assyrian King Sargon had pursued the rebel king of Baby-lon into the southern realms of Chaldaea, meaning the delta of the rivers Tigris and Euphrates, and to Bit-Iakin on the shores of the Bitter Sea. Sargon conquered Bit-Iakin up to the borders of Dilmun. Recounting the history of the campaign Sargon added: 'Uperi, King of Dilmun, whose abode is situated like a fish, thirty double-hours away in the midst of the sea of the rising sun, heard of the might of my sovereignty and sent his gifts.'

Sennacherib, Sargon's son and successor who ruled in about 705 B.C., supplies in his *Annals* further clues to the location of Dilmun. Sennacherib conquered Bit-Iakin and reached the sea, whereupon the inhabitants of the coastal towns took ship and escaped across the sea to Elam. The kingdom of Elam lay on the Persian side of the Arabian Gulf. Bit-Iakin was therefore on the Arabian shore and Dilmun was farther down the coast. Its king lived on an island 'like a fish' in the midst of the sea, about three days' sail from Sargon's probable starting point in lower Mesopotamia, for that seems to be the explanation of a journey of 'thirty double-hours', or sixty hours of sailing. The peoples of Mesopotamia called the Arabian Gulf the Lower Sea, the Bitter Sea and the Sea of the Rising Sun.

That Dilmun was well known as a port and trading centre 2,000 years before Assyrian times is demonstrated by the tablet of Ur-nanshe, the king of Lagash, who stated in about 2520 B.C.: 'The ships of Dilmun, from the foreign lands, bring me wood as a tribute.' An even earlier ruler, Sargon the

Sumerian king of Akkad, referred to his conquest of Dilmun in the 'Lower Sea'.

As more and more cuneiform tablets came to light and were deciphered, it became clear that to the people of Mesopotamia Dilmun had been a land of peculiar importance occupying a unique place in their mythology. Hymns and incantations associated Dilmun with a variety of gods including 'The God Inzak and the God Nabu'. Even more significant was the discovery in 1872 of the Assyrian account of the Flood, and in 1914 of the far older Sumerian version. The connection of Dilmun and the story of the universal deluge requires explanation.

In the Assyrian version, found on a tablet in the library of King Assurbanipal, the semi-mythical king of Erech, Gilgamesh, who has spent many years seeking eternal life, visits the one mortal who has been granted immortality, the survivor of the Flood, Ut-napishtim. He tells Gilgamesh the story of the Flood and how he and his wife had been sent by the gods to dwell in the distance from the mouth of the twin rivers.

The earlier Sumerian version is more helpful. It was found in the temple at Nippur amongst 35,000 tablets dating from before 2000 B.C. The Sumerians were the earliest of the Mesopotamian peoples, the predecessors of the Semitic Babylonians and Assyrians. Sir Leonard Woolley's excavation at Ur, where he found the 15 foot (4.5 metres) layer of mud deposited by a great inundation, places the Flood in Sumerian times, possibly about 4250 B.C.

The Sumerian Flood hero is named Ziusudra. Enlit was the first amongst the gods, the patron god of Nippur. Anu was another god. Ziusudra's story is similar to that told by Ut-napishtim to Gilgamesh. It relates that: 'Anu and Enlit cherished Ziusudra, life like a god they give him, breath eternal like a god they bring down for him. Then Ziusudra, the king, the preserver of the name of vegetation and of the seed of mankind, in the land of the crossing, the land of Dilmun, the place where the sun rises, they caused to dwell.'

While the meaning of the term 'the land of the crossing' is obscure, the epic places Dilmun in the Sea of the Rising Sun, one of the names for the Arabian Gulf, somewhere 'in the distance', as Ut-napishtim describes it, from the mouth of the rivers.

Dilmun is identified as the eternal home of the immortal ancestors of all mankind, where Gilgamesh came to search for eternal life. Another text found at Nippur explains why the gods had chosen Dilmun as the home of the man they had saved from the Flood. This mythological poem is entitled 'Enki [or Enlit] and Ninhursag'. As well as being patron god of Nippur, Enki was also the 'God of the Abyss'.

The Sumerians believed (with some justification as we shall see) that the earth and sea rested upon a lower sea, a freshwater sea which they called Abuzu, or the abyss. The two seas were different. The salt water of one prevented the two from mixing. The Abuzu was the source of all fresh water, of rivers, underground streams and wells. Enki was the ruler and guardian of this fresh-water sea. The events of the myth take place in Dilmun which is described repeatedly as a 'holy land'. There is no predatory beast, no sickness, no old age there.

> In Dilmun the raven utters no cry,
> the wild hen utters not the cry of the wild hen,
> the lion kills not,
> the wolf snatches not the lamb,
> unknown is the kid-devouring wild dog,
> unknown is the grain-devouring boar.
> The malt which the widow spreads on the roof –
> the birds of heaven do not eat up that malt.
> The dove droops not the head.
> The sick-eyed says not 'I am sick-eyed,'
> the sick-headed says not 'I am sick-headed,'
> its old woman says not ' I am an old woman,'
> its old man says not 'I am an old man.'

Dilmun needed sweet water. Enki orders its supply. His daughter, Ninkhursag, causes eight plants to grow, one of which poisons her father. She withdraws from the company of the gods, threatening not to return until Enki is dead. She is persuaded to cure him which she does by giving birth to eight gods and goddesses, the last of whom is named Enshag, the Sumerian name for the god Inzak, the co-god with Nabu of Dilmun.

The myth shows that the Sumerians believed that at the dawn of time Enki had been the original god of Dilmun and had blessed the land with sweet water, with health and eternal youth. It was fitting, therefore, that Ziusudra following his escape from the Flood, should have taken up his abode in the blessed land where death was unknown. There he, or his name-sake Ut-napishtim, is visited by Gilgamesh in quest of the secret of eternal youth. How he finds and loses it bears on the identification of Dilmun.

Ut-napishtim tells Gilgamesh how to find the flower of immortality. It grows on the sea bed in the sweet waters of the abyss. He instructs Gilgamesh to attach stones to his feet and by their aid to sink to the sea bed and there pluck the magic flower. He will renew his youth by eating it. Gilgamesh follows Ut-napishtim's instructions, plucks the flower and surfaces with the elixir of life, the pearl, the ancient symbol of purity and, according to the Indian Atharvan poem, 'our life-producing amulet'. Gilgamesh's story has an unhappy ending, reminiscent of Genesis. He decides to take his flower home to Erech in order to share it with the city's elders. While he sleeps, the serpent comes forth from its water-hole and eats the flower. Thereby he cheats man and gains immortality. Each year the snake sloughs its skin, becoming vigorous again.

These ancient references go far to identify Dilmun as the modern island of Bahrein as Rawlinson had deduced after reading of Captain Durand's discovery there in 1879 of an inscription referring to Inzak, the god of Dilmun. Bahrein is the centre of the world's most ancient pearl fishery, and its Arabic name means, according to the Koran, 'the meeting place of the waters, the one fresh, sweet and pleasant to drink, the other salt and bitter'. Bahrein is famous for the springs of fresh water which well from the seas surrounding the island – the ancient abyss.

Geoffrey Bibby had been intrigued by Rawlinson's tentative identification of Dilmun as Bahrein when he worked there as an oil-company executive. The tens of thousands of burial mounds covering the desert had also excited his interest. As he studied the ancient texts he became convinced that Rawlinson's identification had been correct. But it remained to be proved. That could only be done by excavation. Bibby returned home to Denmark where he interested Professor Peter Glob, the director of the Aarhus Museum, in his theory. They succeeded in raising the necessary finance for the archaeological team to travel to Bahrein in 1953. Bibby has told the story in his book, which he cautiously entitled *Looking for Dilmun.**

The sheik of Bahrein welcomed the archaeologists who hoped to disclose his country's famous past and helped them financially. They found it difficult to know where to begin amongst the 100,000 burial mounds which suggested that the small island had once supported a large and prosperous population. A large mound near the village of Barbar attracted Glob's attention because the villagers called it a *tel*, the Arabic name for a buried city. It stood 16 feet (4.8 metres) high and covered 4,000 square yards (3,344 square metres). Walking around it Glob noticed the ends of two stones protruding from the sand. Clearing it away he found two blocks weighing about three tons each. They stood on a paving of limestone which led into the mound's interior. A trench 16 feet (4.8 metres) wide cut through its centre revealed stumps of ancient walls, beyond them more paving, more walls and a step leading to a raised platform.

Glob had discovered a temple complex, or rather three successive temples which had been built one upon another. A deliberate attempt appeared to have been made to obscure the topmost temple by filling it with sand. The sand was tightly packed and interspersed with gypsum to serve as a binder. It was not the accretion of centuries of drift. Beneath this stratification lay a second, larger temple, shaped like a ziggurat, the typical Mesopotamian religious structure. A stone staircase gave access on one side and a stone ramp on the other. The third and most ancient building consisted of an inner court, surrounded by a wall, within which stood an altar stone. Various objects dated this structure to about 2300 B.C., the period of the peak of the Sumerian civilization. They included pottery bowls of Mesopotamian type, axe-heads, an alabaster vase, copper figurines, earthenware goblets, and a magnificent carving of a bull's head. It showed striking resemblance to a

* Collins, 1970.

87

similar carving which had been unearthed by Sir Leonard Woolley at Ur. Several cylindrical seals, depicting a god seated on a bench, indicated close relationship with the Sumerians. Other seals, square in shape, appeared to resemble the seals of the Indus civilization.

Glob and Bibby refrained from jumping to premature conclusions. The Barbar temple indicated Sumerian influence. They turned to another site, the 250,000 square yard (209,000 square metres) mound at Qulaat. Their attention had been drawn to it by the sheik who suggested that its position on a rise close to the shore would have made an ideal site for a fort or a city. Did the ancient capital lie within the mound? Glob thought it might. The tel measured 600 yards (550 metres) from east to west and 300 yards (275 metres) from north to south. Two years of clearing disclosed successive layers of superimposed buildings. Bibby comforted himself with the thought that Woolley had worked at Ur for twelve years without unveiling more than a fraction of the Sumerian city. The mound at Qulaat was about two-thirds the size of the mound that had cloaked Ur. He had no idea how far it might reach back in time. To learn that would take many years of painstaking excavation.

The team began by digging deep into the mound's centre. Massive walls appeared at 3 feet (.9 metres). As they penetrated deeper, the walls continued downwards. Four years of excavation revealed a palace at ground level. It was a roofless shell into which had sunk artifacts from the higher levels. That made it difficult to date. Objects from the later periods of occupation suggested the date 703 B.C., the period of Assyrian domination in Mesopotamia, the time of Sargon's expedition to the boundaries of Dilmun. The lower palace must have been built 1,000 years before then, in the time of the earlier Sargon, the Sumerian king who knew of Dilmun.

A remarkable discovery beneath the palace's floor seemed definitely to link it with Dilmun's earliest period. The archaeologists unearthed seven bowls containing skeletons of snakes and a tiny bead, a clear association with the flood hero. The snakes were of religious or magical significance, buried beneath the palace floor as a potent insurance against old age and death. The snake and the pearl had been symbols of freedom from sickness and death. At Dilmun the serpent had eaten Gilgamesh's flower of immortality, the pearl. The bowls may have originally contained pearls. Built by the oyster from organic matter, pearls disintegrate in time. Later Bibby found pearls with the skeletons of snakes. Their discovery suggested that Ut-napishtim, or Ziusudra, had been a living legend when the palace had been built. It may have been the flood hero's home.

Another site, on the south-western coast of the island, provided additional confirmation. Close to the beach Bibby found huge piles of oyster shells, the debris of centuries of pearl fishing in the ancient days when the divers brought the shells ashore to dry and open, a custom they later discarded in preference for opening them on ship board, and throwing the useless shells back into the sea.

Many years will be required before the Danes can definitely assert that they have found Dilmun. One of their discoveries has raised controversy, their claim to have found stamp-seals of a type similar to those both of Ur and of Mohenjo-daro and Harappa in the Indus valley (see 'The End of the Harappans' p. 90). They corroborate the belief that the Indus civilizations were influenced by those of Mesopotamia, and that Dilmun served as an entrepôt of trade between them. These seals appear to conform to both cultures, and suggest that the merchants of Dilmun devised their own seals, or trading symbols, to facilitate their international trade. From this sea-going commerce its 100,000 buried dead derived their prosperity, about the time when Ziusudra came to enjoy his immortality in that land. Whoever's skeletons these may have been, his cannot be one. He lives for ever as Dilmun's most famous citizen.

THE END OF THE HARAPPANS

Digging deep into the ruined city of Mohenjo-daro, the excavators found increasing deterioration in standards of building and living. Walls and flooring tended to become more ramshackle and shoddy in the highest and most recent levels. The once well-ordered city had become a slum. Decline had been long drawn out and progressive, the final fall catastrophic. So Sir Mortimer Wheeler described the results of his 1950 excavations. Twenty-five years later, after further excavations, he was less certain about the cause of the decline and fall of the Harappans.

That name is given to the people who created in the Indus valley one of the greatest civilizations of the past, the existence of which was unsuspected until 1921. Two huge mounds concealed the cities of Harappa in the Punjab and Mohenjo-daro in Sind, in what is now Pakistan. Initial excavation disclosed pottery and seals which indicated that the Harappan culture had flourished between 2500 and 1500 B.C.

This was an exciting discovery. Rather than two ancient river civilizations, those of Mesopotamia and Egypt, there had been three, reaching their zeniths about the same time. A new window had been opened on man's past, posing fresh problems for archaeological research. Lack of a bilingual inscription to break the seal of the Harappans' pictorial script makes their culture harder to assess than those which have yielded a wealth of readable texts. The Indus's script remains undeciphered. No other people wrote about the Harappans. Consequently they pose questions which may never be answered. Who were the nameless people who, for convenience, are named after one of their principal cities? From where did they come? Why did their empire decline and vanish as suddenly as it had arisen? Were they overwhelmed by a more virile race, or did they suffer a natural catastrophe? There is another intriguing possibility, as apt today as it may have been then. Did they become tired? Did they fall victim to the 'stress factor', exhausted by the never-ending struggle with their environment and weakened by the terrible uniformity of their lives?

Harappa stood on the Ravi, a tributary of the Indus. Mohenjo-daro lay 350 miles (560 kilometres) to the south on the Indus itself. The twin cities dominated a triangle of territory, 1,000 miles (1,600 kilometres) on each side. We do not know if they were separate city states or the northern and southern capitals of one kingdom. Their citizens lived in comparative isolation from other peoples, and created their own civilization. Their sculptural art has no affinity with any other. The art of their seals is unparalleled elsewhere. The initial impetus, the idea of city building, may have come from without, possibly from Mesopotamia, the roughly contemporary valley civilization on the other side of the intervening mountains, the area from which both peoples may have descended to cultivate the fertile plains.

The Harappan culture arose in mature form. Harappa and Mohenjo-daro did not slowly grow like London or Paris. They were ancient New Yorks and Chicagos, complete cities built in uniform grid-plan blocks. Their architects may have learned from the Sumerian experience at Ur, the straggling Mesopotamian city which had developed according to its peoples' needs. Starting from scratch on the bare plain, the Harappans adopted town planning, laying out streets and building houses by standardized techniques and a rigorously enforced code of practices. Each brick had to be so big, and so laid. Streets intercepted at right angles. They created an elaborately contrived and depressing monotony. Their cities indicate authoritarian rule, a terrible efficiency which may have contributed to their stagnation and decay.

Harappa and Mohenjo-daro have been partly excavated. Another seventy sites have been explored. Their citizens were in possession by 2350 B.C., when they were in commercial contact by land and sea with the Sumerians. The presence of seals of each civilization in the cities of the other prove their trade. Evidence of intellectual borrowing is absent. The Harappans developed a unique and self-sufficient culture based on agriculture.

The mounds at Harappa and Mohenjo-daro have disclosed cities conforming to the familiar Euro-asian pattern, an acropolis or citadel overlooking and dominating a lower city, with a wide gap in between, a plan which suggests concern to overawe the proletariat rather than fear of foreign aggression. The Harappans had a far more dangerous enemy – water. Excavation at Mohenjo-daro has revealed five successive layers of collapse and rebuilding, the results of severe and devastating floods. Rising waters presented a perpetual threat, requiring unremitting vigilance.

The citadel at Harappa forms a parallelogram, 460 yards (420 metres) from north to south and 215 yards (196 metres) from east to west. It rises 50 feet (15 metres) above the plain. Like the other valley mounds it has suffered from the depredations of brick-robbers who, at Harappa, destroyed the staircase which once led to the mud-brick platform. Beneath and around this platform lie six distinct and successive layers of occupation, beginning with a simple village culture, possibly the relics of an aboriginal people. The Harappans constructed their earliest buildings with mud bricks, strengthened with timber, a cheap and primitive form of building which they were forced to abandon when the walls became soaked with water. Learning from experience, they resorted to baking the bricks, giving their cities greater stability at the cost of denuding their forests for fuel, thereby changing the balance of nature. Time and again they were forced to create new platforms as those below became destroyed by water and covered by silt. They succeeded in creating massive walls and huge bastions.

The mound north of the citadel, between it and the river, has yielded information which provides clues to the Harappans' way of life. A range of barrack-like dwellings are flanked by a double row of granaries, the labourers' cantonment and the state storehouse. The 'coolie-quarters', as they have been described, comprised 3 to 4 foot (.9 to 1.2 metres) wide lanes containing little, detached houses, 56 by 24 feet (17 by 7 metres) square, each conforming to its neighbour and consisting of two rooms surrounding a court, an example of uniform planning. They housed the labourers and clerks who transported and checked the grain from the ships in the river. The granaries were arranged in rows of six, each container measuring 50 feet by 20 feet deep (15 by 6 metres), and opening upon a 23 foot (7 metres) wide passage. Airducts made by removing bricks ensured ventilation to prevent the city's wealth from suffering from damp and mildew. The bulk of the population lived in the lower town across the gap from the citadel.

Mohenjo-daro was built on the same plan, and suffered far greater damage from flooding than the more northerly Harappa. Its citizens raised their citadel on an artificial platform 30 feet (9 metres) above the original water level, and protected it by a bund 43 feet (13 metres) wide. It was frequently reinforced and extended, mute evidence of the constantly rising waters. Excavation has disclosed seven successive layers of occupation above the water-table, which remains unprobed to its depths. Five layers show evidence of severe flooding and damage which required abandonment and rebuilding at a higher level.

Around the perimeter of the citadel's platform the citizens built massive burnt-brick walls and towers. It may have served as a fortress-temple. It contained a great bath or tank, 39 by 23 feet and 8 feet deep (12 by 7 by 2.5 metres) reached by steps, and built of brick, interlayered with gypsum to serve as a binder, and lined with a bitumen damp course. A corbelled arched drain 5 feet 5 inches (1.65 metres) high, carried away surplus water. Around the tank, which may have been used for ritual ablutions, were ranked eight small rooms, with bathrooms and lavatories. Their doorways were dispersed so that none opened opposite another, a device to ensure privacy. A separate bathroom was heated by a hot air duct system generated from a furnace. A large building has been described as the high priest's residence, possibly without foundation.

The mound to the north of the citadel was found to conceal the state granary, a grim fortress-like building, 150 feet (45 metres) from east to west, and 75 feet (23 metres) wide. Its inner walls were constructed of criss-crossed bricks to allow air to circulate. Its environs still await excavation. They are believed to contain the usual labourers' cantonment. One building

90 feet (27 metres) square, seems to have contained aisles, which suggests that it may have been a place of assembly.

The lower city, the people's habitation, conforms to the basic grid pattern of main streets, 30 feet (9 metres) wide, running north and south, intercepted by lanes, 5 to 10 feet (1.5 to 3 metres) wide. These thoroughfares partitioned the city into twelve major blocks of equal size, approximately rectangular in shape and covering an area 800 feet (240 metres) from east to west and 1,200 feet (365 metres) from north to south. The houses were prison-like, windowless structures, centred round a court, the focus of family life. Staircases led to upper floors. Each house was served by water from a well. Earthenware drains carried waste from bathroom and lavatory, a seated latrine set against a wall through which a chute carried the matter into the main drain beneath the lane. Brick-built manholes gave access to the drains for inspection and clearing. At the corner of each lane stood a one-roomed house, possibly the shelter of the watchman who kept guard over the 'miles of monotony', as these streets have been described. The houses had been rebuilt on the debris of the past at least five times.

Not all the houses were residential boxes. The greater size of some and their different internal arrangement suggest a palace, with multiple entrances on several lanes and main thoroughfares, a hostel for pilgrims or travellers, with several small rooms or cubicles, and a restaurant with holes sunk in the floor to hold pointed jars. Or they may have been dyeing vats. Another equally conjectural identification describes one building as an artist's studio, for it was found to contain a bearded human head, 6 foot 9 inches (2.05 metres) high, carved in white limestone. The upper lip is shaved, the hair bunched in a bun at the back and bound across the forehead. Part of another head was found nearby. Both images appear to date from a very early period. Another carving represents a seated or squatting man with his hands resting upon his knees. These figures, together with representations on pottery and seals, provide little evidence of the Harappans' physical characteristics. The complete bust shows a man with a heavy lower lip, thrust forward in disdainful, challenging fashion.

No royal tombs have been found at either city. The ordinary

cemeteries have yielded skeletal remains which represent a mixture of racial types, Caucasian, Mediterranean, Indo-European and even Proto-Australoid, the same strain which thousands of years before had migrated from India to Australia. Those that stayed behind may have been the aboriginal inhabitants of the Indus valley, overcome and dominated by the Harappans. The bones of the Harappans' domesticated animals provide clues to their climate and environment. They used horses and oxen, but few camels. This suggests a fertile rather than a desert area. The footmarks, deeply indented in muddy brick, of a cat, overlaid by those of a dog, suggest a pursuit at speed and an abundance of both animals.

The absence of many offensive weapons is a remarkable feature of both cities. It suggests that the Harappans had no powerful enemies. Those weapons that have been found include bows and arrows and sling shot. They possessed the usual implements – saws, axes, knives and razors, made of bronze, copper and iron. Their magnificent seals, with superbly engraved animal figures in negative relief, have been found in Mesopotamia and on the island of Bahrein in the Arabian Gulf the trade entrepôt between the Indus and Tigris and Euphrates valleys. The Harappans' artistry is exemplified by the miniature terracotta face mask found at Mohenjo-daro in 1964. It shows a boldly outlined human face, topped by the ears and horns of some animal. They were skilful modellers in clay and made beautiful pottery as long as the traditional urge lasted.

The Harappan civilization is thought to have ended between 1700 and 1500 B.C. The application of the usual dating techniques, including the test of organic materials by Carbon-14, have failed to confirm any definite date by which Harappa and Mohenjo-daro had been abandoned.

The likelihood that this occurred in the middle of the second millennium B.C. provided grounds at one time for the theory that the Harappans had been vanquished by the conquering Aryans who may have invaded India about that time. There seems to be evidence of violent death. At Mohenjo-daro, thirty-five skeletons of men, women and children were discovered lying in the top layer of occupation in sprawled and contorted positions, their skulls bearing axe and sword cuts. Unfortunately the earlier excavators failed to establish their stratification with any precision. A man and a woman were struck down as they mounted a flight of stairs. Two others had gained the passage above, two more had failed to leave their house. Five skeletons sprawled at the corner of a lane, where they may have been sheltering. Another group of nine lay crowded together in strangely contorted attitudes. Intermingled with their bones were two elephant tusks, perhaps their private and portable wealth. This dramatic archaeological evidence seems to point to invasion, sack and massacre.

It may be supported by the reference in the Vedic literature, the Aryan *Rigveda*, to a place named Hari-Yupuya (Harappa?) as the scene of a battle, and to the invaders' onslaught on fortified cities, a term which could apply in that region only to Harappa and Mohenjo-daro. According to this theory the Aryans overwhelmed the non-Aryan population of the Indus valley, destroying their cities. It rests on the slender assumption that the Aryans reached India about the time when the Harappan empire collapsed. There is no evidence to confirm that.

Another theory has been advanced by Dr G. F. Dales who directed the work of the Pennsylvania University Museum's team at Mohenjo-daro (*Scientific American*, May 1966).

Dales noticed certain topographic anomalies which suggested that the inundations which had left layers of silt had not resulted from river overflows, but rather from an event of much greater magnitude. Had the Indus become stopped up, with the gradual formation of a huge lake upstream from the city? The sudden breaking of the dams could have resulted in the spilling of large volumes of water. That could account, far better than the theory of river overflows, for the nature of the periodic inundations from which the city had suffered. Thick silt deposits had been sandwiched between successive occupational layers. The deposits were characteristic of still water pouring from a lake rather than water surging from a swiftly flowing river.

How could the lake have been formed? Dales was joined by the hydrologist, Robert L. Raikes. His surveys indicated

that an area 90 miles (145 kilometres) from the city had suffered topographic changes, and he observed that certain settlements which had once been seaports were now 30 miles (48
kilometres) inland. This coastal rise indicated tectonic dis-
turbance. Dales found abundant geologic evidence of rock-
faulting. It could have raised a dam, turning the river into a
slow-filling lake. The usual discharge of the Indus, its volume
increased annually by the melting of Himalayan snows, would
have become blocked. As the waters accumulated a huge lake
would have formed. Periodically its banks burst, causing the
citizens of Mohenjo-daro to exert their energy in large-scale
efforts to avert disaster. Each inundation caused the collapse
of walls and floors, requiring extensive rebuilding.

This continual strife with the forces of nature exhausted the
people and their resources. The long period of bourgeois well-
being gave way to a decline of prosperity and led to a squatter
phase. Houses were replaced by shacks made from old and
broken bricks. The traditional red- and black-painted pottery
was replaced by unpainted ware. Mohenjo-daro became a
shanty town, its lower levels engulfed by silt, dying slowly
from decay. The majority of its citizens departed, leaving the
squatters to be massacred by some roving band of mountain
raiders. Harappa survived longer, falling victim in turn to the
barbarian invaders.

There are alternative solutions: internal revolt, climatic or
environmental change, disease, racial degeneration. The evidence of massacre may point to civil strife, possibly the revolt
of the masses against the domineering overlords who condemned them to a life of monotony in drab surroundings.

THE GARAMANTES. ANCESTORS OF THE MODERN TUAREG?

The Italian archaeologist Salvatore Aurigemma made a curious
discovery in 1914. Excavating a Roman villa at the village of
Zliten on the Libyan coast 60 miles (97 kilometres) to the
east of the Roman town of Leptis Magna, he unearthed a

mosaic pavement. Fortunately he photographed it, for the villa and its contents were destroyed during World War I.

One scene in the mosaic depicted a prisoner being torn to pieces by a leopard. Two victims are shown being wheeled into the arena on small vehicles, their hands and feet tied to vertical poles. The animal-keeper pushes one by means of a long handle to meet the advancing, half-starved beast. The handle enables him to turn the victim to face the leopard and another man heads the animal towards the victim.

The prisoners have reddish-golden complexions, long straight hair, aquiline noses and short pointed beards. They seem to be white Caucasians. They have been identified as Garamantes, the people who ruled the Fezzan, that part of the Sahara which lies north of the Hoggar mountains.

Who these Garamantes were is one of the great mysteries of the Sahara. Herodotus, writing in the fifth century B.C., called them a great nation, people who pursued the Negro 'troglodytes who lived in caves' in four-horsed chariots. Rock paintings found throughout the desert depict chariots and their horses, the latter adopting the outstretched legs style of 'flying gallop' which is depicted in the Mycenaean art of Crete. This clue links the Garamantes with the 'Peoples of the Sea', mentioned in Egyptian texts, who, coming possibly from Asia Minor, invaded North Africa in about 1250 B.C. with the object of conquering Egypt. Foiled in this enterprise the Garamantes, if they were these maritime invaders, migrated into the Sahara.

The desert must have been far less arid than it is now. The Tassili frescoes, painted in rock shelters, discovered and copied in the Hoggar and Ajjer mountains by Henri Lhote* depict elephants, giraffes, gazelles, lions, and even hippopotamuses, an aquatic animal. These rock-artists may have been the cave-dwellers conquered by the Garamantes. One or other of these people created the extensive irrigation system which has been found between Garama, the Garamantes' capital, and the oasis of Ghat, modern Rhapsa. Garama, modern Germa, has sunk beneath the sand.

These *foggaras*, as they are called, consist of parallel and interconnecting shafts and tunnels driven through the lime-

* *The Search for the Tassili Frescoes*, Hutchinson, 1958.

stone rock. Rock falls have enabled them to be inspected in places. The tunnels are 10 feet high and 12 feet wide (3 by 3.7 metres). They run in straight lines from the base of cliffs, some for 3 miles (4.8 kilometres). 300 *foggaras* have been found, comprising nearly 1,000 miles (1,600 kilometres) of tunnels. How the irrigation system worked is somewhat of a mystery. Did it draw water from artificial reservoirs fed from gullies in the hills, or did it tap underground springs? Pierre Bellair, the French archaeologist who discovered these *foggaras* in 1933, is uncertain.

This irrigation system indicates the existence of a large population, which is confirmed by the 100,000 graves found in the area. 40,000 of these small, circular, rock-tombs lie close to Garama. Skeletons excavated from them exhibit the characteristics of a white race, possibly the Garamantes who enslaved the negroid cave-dwellers.

Ruined towers and forts, and indecipherable inscriptions have been found throughout the desert. Many of these mud-brick buildings have become silted up by sand and none have been excavated. Archaeological research in the area has been extensive rather than intensive. That may account for our lack of knowledge about the Garamantes. Their tombs have yielded some information. They seem to have borrowed their neighbours' gods and religious rites. The presence of food and drink, dishes, cups, oil jars and lamps in their graves suggest they hoped for a life after death. They may have provided the cavalry, the 'Numidian horsemen' who accompanied Hannibal across the Alps, and who contributed to his defeat in 202 B.C. by refusing to fight the Romans.

Possibly the Garamantes were conquered by the Romans who, following the fall of Carthage, occupied North Africa. More probably they became Roman allies, controllers of the caravan routes which spanned the Sahara and which brought to Rome the riches of equatorial Africa, ivory, gold, ostrich feathers, slaves and wild beasts. They may have been treacherous allies, requiring an occasional punitive expedition. Three Roman armies penetrated deep into the Sahara.

In 19 B.C., as Pliny relates, Cornelius Balbus was accorded a triumph for his conquests. He certainly reached the Garamantes' capital of Garama, 430 miles (690 kilometres) from the coast, and may have progressed much further. In A.D. 70, following a raid by the Garamantes on Leptis Magna (possibly the occasion depicted in the mosaic), Septimus Flaccus spent three months in the desert, reaching the Tibesti mountains. He was followed in A.D. 86 by Julius Maternus.

The extent of Roman penetration of the Sahara intrigued Henri Lhote. He sought the ancient caravan routes established by the Garamantes. Pictures of chariots on the rock walls of the Iforas Massif, near the Arli well, the one-time Tadmekka, showed that the chariot people had crossed the Sahara, a journey of 1,000 miles (1,600 kilometres). The discovery of more pictures of chariots in the Hoggar mountains indicated the line of the chariot route, the great highway from the Fezzan to the Niger river.

Lhote traced many of the names mentioned by Pliny, identifying them with places he himself knew. Two place names seemed familiar, Alasi and Balsa. He identified Alasi as the village named Ilezy by the modern Tuareg tribesmen. They spelt the name both Ilezy and Alasi for their language, Tamasheq, is written with consonants only. Balsa seemed to be Abalessa in the Hoggar mountains. There Lhote found a ruined fort containing Roman coins, vases and lamps. Significantly, it lay on the caravan route.

Balbus had marched southward from Abalessa, reaching 'Dasibari'. The name kept running through Lhote's head. He got out his maps and books. The Niger, he recalled, was named by its riverside peoples the Isabi, 'Isa' meaning river, and 'bari' big. These Songoli people called the Niger the 'great stream'. Lhote remembered that they called themselves the 'Das', the lords of the river, and that the Niger was sometimes described as 'The great stream of the Das', possibly the Dasibari of Balbus's triumph. This indicated that the Romans and the Garamantes had crossed the Sahara desert, an amazing feat.

Whether or not the Garamantes became a Roman subject people, they were converted to Christianity when it became the official religion of the Empire in A.D. 325. On the collapse of the Roman Empire, they fell easy victims to the Arab conquest. The Arab general, Okba ibn Nafi, subdued the Fezzan in A.D. 668 with 400 tribesmen and 400 camels carrying 800 goatskins of water. Weakened by their servitude to Rome, the Garamantes collapsed without opposition. The Arab historian Ibn-Khaldoun (*History of the Conquest of Egypt*) describes Okba's conquest:

Having cut off the ear of the king of Waddan and exacted a tribute of 360 slaves, he desired to know what kind of country lay beyond Waddan. They told him of Germa, capital of the whole Fezzan. Leaving Waddan, he arrived after a march of eight nights on the outskirts of Germa whose inhabitants he invited to embrace Islam. They agreed, and he called a halt six miles from the town.

When the king of the Garamantes came out from Germa to meet Okba, the Arab horsemen rode in between the king and his escort, forcing them to dismount and to walk on foot, the six miles to where Okba was camped. Since the king was sickly, he arrived in an exhausted state, spitting blood.

'Why do you treat me like this after I have yielded to you?' the Garamantian king asked.

'It will teach you a lesson not to make war on the Arabs,' Okba replied as was his custom; and he sent the king back to Egypt in chains.

The Garamantes are not heard of again. Okba marched from Garama, possibly for another 300 miles (480 kilometres), to the great rock fortress of Kouar. Failing to capture it by siege, he entered it by night. Its defenders had retired to their underground chambers. Okba cut the throats of all men capable of bearing arms and took the children into slavery. In A.D. 712, at the order of the Caliph Omar II, the peoples of the desert were forced to adopt the Moslem faith.

What happened to the survivors of the Garamantes, the white race who once ruled the Sahara? Some travellers believe that the Tuaregs of the Hoggar and Air mountains are their descendants. This theory does not command complete acceptance, but is nonetheless intriguing. There seems to be much to be said for it.

Until the end of the nineteenth century, by when they had been subjected to French administration, the veiled Tuareg were the lords of the desert, the masters of the caravan high-way from the Fezzan to the Niger. They were strikingly dis-similar to other desert peoples. They did not know themselves why their men, but not their women, veiled their faces. As far as can be discerned beneath their veils, their complexions are copper-coloured, resembling those of the prisoners in the Roman mosaic. The Tuaregs are very tall and slim, averaging 6 feet (1.8 metres) in height, whereas the other desert dwellers, the Berbers and Arabs, are dark and of medium height. The Berbers are powerfully built.

The Tuaregs have other peculiarities. They have retained their own language, Tamasheq, and their own written script called Tifinagh, which they can no longer read. Was this the speech of the ancient Garamantes? Only the decipherment of their inscriptions can tell.

The Tuaregs were divided into three classes, the nobles, the serfs who were camel breeders and merchants, and Negro slaves. Women were held in high esteem, even idolized, in strik-ing contrast to Moslem custom. The Tuareg weapons, sword, dagger, lance and shield were similar to those described as owned by the Garamantes by the historian Corippus in the sixth century. Even more striking is the Tuareg employment of the symbol of the cross, unique amongst Moslems, with which they decorate their weapons and equipment. They were desert brigands when the French encountered them, filling exactly the same role as the Christian Father, Augustine, attributed to the Garamantes.

One story seems to link the Tuaregs even more firmly with the Garamantes. According to Tuareg legend, their ancestor, Queen Tien-Hinane, was buried in a stone tumulus near the Abalessa fort, to the south of the Hoggar mountains. Their curiosity aroused, French amateur archaeologists excavated the tumulus in 1926. They found it to contain a stone mauso-leum, comprising passages and chambers, the walls decorated with indecipherable signs and inscriptions. They unearthed the skeletons of twelve noble retainers of the famous queen. 6 feet (1.8 metres) further down they reached a central chamber. On its floor lay a tiny bead, similar to those unearthed from the ruins of Carthage. In a corner they found a bowl bearing the insignia of the Emperor Constantine who recognized Christianity in A.D. 325. In the chamber's floor they discovered a sepulchral slab. Raising it, they found the skeleton of a woman, round her neck a jewel-encrusted necklace, ending in the reproduction of a Greek column and fashioned from solid gold. Her wrists were encased in golden bracelets. Dr Leblanc of the Faculty of Medicine of the University of Algiers, to whom the skeleton was eventually brought, described it as that of a 'woman of the white race'. Queen Tien-Hinane is believed to have died in the fourth century of our era.

Her identification as a white woman led the novelist Benoît to create his Antinea, queen of Atlantis, Plato's state. He based his belief on Herodotus's reference to a North African tribe which he called the Atlantes, and to the location of the lost continent in the Sahara by Professor Berlioux of Lyons University. He ignored the unfavourable geological history of the region. The Sahara has not experienced the tectonic disturbances reputed to have destroyed fabled Atlantis in a day and a night.

CARTHAGE.
THE CHILDREN WHO MUST NOT CRY

The Carthaginians left a legend which has stirred our imagination. A small, seafaring nation, they established colonies throughout the western Mediterranean where, inevitably, they clashed with the powerful Romans. The great Carthaginian general, Hannibal, crossed the Alps, campaigned for sixteen years in Italy, won great battles, but failed to conquer Rome. On his defeat in 202 B.C. Carthage was razed to the ground, destroyed as the victors had demanded. For 500 years Carthage had been the greatest city of the western world, situated on the African shore, close to modern Tunis. The Carthaginians were merchant-adventurers, courageous seamen, like their ancestors the Phoenicians of Tyre and Sidon. In the fifth century B.C. Hanno had ventured into the Atlantic and explored the west coast of Africa, Himilco had sailed up the coast of France, possibly to Britain. But the Carthaginians had also a darker reputation.

Only a fragment of the Carthaginians' own history has survived. We know of them from the writings of their Greek and Roman enemies, hostile, biased witnesses. Plutarch, writing long after their disappearance, called the Carthaginians 'a hard and gloomy people, subservient to their rulers, harsh to their subjects'. Compared with earlier historians, he was almost a flatterer. They described the Carthaginians as cowardly and cruel, obstinate and superstitious, under the thraldom of their priests, and observers of hideous religious rituals. To nineteenth-century European historians, the story told by the Greek historian, Diodorus of Sicily, seemed almost beyond belief.

In 310 B.C. an army of Greeks and their allies, 14,000 soldiers led by Agathocles, the tyrant of Syracuse, invaded Africa, bent on the destruction of Carthage. Defeating Hamilcar's far more numerous Carthaginians, who were rent by internal jealousies and dissensions, Agathocles laid siege to the city. Its fall seemed imminent. Seeking reasons for their misfortune, the Carthaginians attributed it to divine wrath, due to their impiety. Agathocles was the chosen instrument of their god's revenge. They had angered their god, Baal Hammon. Diodorus tells the nightmare story: 'Lately, instead of sacrificing children from the best families to the god, they had been buying children from other nations, rearing them in secret and then sacrificing them. When the matter was looked into, it became apparent that the greater part of the children immolated were substitutes.'

Diodorus, it was thought, had repeated ancient legend, the creation of some atrocity-monger, a typical example of a slur campaign against a hated enemy. The very savagery, indeed the poignancy of the story, appeared to invalidate its truth. No ancient people could have been that cruel or superstitious, especially the courageous Carthaginians. The historians forgot that the Jews (2 Kings 23: 10, and Jeremiah 7: 31) had built in the valley of Hinnom (which surrounds the southern walls of Jerusalem) a high place called Tophet where 'to burn their sons and daughters in the fire'.

The angry historians lashed out at the novelist Flaubert, subjecting him to a storm of abuse and mockery when he published in 1862 his *Salammbô*. Heatedly but vainly Flaubert quoted his source, Diodorus, who had described how these child sacrifices were performed. 'There were in Carthage several brass statues of Baal Hammon. The outstretched hands were inclined towards the earth so that a child placed on them could not lie there but rolled off and fell into the fiery pit below.'

Drawing upon a novelist's licence, Flaubert improved the story:

A man who staggered, pale and ugly with fright, pushed forward a little child. A small black form appeared in the hands of a Colossus; then it sank into the dark gulf wrapped in the red mantle of the priests of Moloch. Hamilcar stood at the right foot of Baal. When the fourteenth child was brought, everyone could see the shudder of horror he gave. The brass arms moved faster. They never paused now. Every time a child was placed in position, the priests laid their hands over him to lay upon the little body the sins of their race. The victims hardly reached the edge of the pit when they disappeared – like a drop of water on a red hot iron – and a plume of white smoke rose above the scarlet glow.

But the appetite of the god was not appeased; he wanted still more. To satisfy him, they piled the victims on to his hands and bound them with a great chain. At first the devotees wanted to count them, to see that their number corresponded to the days of the solar year. Then, as the pile mounted, the movements of the terrible arms made their heads reel, and it became impossible to distinguish the victims.

This went on for hours, right up to the evening. The inner walls took on a darker glow and the burning flesh became visible. Soon people even thought they could recognize heads of hair, limbs or whole bodies.

Daylight failed, clouds gathered above Baal. The flames of the funeral pyre died away and only a pyramid of black ashes rose about the god's knees. His body was red, like that of a giant who has bathed in blood, and with his head tilted back, he seemed to stagger as if weighed down by a terrible drunkenness.

Was Flaubert's source impeccable? Had Diodorus told the truth? Could the terrible legend be substantiated? Had the Carthaginians sacrificed children to appease their gods?

Archaeologists began to unearth the ruins of ancient Carthage in 1921. Little remained, for the Romans had destroyed and fired the city. One spot, it was thought, might yield results. On the strip of land enclosing the ancient harbour had lain Tanit's sanctuary, the precinct sacred to that goddess whom the Carthaginians had called the 'face of Baal'. There had landed Carthage's founder, the Phoenician princess Dido. The Roman poet Vergil repeated the legend. She fled from Tyre in 814 B.C. on the murder of her husband by her brother, King Pygmalion. A powerful African king demanded Dido's hand in marriage, threatening destruction of the colony. She refused, vowing fidelity to her dead husband. Rather than sacrifice her fellow citizens, Dido had a pyre erected on the shore. She was burnt alive, following other victims.

Dido's end deeply impressed the Carthaginians. Only by re-enactment of her death could they ensure the safety of their city. They employed the ancient legend of Dido's fate to justify human sacrifice at the place where she had died.

The archaeologists of the Tunisian department of antiquity sought the ancient necropolis at Le Kram lagoons, the site of the Carthaginians' harbour. A clue, the chance discovery by a workman, led to the right spot. This engraved *stele*, a long narrow stone, portrayed a priest carrying a young child on his arm. It is preserved in the Musée Nationale du Bardo in Tunis.

Excavation took many years. The archaeologists uncovered layer below layer of ancient occupation, the topmost yielding the burned bricks of the Roman conflagration, the lowest layer contemporary with the foundation of the city. They dug in hopes of finding Dido's tomb. They found scattered and tumbled together the burnt bones of little children, thousands of tiny bones, some those of mere infants, others of children up to twelve years of age. Mingled with the bones were the ashes of the vast pyre on which they had been sacrificed, to appease the wrath of Baal, to ensure the Carthaginians' safety.

Diodorus had told the truth about the Carthaginians' hideous ritual. Legend had been confirmed by archaeology. Gilbert and Colette Picard have told the story in their book *The Life and Death of Carthage** and Colette Picard in *Carthage.*†

Child sacrifice at Carthage did not cease with the Roman destruction of the city. It continued for hundreds of years, as Tertullian, the second-century Christian Father, himself a native of Carthage, shows. He stated that in Africa children were sacrificed to Saturn in public until the pro-consulship of Tiberius, in the Augustan age. Tiberius, the future emperor (A.D. 14–37) caused the priests of the god to be crucified.

But, says Tertullian, this execrable sacrifice continued to be performed in secret until his own day. The parents themselves brought their children to the blood-thirsty god. 'They comforted their children so that they should not cry when they were sacrificed.' Another Christian writer, Minucius Felix, relates that the parents 'stifled the cries of their children with kisses and caresses so as not to immolate sleeping victims'.

The holy place of Carthage, Baal's sanctuary, has been made into a sunken garden, planted with pelargoniums and surrounded by cypress trees. The bones of the little children 'who must not cry' have been collected and buried together.

THE ETRUSCAN ENIGMA

Even in antiquity the Etruscans were surrounded by an aura of mystery. Their Greek contemporaries were puzzled by their sudden emergence as a maritime and trading power. Their later Roman conquerors and successors benefited from their achievements and never lost their jealousy of the people they had supplanted. Despite two centuries of scholarly inquiry and the discovery and excavation of their buried cities and forgotten tombs, the problems remain. From where did the Etruscans come? Was their art their own, or a mere copy of the greater Greek achievement?

The Etruscans were at the zenith of their power and prosperity in north-western Italy when Herodotus wrote his his-

* Sidgwick and Jackson, 1968.
† Elek Books, 1964.

107

tory in the fifth century B.C. He related that they had migrated from Asia Minor in about 1000 B.C., as refugees fleeing from the great famine which had struck the kingdom of Lydia. Writing five centuries later, Dionysius of Halicarnassus was fully convinced that they were a very ancient indigenous people who 'do not resemble any other in its language and its customs'.

The Etruscans were unlike any other people. They evoked the envy of their contemporaries and the admiration of the people who can now gaze upon their frescoes and their sculptures. D. H. Lawrence (*Etruscan Places*) may have discerned their *joie de vivre*. Standing in one of the underground tombs, its paintings partly obscured by time, he wrote:

Fragments of people at banquets, limbs that dance without dancers, birds that fly into nowhere, lions whose devouring heads are devoured away! Once it was all bright and dancing; the delights of the underworld; honouring the dead with wine, and flutes playing for a dance, and limbs whirling and pressing. And it was deep and sincere honour rendered to the dead and to the mysteries. It is contrary to our ideas; but the ancients had their own philosophy for it. As the pagan old writer says: 'For no part of us nor of our bodies shall be, which doth not feel religion: and let there be no lack of singing for the soul, no lack of leaping and of dancing for the knees and the heart; for all these know the gods.' Which is very evident in the Etruscan dancers. They know the gods in their very finger-tips. The wonderful fragments of limbs and bodies that dance on in a field of obliteration still know the gods, and make it evident to us.

Perhaps unfairly the Romans attributed to the Etruscans unbridled sexual licence, describing them as people without shame who indulged in sexual acts, making love and taking their pleasure in full view even of passers-by, and calling the act impudently by name. They were great wine-bibbers and beautiful to behold, according to the fourth century B.C. Greek historian Theopompus who delighted in malicious gossip. The Greek philosopher Posidonius gave them credit for manly courage. The poet Vergil admired their fertile genius and artistic vigour.

Diodorus of Sicily who wrote his *University History* during the reign of the Roman Emperor Augustus, when the Etruscans were only a memory, provided a more balanced view.

The Etruscans, who formerly were distinguished for their energy, conquered a vast territory and there founded many important towns. They also disposed of powerful naval forces and for a long time enjoyed mastery of the seas, so much so that the one which washed the western shores of Italy was called by them the Tyrrhenian. They perfected the equipment of their land forces by inventing what is called the trumpet, which is of the greatest utility in war and was named by them Tyrrhenian; they also devised marks of honour for the generals who led them, assigning to them lictors, an ivory throne and a toga bordered with purple. And in their houses they invented the peristyle which is a great convenience in that it deadens the uproar caused by their great crowds of servants. The majority of these discoveries were imitated by the Romans, who perfected them and introduced them into their civilization. They encouraged the progress of letters, science, nature and theology and developed to a higher degree than any other people the interpretation of thunder. This is why today they still inspire those who are masters of nearly all the world (the Romans), with such deep admiration, and why they are employed today as interpreters of the celestial signs. As they inhabit a land fertile in fruits of all kinds and cultivate it assiduously, they enjoy an abundance of agricultural produce which not only is sufficient for themselves but by its excess leads them to unbridled luxury and indolence. For twice a day they have tables sumptuously dressed and laid with everything that can contribute towards delicate living; they have coverings embroidered with flowers and are served wine in quantities of silver bowls, and they have at their call a considerable number of slaves. Some of the latter are of a rare beauty; others dress themselves in clothes more magnificent than befits their station of servitude, and the domestic staff have all kinds of private dwellings: as have indeed most of the freed men. In general they have abandoned the valiant steadfastness that they prized so much in former days, and by their indulgencies in banquets and effeminate delights they have lost the reputation which their ancestors won in war, which does not surprise us. But what served more than anything to turn them to soft and idle living was the quality of their land, for, living in a country that produces everything and is of inexhaustible fecundity, they are able to store up large quantities of fruit of every kind. Etruria is indeed very fertile, extending for the most part over plains separated by hills with arable slopes and it is moderately well-watered, not only in the winter season, but also during the summer.

Under the influence of a too-generous climate, with their love of idleness, the Etruscans had become degenerate and had fallen victims to Roman discipline and moral character. This Roman opinion is being challenged by the archaeologists who are slowly revealing the full extent of Etruscan civilization and interpreting their culture. But excavation alone is unlikely to solve the problem of Etruscan origins. The craniological study of Etruscan skulls has failed to elucidate the mystery. The blood grouping of their descendants, those who have been little ethnologically disturbed, has proved equally inconclusive. The slightly higher proportion of groups A and B than amongst their neighbours seems to connect them with certain oriental peoples. The Etruscan language is considered not to belong to the Indo-European group of languages, the speech of their Greek and Roman contemporaries. The French linguist Zacharie Maigani believes they originated in Albania. The German scholar, Barthold Geog Niebuhr, asserts that they came from beyond the Alps.

No theory commands complete acceptance. It seems possible that both Herodotus and Dionysius were partly correct. The Etruscans may have been herdsmen who descended into the fertile valleys and created their own culture, helped possibly by the infusion of an alien race, perhaps the survivors of the Lydian refugees who, according to Herodotus, 'coasted along among many nations' before reaching Italy. Etruscan art and some of their religious practices seem to have been influenced by oriental ideas.

Following their absorption by the Romans, the Etruscan cities and tombs were submerged and lost to view. Several of their statues and tombs were found during the period of the Renaissance. Some art historians have detected Etruscan motifs in fifteenth-century Italian sculptures. The rediscovery of two great bronzes, the famous Capitoline wolf and the statue of the orator, excited interest and led to the search for the subterranean dwellings of the Etruscan dead.

The first excavations were made in 1728 at Volterra where the tomb of the illustrious Cecina family was disclosed. The chance discovery ten years later of a tomb at Palestrina revealed the Ficoroni coffer, depicting various episodes of the voyages of the Argonauts, one of the ancient masterpieces of engraving in bronze. By mid eighteenth century the excavators had penetrated the frescoed tombs of Corneto (present-day Tarquinia). Archaeologists, mostly amateurs, scoured the Etruscan countryside searching for more evidence of their lost art. In 1828 a team of oxen fell into a tomb at Vulci. In 1834 a beautiful sarcophagus was found in a tomb at Tuscania. During the next hundred years, subterranean tombs were entered at Cerveten, Vulci, Tarquinia, Veio, Orvieto and many other places. An amazing, forgotten world had been revealed. Etruscan history has been partly recreated.

A series of princely tombs filled with golden ornaments and statues and decorated with frescoes symbolize a sudden, prodigious increase in wealth in the region between the rivers Arno and Tiber, the Apennines and the Tyrrhenian Sea. By the seventh century B.C., the Etruscans had founded a confederation of twelve city states, united more by religious solidarity than by political union, probably at Veii, Caere, Tarquinii, Vulci, Rusellae, Vetulonia, Volsinii, Clusium, Perugia, Cortona, Arretium and Volateera. They extended their domain by a series of conquests, subjugating other Italian tribes including the Latins. The Etruscan dynasty, the Tarquins, ruled Rome from 616 to 509 B.C. Uniting their naval strength with that of the Carthaginians, the Etruscans held in check the Greek colonists of southern Italy, defeating the Greeks at the battle of Alatia in 535 B.C. That was the apogee of Etruscan power. The slow decline set in. The Etruscan fleet was defeated by the Greeks at Cumae in the Bay of Naples in 474 B.C. The republican Romans destroyed Veii in 396, Volsinii in 265. The first Italian civilization had been vanquished and according to the poet Horace, it 'vanquished its vanquishers'.

Many theories have been advanced to explain the Etruscans' decline and fall. They may have failed to weld themselves into a nation. They suffered from social stagnation, from over-rigid class distinctions. All power was held by the ruling families. The working class had no rights, only duties. They pampered their women, they clung to obsolete customs. They guarded their ancestral habits too jealously. They were too conservative, fearing change. They suffered from slavish obedience to their soothsayers, the haruspices, the priestly caste who divined the will of the gods from the clap of thunder, the flight of a bird, the scrutiny of livers. They gave the Etruscans false hopes of greatness, too strong a certainty of their destiny.

According to the Roman historian Livy, the Etruscans were more addicted to religious practices than any other nation. They passed their practice of liver-reading on to the Romans. It suggests an oriental influence on Etruscan life, derived from Canaanite beliefs, or the Assyrian Magi. A bronze model of a liver found at Piacenza is divided into forty-five areas, each inscribed with the name of the presiding divinity. The Etruscans were equally concerned with the after-life. Therein lies the paradox of their culture. Gay, pleasure-loving, self-indulgent, they were obsessed with death. Nearly all knowledge of the Etruscans is derived from their mausolea. They revealed their activities in their art, the shape of their temples, the plans of their houses, the streets of their cities, their banquets and games, their hope of resurrection. They created an image of the present as a stubborn challenge to the future. No other ancient people equalled the Etruscans in self-esteem.

THE HAIRY AINU

The Japanese are reluctant to admit that the Ainu are the aboriginal inhabitants of their islands. They prefer to believe that the sun goddess, Amaterasu, created the land expressly for them. It hurts, too, that the Ainu are classified as Caucasians, members of the white, barbarian race which inhabits Europe. In contrast to the yellow-skinned, Mongoloid Asiatics, the Ainu are fair-skinned with the characteristic Caucasoid long head and square face, and hirsute, heavily-built bodies. They are no more hairy than Europeans. They lack the Mongolian 'eye-fold' and they describe their own people as 'of the same eye-socket'. Carleton Coon, the American anthropologist and authority on the races of man, standing beside an Ainu, remarked that, except for the other man's more widely-set eyes and lower nose bridge, they might have been brothers. How the Ainu's ancestors reached Japan is one of the mysteries of migration, which archaeology alone is unlikely to solve.

When the Yayoi, the ancestors of the Japanese, invaded the islands in about A.D. 300, they found an earlier people whom they called the Emishi, meaning 'the barbarians'. These Ainu, a word meaning 'man', were simple hunters and fishermen. They were forced to retreat northwards, the Japanese exerting relentless and increasing pressure as their farming and herding population expanded. Settled agriculture and animal husbandry gave them irresistible superiority over primitive food-gatherers.

A memorial presented to the emperor in 805 refers to the drain on the treasury caused by the constant fighting with the Ainu. It recorded that they 'gathered together like ants, but dispersed like birds'. Even then the Japanese were loath to accept the Ainu's indigenous origin. When, in 839, a number of arrow heads were found on a beach, their presence was attributed, not to the long-time existence of the despised aborigines, but to a flight of geese which had carried them in their bodies from the mainland where they had been shot by other Mongols.

The Ainu, driven into the colder islands of Hokkaido and Sakhalin, retained their independence until 1799 when these islands were colonized by the Japanese in order to forestall Russian aggression. The Ainu were accorded humble status and treated as under-dogs, until the twentieth-century by when many had become assimilated with the Japanese or intermarried. About 14,000 pure Ainu live in small villages on the coast of Hokkaido. Other peoples of similar racial strain inhabit the Kurile and Aleutian islands, farther to the north, and still others the basin of the Amur river in Manchuria. These Ainu people may have migrated from the west in remote antiquity. One theory suggests that eastern Asia was peopled by Caucasians before the arrival of the Mongolians. Another suggestion accounts for the legend of white, bearded men in

Mexico and Peru by an Ainu crossing of the Bering Straits at the time of the Mongoloid invasion which peopled the American continents shortly before, or soon after, the last Ice Age. Some support for this theory is gained from the discovery in 1958 on the coast of Ecuador of pottery of similar design to that made by the Ainus' ancestors.

The modern Ainu have no traditions relating to a migration from an original homeland. None of their customs or ideas mirrors typical Caucasian spiritual beliefs or values. The Ainu appear to have lived in Japan since 3000 B.C., the date attributed to the earliest forms of Jōmon culture, as it is named. The term is derived from the corded design found on pottery excavated from ancient habitations. This pattern was achieved by pressing the soft, unfired clay with small sticks or rollers on which plaited cord had been closely wound. Or the vessels may have been placed in plaited baskets which were burnt away in the firing. It is a distinct design, not used by any primitive people other than the Ainu who, until the nineteenth century at least, employed it in the carving of wooden ornaments and in textiles.

This is not the only link between the Ainu and the primitive culture which existed in neolithic times. The Jōmons sunk their houses several feet below ground, digging post-holes and constructing steep roofs rising to an apex, exactly as the Ainu did until recent times, when they abandoned the sunken floor, replacing it with stone slabs and open hearths. The Jōmons built huge mounds of shell, their food refuse, another Ainu characteristic derived from their fishing industry.

The bones of animals, their stone spearheads, harpoons, fish hooks and hand-axes identify the Jōmons as simple hunters and fishermen who, like the early Ainu, created a rudimentary social organization. The discovery of carved stone staffs, emblems of authority, suggests that they were ruled by chiefs or family head-men. The presence in their primitive graves of small female figures, possibly the representation of a mother goddess, indicate their worship of a fertility cult. The lack of grave goods and of organized cemeteries points to the absence of a cult of the dead, which the Ainu developed. Divergences between Jōmon and early Ainu skeleton remains, due possibly to mixtures with related peoples from the remote islands, are not considered by anthropologists as an obstacle to the relevance of Jōmon and Ainu cultures. Whoever these Jōmons were, they appear to have replaced an even earlier, unknown race which left primitive artifacts beneath the layers of volcanic ash which cover much of the region of Tokyo, because of the many eruptions of Mount Fuji. The bronze-tool and weapon-making Yayois bear no similarity to the far more ancient Neolithic Jōmon culture.

The Ainu were described by the Christian missionaries who visited them in the late nineteenth century as content to follow the old paths and indifferent to the higher standards of economic and cultural life of their Japanese neighbours. They were content to hunt and fish, to sustain life and to worship their gods. They seldom lacked food. Land and sea supplied their simple needs. They were expert fishermen, netting salmon and trout, spearing the sea fish from their dug-out canoes. They trained their dogs to swim offshore, divided into two groups in single file. A cry from the shore made them converge into a crescent-shaped formation, trapping the fish and forcing them shorewards where they could be caught. They collected several varieties of shellfish, and harpooned walrus and whales. Like the Arctic Eskimos, the Ainu invented a detachable head, held by a rope, which was dislodged on impact. It prevented the animal's escape.

They hunted with bows and arrows, mimicking the cry of an injured animal to delay the flight of the rest of the herd of deer and bring them within range. They made traps and pit holes to catch unwary beasts. To detect a hibernating bear, they watched for the telltale yellow discolouration of the snow made by the sleeper's breath. A hunter crawled into the den, carrying only a stone knife, with his head protected by skins. His job was to rustle out the bear amongst the waiting band of hunters. Young cubs were carried home to be reared for the sacrificial ceremony, the occasion of a great annual feast, when they were killed to enable them to act as messengers to the gods, to assure them of the Ainus' devotion and to counter adverse rumours carried by other animals.

The Ainu believed in the existence of spirit beings, descended in a hierarchy from the supreme god, the creator of life. Their religion was not formalized. There were no Ainu priests, only medicine men who practised magic. While they believed in rebirth after death, the Ainu had no clear idea of rewards and punishments. Each human being was afflicted by demons, who were personified by dwarfs, the earliest inhabitants of the land.

Even the most bigoted missionaries failed to find evil in the Ainu religion. They observed their high standards of morals and of justice. Offenders against customary behaviour were tried by the council of elders, who considered each case carefully. A man might be required to test his innocence by extracting a stone from boiling water or picking a coal from a burning fire. Scorched skin betrayed his guilt, a form of judgement which was practised in medieval Europe. The guilty man was never killed. He might be fined, beaten or driven from the community, according to the nature of his crime.

The Ainus were ruled by etiquette. Within the house, a single unpartitioned room about 20 feet (6 metres) long, everyone had his or her allotted place; the honoured guest by the wall farthest from the door, the lesser guest nearer the entrance, the husband and wife by the hearth. There was no furniture. Everyone sat or lay on mats. By the middle of the nineteenth century the Ainu had adopted the Japanese custom of the kimono for ordinary wear. Their bark-cloth garments were kept for ceremonial occasions. Their women wore ankle-length gowns. They held an inferior status but were permitted freedom of choice in marriage. A man could marry as many wives as he could support. The possession of several wives was considered to be proof of virility.

The Ainu had no written script. Their language is quite unlike any other and defies classification. Like their customs, it supplies no clues to their origin.

Prior to the arrival of the Japanese, the Ainu lived in comparative isolation, having little contact with other peoples, possibly the reason for their failure to progress. They were content with their hard life, their daily struggle for subsistence, and with their gloomy, cold and draughty houses. The missionaries found them suffering from the shock of civilization.

An Ainu told the Venerable Dr John Batchelor: 'Our fathers had an easy time of it, without care and anxiety. They lived in great contentment and general happiness. But now all is changed, and the struggle for existence is wiping us out.'

THE KHYMERS ABANDON ANGKOR

Floundering across swamps and hacking a path through the green jungles of Cambodia in 1850, the French missionary Charles Bouillevaux came upon a huge lake. On its shores rose towers and temples, their crumbling stones engulfed in forest, their foundations clutched by tree roots, their walls ascending in precipitous steps like the slopes of a mountain range. Monkeys played in the ruins. Orchids grew from the sculptured walls. Lichens masked the friezes. The dank smell of death pervaded the air. Coming closer, Bouillevaux saw a vast complex of buildings some of gigantic size, of singular beauty and exquisite proportions, deserted and abandoned. He had discovered the lost city of Angkor. The French naturalist, Henri Mouhot, made it known to the western world. He thought Angkor grander than anything left by Greece or Rome. It must have been designed by some ancient Michelangelo.

The work of restoration and conservation took half a century. Angkor rose from the dead in 1907. This sudden emergence of a forgotten civilization gave rise to fanciful and far-fetched theories. Angkor was a city of fabulous antiquity and unknown origin. Its people had disappeared as the result of some mysterious catastrophe, leaving no trace of the city's inhabitants and builders. It could have been lost Atlantis.

The romance of Angkor, says Christopher Pym 'lies in the story of a civilization which flowered brilliantly for six centuries and then suddenly disappeared into the forest'.* The mystery is why? 'Why did such an accomplished and vigorous people suddenly stop building their beautiful temples? Why did the great Khymer Empire collapse?' Spiritual imagination made the Kymer civilization one of the most remarkable of the

* *The Ancient Civilization of Angkor,* Mentor Books, 1968.

ancient world. Bernard Groslier* calls the Khymer culture one of the most brilliant of South-East Asia. Our knowledge of the Khymers, he says, is far from complete. Many surprises may be in store. Nothing is known of the prehistory of Cambodia. He describes the story of the Khymers' rise and fall as a tale of mystery and imagination.

The Khymers were one of several tribes which inhabited South-East Asia. They had become 'Indianized', and had adopted the Hindu religion with its trinity of gods, Siva, Vishnu and Brahma. They established their capital at Angkor in A.D. 802. In the course of the next six centuries they expanded their rule over all Cambodia and much of Thailand and Laos, and their influence over modern South Vietnam and parts of Burma. They created great material prosperity from the fertility of their well-watered land.

King Jayavarman II established Angkor, Yasovarman I built the city. Indravarman in 881 created the Bakong, the first artificial temple-mountain, and Suryavarman II (1113–50) added to the complex of temples. In 1177 the Chams, another Hinduized people, sailed their ships up the Mekong river, across the Great Lake and up the Siemreap river. They took the Khymers by surprise, pillaging and sacking the city. They departed, their ships weighed down with the rich spoil. King Jayavarman VII took revenge. In 1199 he won a decisive battle and captured the Cham capital. The Khymers under his rule enjoyed their greatest period of prosperity and temple building. He extended the empire from the lower Annamese coast on the east to the borders of Burma on the west, into Laos on the north-east and down the Malay peninsula. He rebuilt the capital, surrounding it with walls and a great moat 8 miles (13 kilometres) in perimeter.

Each god-king was buried beneath the temple he had built during his lifetime. His successor raised his own mausoleum or 'god-mountain'. The Bakong, the most celebrated of the many temples which comprise Angkor Wat, rises in tiers of terraces surmounted by a shrine. It symbolized Mount Meru, the Hindu mythical mountain, the centre of the universe. Angkor *was*

* *Angkor, Art and Civilization,* Thames and Hudson, 1966 (second edition).

Mount Meru. Each successive ruler developed the same formula, building pyramids in mountain form crowned by towers and surrounded by an elaborate system of galleries and pavilions. Jayavarman VII built the Bayon temple, in a series of apparently rotating towers, each spinning on its own axis as if some important operation is taking place. And so it is. The towers and their sculptured designs represent a message in spiritual form, the guarantee of health, wealth, happiness and the permanence of the Khymer empire. The feeling of movement had been adapted from the Vishnuite legend called the Churning of the Sea of Milk. The Khymers repeated it again and again in their sculptures.

Teams of giants are depicted having a tug-of-war with snakes' bodies for rope. To understand the act's significance it is necessary, says Christopher Pym, to understand the thought behind it.

In the churning legend Vishnu is supposed to appear in the form of a tortoise to recover things of value, ambrosia for example, which have become lost. He seats himself at the bottom of the Sea of Milk, and offers his shell as the base on which a mountain may be pivoted. The gods and demons twist a great serpent around the mountain, and proceed to churn ambrosia. The churn operates like a boy's top, but whereas a boy spins his top, then detaches the piece of string, the string in the churning legend, represented by a snake, is pulled backwards and forwards by two teams and remains coiled round the pivot.

The legend is easily understood if one equates ambrosia with health, wealth and happiness. The Khymers believed they would obtain these desirable gifts by representing the legend in sculpture. The most striking examples are the sculptures at the city gates, where the gods straddle the moat. The moat represents the Sea of Milk, or was the Sea of Milk, just as the Khymer god-king was the source of the ambrosia. To see his sculptured face was a guarantee of future happiness. But only if his subjects fulfilled his commands. They were forced to labour building temples and constructing and maintaining the irrigation system which ensured the fertility of the soil. The system's efficiency guaranteed prosperity. The pools and temples were linked in magical relationship. Neither could exist without the other. It would have been unthinkable for the Khymers to have built temples without pools, or pools without temples. Together they formed the magical basis of the absolute power of the king, the incarnation of God.

The Khymers were obsessed with water. Without water there was no life. They took advantage of a natural phenomenon, the back-flooding of the Mekong river. Each spring its waters were augmented by the melting of the Himalayan snows and the torrential monsoon rains. There was more water than the Mekong could cope with. The water backed up, the flow reversed. The river flowed into the great lake, the Tonle Sap, on which Angkor had been built. To overcome the danger of excessive flooding, the Khymers erected dykes and created the temple pools. Two such reservoirs held 1,000 million gallons each. From them the muddy water was drained into the fields, carrying a deposit of rich alluvium. Thereby the Khymers were able to reap three rice crops a year. The system required constant enlargement and vigilance. Each new pool required the building of another temple. According to one theory, the Khymers exhausted themselves building temples.

Angkor was bursting with riches in 1296 when it was visited by the Chinese traveller Chou Ta-kuan. He spent a year at Angkor, and provides the only written source of information about its people.

When the king rides forth soldiers march at the head of the procession, followed by the standards, banners and musicians. Next comes a column of three to five hundred palace maidens, clad in robes of floral pattern, with flowers in their hair and bearing candles, lit even in broad daylight. These are followed by another troop of maidens carrying the royal plate of gold and silver and a whole series of ornaments and insignia. Next come Amazons armed with spears and shields forming the private palace guard, and goat and horse-drawn carriages, all decorated with gold. Then, preceded by innumerable red parasols, visible from afar, come the ministers and the princes, all mounted on elephants, followed by the wives and concubines of the king, borne in palanquins and carriages, or mounted on horseback and elephants, their gold-spangled parasols assuredly

KNOSSOS—CRETE: The Hall of the Double Axes in the Palace of Minos

THE GREAT PYRAMID:

Chambers and Passages in The Great Pyramid

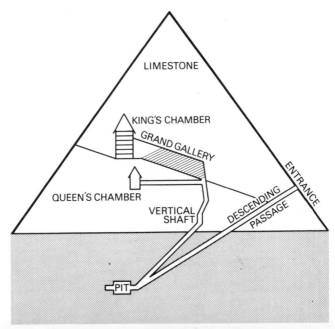

LIMESTONE

KING'S CHAMBER

GRAND GALLERY

ENTRANCE

QUEEN'S CHAMBER

VERTICAL SHAFT

DESCENDING PASSAGE

PIT

MALTA: The rock-cut Hypoqtum of Halsaflitri showing the Main Hall and the Holy of Holies

MALTA: Pre-historic tracks made by sledges

EASTER ISLAND: Images outside the crater of Rano Raraku

RHODESIA: The massive outer wall of the Elliptical Temple in the Zimbabwe ruins

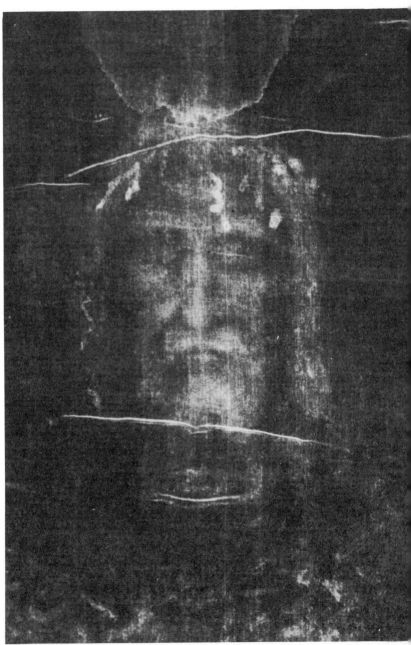

The Holy Shroud of Christ: This incredible portrait of Christ appears on the negative plate or film when the inverted (negative) image of the Shroud is photographed. (Fig 14, THE MAN IN THE SHROUD)

A view of the well-planned Mohenjo Daro city in the Indus Valley. On the left are the bases of pillars supporting the roof of the Great Bath

CARTHAGE: The Punic 'Tophet' Crematorium

ITALY: The Etruscan Necropolis at Cerveteri, showing the tombs which bear a curious resemblence to African huts

JAPAN: Ainu fishermen

THE BAYON TEMPLE in the city of Angkor

Stonehenge

Sutton Hoo: A view of the boat after excavation

Mystery Hill: The Hut and the Sacrificial Stone

The Kensington Rune Stone

The Parahyba Inscription

numbering more than a hundred. Finally the sovereign. He stands erect on an elephant whose tusks are sheathed in gold, and holds the precious sword of state in his hand. He is escorted by more than twenty white parasols, spangled with gold. Numerous elephants mill around him and yet another troop of soldiers provides him protection.

Twice a day the sovereign holds an audience for the affairs of government. After waiting some time, one hears music far away within the palace. Without a fanfare on conch horns greets the sovereign and an instant later two palace maidens raise the curtain with delicate fingers and the king, sword in hand, appears standing at the window of gold. Ministers and people join their hands together and bow their foreheads to the ground. Only when the noise of the conches ceases are they permitted to raise their heads. When the audience is over the king leaves, the two maidens let the curtain fall and all rise. From this it can be seen that a kingdom of barbarians though this may be, they know full well the meaning of royalty.

Both men and women, including the king, wear their hair in a chignon and have the upper part of the body bare, wearing only a small piece of cloth around the loins. Both use perfumes of sandalwood, musk and other essences most liberally. The pattern and quality of the cloth varies according to the status of the person. Among the stuffs worn by the sovereign are some worth three or four ounces of gold. Although cloth is woven in the country itself, it is also imported from Siam, Champa and India, the latter being generally the most prized for its fine workmanship.

The king usually wears a crown of gold. Occasionally, however, he is adorned only with a garland of sweet-smelling flowers similar to jasmin, entwined in his chignon. Around his neck he wears about three pounds of large pearls and around his wrists and ankles, and on his fingers, bracelets and rings of gold set with cats' eyes.

Even the king goes bare-footed. The soles of his feet and the palms of his hands being tinted with red dye. Among his subjects, only the women dye their soles and palms red. The men would not dare.

The king has five wives, one for the principal chamber and one each for the four cardinal points. As for concubines and palace maidens, I have heard a figure of three to five thousand mentioned. When a family has a beautiful daughter they never fail to send her to the palace.

The freedom accorded to their women by the Khymers surprised and even shocked the Chinese traveller. The daughters of the upper classes were as well educated as the sons. They became counsellors, royal secretaries, professors and even judges. Many were skilled in science, and others engaged in trade. Chinese merchants took Khymer wives to benefit from their experience. Chou Ta-kuan thought the Khymer women were extremely lascivious.

A day or two after they have given birth they sleep with their husbands. If a husband does not respond to their desire, he is abandoned. Again, if he is called away on some business, all goes well for a couple of nights, but very soon they are sure to say 'I am not a spirit. How can I sleep alone?'

He was told about the puberty rites which he was not allowed to see. Young maidens, on reaching the age of between seven and nine years, were taken on the appointed day to the temple where each girl was given a taper. It was lit at nightfall at the start of the ceremony. When it had burned to its socket, the girl was taken to the priest, with whom her family had made a contract.

On the chosen night a great banquet is given, and the parents seek out the priest with palanquins, parasols and music. Two pavilions are constructed of vari-coloured silk. In one the young girl is seated, in the other the priest. So deafening is the music that it is impossible to hear a word that is said. When the chosen moment has arrived, the priest enters the pavilion of the virgin, deflowers her with his hand and collects the first fruits in some wine. It is averred that the parents, relatives and neighbours mark their foreheads with it, and even that they taste it. Some claim that the priest actually unites with the young girl but others deny this. Since Chinese are, however, not permitted to witness the event, it was impossible for me to determine the precise truth in this regard.

Chou Ta-kuan observed that the women aged very quickly. At twenty or thirty they resembled Chinese women of forty or fifty. He found the country to be 'frightfully hot', and, 'one

cannot spend a single day or night without taking several baths.'
Each family, or group of families, had their own pool.

Both sexes enter the pool together. The only restriction is based on age. The older members of the family do not bathe with the young. Often, small groups of women go off together to bathe in the great river outside the town. They take off their clothes on the river bank. Sometimes there are thousands of them in the water, including women of the noble families, who incur no disgrace whatever, even though everyone can see them naked from head to foot. The Chinese, in their leisure hours, often have fun going to see this. I have even heard it said that there are those who enter the water to take advantage of the occasion.

Chou Ta-kuan noticed, without fully realizing its significance, another feature of Khymer life, the presence of yellow-robed priests in the temples. A point to which we shall return.

Chou Ta-kuan saw Angkor in its decline. The power of the Khymers was waning. After Jayavarman VII's death they were defeated first by the Annamites of North Vietnam, and later by the Thais. They captured and sacked Angkor in 1431. The jungle closed over its ruins.

Why did the prosperous and courageous Khymers fall such easy victims to these invaders? Several observers believe that the Thai invasion was the result, not the cause, of the Khymers' decline. The Khymers genius was already dead, believes Bernard Groslier.

They had reached a stage of spiritual paralysis. The basic cults fell into neglect. The vast irrigation system deteriorated. The fields suffered a catastrophic disaster from flooding. With their fields no longer fertilized by alluvium, the Khymers were forced to turn to dry-rice cultivation. That required the clearing and burning of forest. That led to soil erosion and the creation of dead savannahs. The economy collapsed, the population declined. Angkor was swallowed up in the green silence of the forest.

The cause of this decline was over-centralized rule. The king became cut off from his people, the prisoner of the great priestly families, a tiny, sterile elite. The country was milked dry for the sole benefit of the king. The Khymer culture from its start had contained the seeds of its own destruction. It was beautiful but barren, doomed to failure because the Khymers were incapable of evolving a philosophy of man and his destiny. They accepted what the gods gave and failed to formulate a theory of public welfare.

Christopher Pym examines the many factors which may have contributed to Angkor's decline. The Siemreap river may have changed its course. He noted an ancient bridge spanning a dry channel. A massive inrush of water from the overflowing lake may have overcome the defences. The Khymers may have become exhausted by the royal megalomania of temple building. One fact only was certain. The irrigation system stopped working in the fourteenth century. Pym sought deeper reasons. He found them in the human and spiritual factors of Khymer life.

He noticed that Jayavarman VII's death had been marked by violent reaction from the people. His temple had been thrown down, the sculptures defaced. The Khymers had become affected by some kind of mania. According to the accepted theory, the king exhausted his subjects by the creation of yet another reservoir, and by the building of even more temples. But Jayavarman had been a very level-headed ruler who had acceded to the throne in middle age. Pym sought a deeper reason. Chou Ta-kuan, he recalled, had remarked the presence of yellow-robed, Buddhist priests at Angkor.

Since 802, at least, the Khymers had worshipped the Hindu gods, Vishnu, Siva and Brahma. They had built their temple-mountains to symbolize Mount Meru. Jayavarman VII had placed statues of Buddha in his temples. The new religion, Pym believes failed to satisfy the people's demands. Jayavarman's innovation was a spiritual catastrophe. The Khymers had worshipped their king as a god. The particular sect of Buddhism Jayavarman had embraced revered Buddha but did not worship him as a god. The Hinduized king had demanded obedience and had guaranteed prosperity. Theravad Buddhism demanded humility and promised suffering. The Hindu god-king dressed himself in gold and lived in sumptuous palaces. The Buddhist monks preached that the king should give up his powers and clothe himself in rags. The old faith had been obsessed with material prosperity. The new one required resignation to poverty. Hunger was a virtue. The new religion loosened the Khymers' loyalties. The irrigation system was allowed to fall into disrepair. They became too weak to resist the Thais.

The Khymers abandoned their temples and fled into the jungle. Their descendants inhabit Cambodia to this day, content to eke out a living from their dry-rice cultivation. Staunch Buddhists, they take small interest in Angkor's glorious past.

THE PANAGYURISHTE TREASURE

The department of antiquities of the Bulgarian National Archaeological Museum at Sophia, and in particular the curator in chief, Ivan Venedikov, can take pride in their achievement in dating and identifying a hoard of golden vessels which were found in 1949.

Digging for clay at Panagyurishte, between the towns of Sophia and Plovdiv, the ancient Philippopolis, workmen unearthed eight vases and a cup, all made from solid gold. They weighed $12\frac{1}{2}$ pounds (5.6 kilos). The region where they were found had been ancient Thrace, the rich and turbulent land subjugated in 350 B.C. by Philip of Macedon, the father of the more famous Alexander the Great. Following Alexander's death in 323, the Thracians exhausted themselves in their attempt to throw off the Macedonian yoke. They fell easy victims to the Celts who conquered Thrace in 278 B.C. The Panagyurishte treasure had been buried during one of these periods of upheaval.

The designs on the cups and drinking vessels portrayed episodes from Greek mythology. Yet they did not appear to be of Grecian manufacture. They represented oriental love of ostentation, rather than Greek simplicity.

The treasure consists of eight rhytons, or vases with wide mouths and a small hole for drinking, and a phiale, a shallow bowl used for libations at banquets and religious ceremonies.

They had been made by the ancient method of hammering the gold sheet on which the designs had been chiselled.

The first rhyton is $5\frac{1}{2}$ inches (13.5 centimetres) high and weighs about $21\frac{1}{2}$ ounces (674.6 grams). Its lower end is shaped to represent a stag, its snout, mouth, nose, eyes and eyelashes all artistically chiselled. In the lower lip is the drinking aperture, a small, round hole. The handle ends in the shape of a female head. The upper end is worked in the shape of a lion resting its front paws on the mouth of the rhyton. Four figures decorate the neck. The goddess Pallas Athene is clothed in a long sleeveless gown; by her sits Paris, dressed in a short coat and pointed shoes. Next comes Hera, enthroned and holding her mantle across her lap. Aphrodite stands erect, draped in a long mantle. These garments are peculiar, not those in which these mythological gods and goddesses are usually depicted. Had it not been for the names inscribed above their heads, they might not have been identified.

The second rhyton is about 5 inches (13 centimetres) high and weighs 22 ounces (689 grams). It is similar in shape to the first and shows two groups of figures: Heracles battling with the roe of Cyrenaica, and Theseus fighting the bull of Marathon. The animals are delineated in great detail, even to the hair of their fur. Heracles is naked; Theseus is dressed in a short cloak. Both heroes press the defeated animal to the ground. Their front legs are unnaturally twisted and out of proportion.

The third rhyton is 5 inches (12.5 centimetres) high and weighs $16\frac{1}{2}$ ounces (506.05 grams). Its lower part represents the head of a ram. Above its muzzle, Dionysius, seated on a throne, holds the hands of Eriopis. His body is covered with a heavy mantle. Two maenads dance, both garbed in trailing robes.

The fourth rhyton is $5\frac{1}{2}$ inches (14 centimetres) high and weighs 14 ounces (439.05 grams). Lighter than the others, its shape is also different. Its lower part represents a he-goat, displayed in great anatomical detail. Four mythological figures, all garbed and shod, decorate the vase's neck. They are named as Hera, Artemis, Apollo and Nike, the goddess of victory.

The fifth rhyton is $8\frac{1}{2}$ inches (21.5 centimetres) high and weighs 15 ounces (460.75 grams). It is shaped as a woman's head, her hair finely chiselled. The sixth rhyton is 9 inches (22.5 centimetres) high and weighs 15 ounces (466.75 grams). It represents another woman's head. The seventh rhyton, 8 inches (20.5 centimetres high), weighs $12\frac{1}{2}$ ounces (387.3 grams). It is shaped as a woman's head, but this time she is unveiled and wears a helmet, ornamented by two griffons.

The amphora, the drinking vessel, is $11\frac{1}{2}$ inches (29 centimetres) high and weighs 55 ounces (1695.25 grams). Venedikov calls it the most interesting of the collection. It has two handles shaped as human-headed beasts, gripping the spout. Under each handle are Negroes' heads represented with typical curly hair, wide-open eyes, broad flattened noses and open mouths – the drinking apertures. Below two men converse calmly. They wear mantles and swords. Other warriors are bearded. Heracles is represented as a child fighting with two serpents. The amphora is inscribed with Greek letters, denoting numbers, and indicating the vessel's weight. There is one peculiarity. The weight is shown both in gold and in silver units of measure.

The phiale, the libation bowl, is made of pure yellow gold. It is a round dish, $1\frac{1}{4}$ inches (3.5 centimetres) high, 10 inches (25 centimetres) in diameter, and weighing 27 ounces (845.7 grams). It bears the Greek letter H, denoting the number 100.

Beginning their examination of these vessels, the Bulgarian archaeologists noticed certain remarkable features. The scenes depicted derived from Greek mythology, yet the workmanship was below the Greek standard. It contained errors of anatomy and of perspective, blunders foreign to Greek art. The gods and goddesses were modestly dressed, whereas in Greek art the human form was usually portrayed nude. These peculiarities suggested that the vessels had been made in a country influenced by Greek art and by another culture. They contained Persian as well as Greek elements. The clothed figure, so alien to Greek tradition, was a familiar feature of Persian art.

Summing up, Venedikov says that the preference for the garbed figure, the frequent errors in portraying the nude figure, the attempt to reproduce characteristic details of costume fabrics, including their surface patterning, the very characteristics of the apparel itself – all these are indications that the Panagyurishte treasure was produced not in a country with ancient Greek traditions of art, but somewhere in the Hellenistic East, which had not yet rid itself of its Persian traditions.

The types of vessels held by the gods and goddesses dated the ornaments in the early years of the third century B.C. Venedikov concluded they had been manufactured in Asia Minor, modern Anatolia. The Greek language inscriptions, letters and certain linguistic peculiarities gave additional clues to their origin. For example, the name Hera had been written in Ionic, a Greek dialect spoken in Asia Minor. Had the inscriptions been made in Greece, they would have been written in Attic forms. In Asia Minor, Attic began to replace Ionic early in the third century B.C.

The inscriptions on the phiale and amphora, the two largest vessels, indicated their weight. These had been written in the old phonetic system, a practice which had been discontinued after the death of Alexander the Great. The new system of representing numbers alphabetically had been introduced early in the third century. The vessels' weight had been written according to this new system. These weights are the key to the vessels' place of origin, a Greek centre in Asia Minor.

The Greeks used coins as a standard of measure, for gold – their gold coin, the stater. For silver – their silver coin, the drachma. Smaller weights were denoted by subdivisions. The Persians had their own monetary and weight system. Both systems were used in the Greek cities of Asia Minor.

Two inscriptions on the phiale denote its weight. The first number, 100, showed that it weighed 100 units of a given unit. Divided by 100, the vessel's weight of 845.7 grams produces a unit of 8.457 grams. Consequently the gold standard used for measurement weighed that amount. The Persian gold stater weighed 8.40 grams. Thus the unit employed was some five-sixths of a centigram heavier than the normal Persian gold coin. On the coast of Asia Minor only one city used stateres weighing more than the Persian. That was Lampsac, the modern Layseki, on the Asiatic shore of the Dardanelles. That town's stateres weighed 8.44 grams, close to the unit used to weigh the phiale. Its weight had also been calculated and marked in drachmae, the silver unit of measure. Division of the number of grams (845.7) by 196.042, the number of drachmae, produced the figure 4.313, approximately the weight of the Attic drachma.

Why had the phiale been weighed by two units of measure? That, believes Venedikov, could only have been possible in Asia Minor where the Attic system replaced the Persian one, after Alexander's conquests. The phiale had been measured for a second time to the new unit, by drachma measure.

Venedikov found the inscription on the amphora even more interesting:

At present it weighs 1695.25 grammes or, according to the inscription, 200 stateres $\frac{1}{2}$ drachma and 1 obol. Half a drachma plus 1 obol equals 2.8 plus 0.94 or 3.74 grammes. Subtracting this number from the total weight, we get 1695.25 minus 3.74 grammes, which equals 1691.51 grammes. This corresponds to 200 stateres. Hence one stater would be equal to 1691.51 divided by 200, or 8.457 grammes approximately. In other words, the unit of weight used for the amphora weighed just as much as that used for the phiale – 8.457 grammes, which is the weight of the Lampsac stater. We are therefore quite justified in assuming that the amphora too was manufactured in Lampsac.*

The epigraphic evidence, he points out, coincides completely with the results of a stylistic investigation. On the one hand, the inscriptions containing the names of the gods clearly testify to an Ionic origin of the treasure, with the first half of the third century B.C. as the most probable date. On the other hand, the weights of the vessels with their Persian system of measurement point to a centre in Asia Minor, while the use of the alphabetic system of numeration makes it pretty clear that the date of origin was the third century B.C. And so it was duly established that the treasure hailed from the city of Lampsac.

The treasure had been gradually amassed, the items purchased at intervals. The buyer built his collection slowly, starting with several rhytons. The phiale was purchased to serve as

* *Panagyurishte's Golden Treasure*, Bulgarian Publishing House (Sofia), 1961.

a salver for these vessels. Finally, he acquired the further rhyton and the amphora. He completed his collection in Asia Minor where he may have been a follower of the Thracian general Lysimachus. Following Alexander's death, and the break-up of his empire, the owner returned to Thrace. He must have been a very rich man to acquire a treasure weighing 5.6 kilogrammes, or $12\frac{1}{2}$ lbs. He may have desired to safeguard his wealth in easily transportable valuables. He may have foreseen the troubled times that lay ahead.

The old order collapsed. The Celts invaded Thrace in 278 B.C. Fleeing from the invaders the owner sought safety in the mountains. Waylaid by his pursuers or fearing an ambush, the fugitive dug a hole and buried his treasure. That he did not return to recover his hoard suggests that he was caught and killed. It was revealed by accident, and it now reposes in the museum at Plovdiv.

The identification of the Panagyurishte's golden treasure's place of origin and date of manufacture makes a wonderful story of archaeological detection.

British Mysteries

THE ENIGMA OF STONEHENGE

Diodorus of Sicily, who wrote his Universal History in about 50 B.C., and who based his information on the lost book by the fifth-century Greek historian Hecataeus, may have provided a clue to the chief enigma of Stonehenge – its purpose.

Referring to the Hyperboreans, the people who inhabited an island in the north of Europe 'beyond the point where the north wind blows', Diodorus says they possessed 'a magnificent sacred precinct' and a 'notable temple', dedicated to the sun god, Apollo, which was spherical in shape. The moon god visited the island every nineteen years, 'the period in which the return of the stars to the same place is accomplished'. By the term 'spherical' Diodorus is thought to have meant not the temple's shape but its purpose. That was to study the courses of the celestial bodies. Diodorus's statement may be significant if, as seems certain, he was describing Stonehenge, Europe's most famous stone monument.

Diodorus's source, Hecataeus, had gathered his information from Greek travellers who, we believe, left their mark on Stonehenge by carving symbols of Mycenaean daggers and axes on the stone uprights. These early visitors believed that the great stones had been erected to serve as an astronomical observatory, the conclusion reached by some modern astronomers.

That is one of the reasons Stonehenge is so fascinating and frustrating. Its huge stones pose problems which may be beyond solution. Who transported and erected them on Salisbury Plain in Southern England. How, when and above all why?

Stonehenge is far more ancient that was once thought. It is a composite structure assembled over several centuries. The ancient Druids have been eliminated as the creators of the precinct they may have used. Their cult arose 1,000 years after Stonehenge had been completed.

True archaeological investigation of Stonehenge began in 1919. Its age was determined by the cross-dating of fragments of pottery found on the site with similar pottery of known period found elsewhere, and was assessed at about 1400 B.C. That approximate date seemed to be confirmed in 1953 by the chance discovery of carvings on the upright stones of daggers and axes of Mycenaean type. This suggested that the monument had been designed by Greek architects.

Then archaeologists acquired a new tool: carbon dating. By this method it is possible to determine the rate of the radioactive decay of organic matter and to calculate the time that has elapsed since the sample lived or grew. Some uncertainty, however, remained owing to possible contamination of the sample, and the variations of the intensity of cosmic radiation reaching the earth (see p. 27, 'The Temple Builders of Malta').

The discovery in 1967, from the examination of ancient trees, that the concentration of cosmic radiation in the atmosphere has varied considerably over the last 6,000 years, has led to the revised dating of many European structures by several hundred years. By this new technique samples of ash taken from the 'cremation cemetery', from the depths of the Aubrey Holes at Stonehenge, have been dated about 2500 B.C., or 1,000 years or so before any Mycenaean could have visited Britain. That date indicates the period when Phase I was constructed.

To the casual observer Stonehenge may seem to be one structure, a circle of huge horizontal stones, some carrying massive stone lintels. Some stones now lean from the perpendicular, others have fallen or lie half buried in the soil. The whole structure is surrounded by a bank and ditch and is approached by a causeway. Hundreds of tumuli, ancient graves, show that the area was once densely populated. Its people supplied the millions of man-hours required to transport, tool, and erect the original 112 large stones and many smaller ones. Why did these busy hunters and farmers devote their time and energy to what may seem to have been an unproductive task? To them it was all-important, so vital that as time went by they added to and improved the structure. Stratigraphic excavation has revealed the various stages of construction.

Phase I is represented by the earthen bank and the ditch surrounding the perimeter, and the fifty-six Aubrey Holes, the 30 to 70 inch wide (76 to 177 centimetres) cavities, 24 to 45 inches deep (60 to 114 centimetres), set in an accurate circle 288 feet (88 metres) in diameter. The discovery within these cavities of burnt bones and ash suggested they had been used as a cremation cemetery. They are named after John Aubrey, the sixteenth-century antiquarian who discovered them. They form one of the most puzzling and controversial features of Stonehenge. A recent investigator has suggested they provide a 'digital computer' for the prediction of eclipses. Phase I included also two Station Stones and the Heel Stone. Seen from the centre of the circle the Heel Stone aligns with sunrise on Midsummer Day.

Whatever may have been the purpose of the original architects, their successors improved the design. They undertook the herculean labour of transporting eighty-two Blue Stones from the Prescelly mountains in Pembrokeshire, South Wales, 200 miles distant from Stonehenge. They weighed four tons apiece. It is assumed that they were brought part of the way by water, by boat and raft, from the site of Milford Haven on the Welsh coast, up the Bristol Channel and across the river Severn. From there they could have been conveyed on the Bristol river Avon to its headwaters, and thence across six miles of country to the river Wylye. They were carried on its waters to its confluence with another river named Avon at the town of Amesbury. That left an overland journey of 2 miles (3.2 kilometres) to Stonehenge. The feasibility of this route was tested in July 1954 by the B.B.C. Television Service. Heavy blocks of concrete weighing approximately four tons each were transported on rafts, and across country by sleds and wooden rollers, assisted by schoolboy rope haulers. The test established that sixteen men would have been required per ton weight, and 110 haulers would have been needed to drag the larger stone, the so-called Altar Stone.

The eighty-two Blue Stones, so named from their slightly bluish colour, were erected in two concentric circles, oriented on the sunrise and sunset at summer and winter solstice respectively, and within the Aubrey Holes circle. At the same time, in about 2000 B.C., the two Station Stones were dismantled, and the causeway was constructed. Subsequent generations became dissatisfied with this design.

Phase III of the operation may have begun in about 1750 B.C. It occupied many years when further minor changes were made. The Blue Stones circle was dismantled, and a circle of Sarsen Stones with hanging lintels was set up in the shape of a horseshoe, with five freestanding trilithons (two uprights supporting a lintel) in the centre. Later, the Blue Stones were reset, forming a circle within the sarsens.

The transportation of these thirty sarsens, each weighing fifty tons, was another astonishing feat. They were brought from the Marlborough Downs between 18 and 24 miles (30 and 39 kilometres) to the north of Stonehenge. They were cut from the parent blocks and roughly shaped, probably by splitting large sections on the line of natural cracks, aided by the insertion of wooden wedges. When these wedges were soaked in water they swelled, splitting the stone in two. The transportation of a single stone, Professor R. J. C. Atkinson believes on sleds on rollers,* would have required a labour force of 1,500 men and have taken seven weeks. To complete the job these men must have worked continuously for five and a half years.

The Blue Stones and the sarsens (possibly a corruption of 'saracen' meaning a foreigner), before erection, were dressed and shaped by pounding and grinding with heavy stone mauls and polishers. A professional stone mason who visited Stonehenge in 1923 estimated the process of pounding would have removed six cubic inches an hour. Taking an average thickness of two inches on each stone, the volume of stone removed would have amounted to 3,000,000 cubic inches. The shaping of the sarsens alone would have taken a force of fifty modern masons, working ten hours a day, seven days a week, two and a half years. Final polishing and the cutting of mortices to carry the lintels would have taken even more time.

How were the stone uprights erected and the lintels raised?

* *Stonehenge*, Hamish Hamilton, 1956.

An experienced engineer, E. H. Stone (*Stones of Stonehenge*, 1924), worked out the problem using models. His contentions have not been seriously questioned.

First the designer aligned the axis of the intended structure upon the point of midsummer sunrise. He did that by finding the centre of the circle. That could have been achieved by swinging a measuring line from an assumed centre, and shifting it until its circumference coincided with the circle of the Aubrey Holes. That would have been an easy trial-and-error method. He may have employed more sophisticated methods, such as the use of a plumb line.

Once the circumference had been determined, marks were made to position the holes at intervals of $10\frac{1}{2}$ feet (3.2 metres) round the circle. The depths of the holes needed to be varied to allow the tops of the uprights to be level. Stone assumed that the sarsens were rolled and levered into position, one end being allowed to overbalance squarely into the hole. The final stage could have been achieved by hauling the stone upright by brute force. Or possibly the builders employed a wooden cradle by which the stone could be lifted into the hole. Once the stone was in position, the space between it and the sides of the hole was packed with stone fragments and rammed chalk.

The stone lintels could have been raised to the level of the top of the sarsens by means of earthen ramps built against each stone. That may have been the method adopted by the Egyptians to raise the stones of the Pyramids. Alternatively, the builders could have erected timber ramps, or built a timber crib, a structure of alternate layers of parallel timbers laid horizontally. This method is used today to lift heavy objects when cranes are not available. The lintels would thereby have been raised by means of a wooden lever while another man thrust a fresh piece of squared timber beneath it. Stone calculated that the force required could have been exerted by a gang of seven men. It seems possible that this was the method employed, to avoid the construction of many separate earthen banks. No sign has been found in the earth to suggest that timber ramps were made.

All these operations would have required skilled labour, many hundreds of men working under the supervision of an architect who knew exactly what he wished to achieve.

Archaeologists cannot precisely define the identity of the peoples who created Stonehenge in its various phases, because the revolution in carbon dating techniques has reduced the study of pre-history to a state of chaos. It can be assumed only that the early generalities may still apply. On that basis the builders of Stonehenge I were people of the Windmill Hill culture who may have reached Britain as early as 2500 B.C. They are known from their characteristic collective burials in long barrows, which varied from 100 to 300 feet (30 to 90 metres) in length. They were farmers and stock raisers.

They were succeeded or supplanted by the Iron Age Beaker People, so called from their characteristic pottery. They may have come from Central Europe. They erected chamber tombs in round barrows for individual inhumation. The contents of their graves show deference for wealth and status, and suggest that they were ruled by a warrior aristocracy. They redesigned and created Stonehenge II.

Stonehenge III is believed to have been the work of people of the Wessex culture. They may have derived from a fusion of indigenous peoples. They possessed bronze tools and weapons and built elaborate tombs. The discovery of faience beads was once thought to link these Wessex people with the eastern Mediterranean, until analysis proved their high content of tin, which indicates local manufacture. It was this Cornish tin which brought the Phoenicians and Greeks to Britain after Stonehenge had been completed. Stonehenge, in all its phases, was the product of Britons. Did they create its circles and stone markers to predict the cycle of the seasons?

It is generally accepted that the Stonehenge axis is aligned to the point of midsummer sunrise for, seen from the centre of the circle, the sun rises over the Heel Stone on Midsummer Day. We do not know whether the designers accepted sunrise as the moment of the first glint of the sun or the appearance of the full sun. Doubt of their intention prevented the astronomer Sir Norman Lockyer in 1901 from calculating the precise year of the origin of Stonehenge. He was followed in 1963 by a Mr C. A. Newman who discovered certain significant alignments which did not appear to be coincidental.

Professor Gerald Hawkins, an American astronomer, also visited Stonehenge in that year. He published his conclusions in *Nature* (26 October 1963 and 27 June 1964), and in his book *Stonehenge Decoded*.* He claimed to have found a series of astronomically significant alignments from which a computer calculated the positions of sun, moon and stars. From these results Hawkins concluded that: 'The monument could certainly form a reliable calendar for predicting the seasons. It would also signal the danger period for an eclipse of sun and moon.'

Hawkins accepted that lunar eclipses could have been predicted by use of the fifty-six Aubrey Holes which form a circle. The ancient astronomer could have achieved this by inserting a stone in one hole, and by moving it from hole to hole each year in clockwise direction, in conformity with the erratic movements of the moon, which rises and sets at different places on the horizon, returning to its original position almost exactly every fifty-six years.

What, therefore, did Diodorus mean by saying that the moon god returned every nineteen years, Hawkins asked himself. Could the moon do something spectacular at Stonehenge every nineteen years? When was the eclipsed moon most spectacular? The answer seemed to be when it was over the Heel Stone, or in the archway of the Great Trilithon. To primitive men lunar eclipses had been a frightening phenomenon.

Van den Bergh's *Eclipses in the Second Millennium B.C.* (1954) showed where lunar eclipses had been, and that an eclipse of the moon or sun always occurred when the winter moon, that is the full moon nearest the winter solstice, rose over the Heel Stone. Some of these eclipses would have been visible at Stonehenge. The interval between nights of winter moonrise over the Stonehenge axis occurred about every nineteen years, or in a cycle of 18.6 years. The priests, in order to track the moon and predict an eclipse, had used a simple nineteen-year interval. But by rigid adherence to that cycle they would have drifted into hopeless error. 'The smallest time that would have remained accurate for many years would have been the triple interval measure, 19 + 19 + 18, or a total of 56

* Fontana, 1970.

years, the number of Aubrey Holes. 'Professor Hawkins' graph showed that the Stonehenge moon phenomenon repeated every fifty-six years with good uniformity. Thus Diodorus was correctly informed that Stonehenge had been designed as an astronomical observatory.

Hawkins admitted his failure to prove beyond all doubt that Stonehenge had been used as an astronomical observatory, but it 'would be strange indeed if Stonehenge had no astronomical connotation'. His findings had a mixed reception. Professor Atkinson reviewing his book in Antiquity (40) under the heading 'Moonshine in Stonehenge' and in Nature (210) as 'Decoder Misled' called them 'tendentious, arrogant, slipshod and unconvincing'. Other reviewers thought that Hawkins had something worth saying, even if some of his findings were implausible.

'Stonehenge is not only an astronomical observatory, but also a monument constructed geometrically, using giant ellipses, spirals and circles laid out on the ground,' concludes Professor Alexander Thom. He and his collaborators surveyed the site in April 1974 (*Journal of the History of Astronomy*, vol. 5, pt. 2, pp. 71–90). Professor Thom is justly famous for his surveys of the lunar observatories which exist along the west coast of Scotland.

The difficulty in deciding Stonehenge's purpose partly arises from the removal and destruction of certain possible marker stones during the course of centuries. As Diodorus suggests it was probably built as a temple dedicated to the sun god, where the motions of the heavenly bodies could be observed.

WHO WASN'T BURIED AT SUTTON HOO?

The mounds on her estate at Sutton Hoo, Suffolk, aroused Mrs Edith May Pretty's curiosity. The old story of the ploughman who had turned up a golden brooch in 1800 hinted at buried treasure. A previous owner of the estate had set his gamekeeper digging into one of the mounds. Finding only a rabbit warren he had given up. The mounds, eleven in number, rose on the scarp above and 450 yards (410 metres) from the eastern bank of the river Deben, a tidal estuary 9 miles (14 kilometres) from the North Sea. Mrs Pretty, a justice of the peace, contacted Ipswich Museum. Its curator, Guy Maynard, sent the museum's field surveyor, Basil Brown, to inspect the mounds. He recognized them as ancient tumuli, possibly containing burials.

Assisted by two of Mrs Pretty's gardeners, Brown started work in 1938. The first three mounds yielded comparatively uninteresting results. One contained a cremation burial and had been looted. Enough objects, the remains of an ornamental shield and the tip of a sword, were found to identify the site as an Anglo-Saxon grave. In the second mound Brown detected the outlines of a small rowing boat, which may have been 18 to 20 feet (5.5 to 6 metres) long. Two small clench nails were similar to those that had been found within a mound 9 miles (14 kilometres) away at Snape in 1862. That mound had yielded the outline of a smaller boat. The third mound contained pieces of bowls and pottery of Anglo-Saxon type. All three mounds had been entered and ransacked. While these early discoveries confirmed that the mounds contained Anglo-Saxon burials, there was no hint that another would yield what Sir Thomas Kendrick, the director of the British museum, would call 'the most remarkable archaeological discovery ever made in England'.

Work was resumed in May 1939. Doubtful which mound to excavate next, Brown turned to Mrs Pretty. 'What about this one?' she asked, pointing to the largest mound, the one closest to the river, which was now obscured by a clump of trees. The mound was 9 feet high, 100 feet long and 75 feet wide (2.7 by 30 by 23 metres). Starting from the eastern end, Brown began to dig a trench 6 feet (1.8 metres) wide, through the mound. The gardeners' spades soon turned up clumps of corroded clench nails, evidence pointing to another ship burial. Leaving the nails in position, Brown carefully cleaned the earth around them, disclosing the outline of the forward part of a ship, a vessel clearly of considerable length. A layer of displaced earth, and the find of a tiger-ware jug and remains of a fire, showed that the mound had been previously entered. Fortunately the sixteenth-century robbers had missed the ship and had penetrated only to ground level. They had cooked a meal before departing.

By 11 June Brown had cleared sufficient earth to disclose the ship's frames, or rather their outlines in the sandy soil. Its timbers had decayed, leaving the clench nails which had fastened the planks to the frames. Had the central portion of the ship been used as a burial chamber? That was a fair inference because the burial of a chieftain or king within his ship had been a pagan custom adopted by both Anglo-Saxons and Norsemen. The size of the mound and the length of the ship suggested a unique discovery. Brown called a halt and informed the British Museum and the Inspectorate of Ancient Monuments. C. W. Phillips, a fellow of Selwyn College, Cambridge, and secretary of the Prehistoric Society, an experienced excavator, was sent to supervise the work. He was soon joined by a team of specialists.

The archaeologists faced a task of unprecedented difficulty. No one in England had previously attemped to excavate a ship, especially one of which the timbers had disintegrated. The Viking ships discovered at Oseberg and Gokstad in Norway and at Ladby in Denmark had been recovered intact. Brown had found a much older vessel, one dating from the early years of the Anglo-Saxon conquest, a discovery unparalleled in British archaeology.

The vessel had left a perfect impression of its hull in the sand. It had been 89 feet long and 14 feet wide (27 by 4 metres), and had been clinker built, with overlapping planks of oak. It had been rowed by thirty-eight oarsmen. The helmsman had steered by means of a broad-bladed oar affixed to the starboard quarter. Its construction showed advances in technique from the row-gallery which had been unearthed at Nydam Moss in Schleswig in Denmark in 1863. The Nydam ship had been built about A.D. 400 and had been 73 feet 9 inches (22.5 metres) long. It is housed at Kiel Museum. Another somewhat smaller vessel had been found near Utrecht in Holland. Both these vessels had lacked proper keels, whereas the Sutton Hoo ship had had a primitive horizontal plank, enabling it to be sailed with a following wind. Its greatest depth had been 4 feet 6 inches (1.3 metres), and it had drawn 2 feet (.6 metre) of water. It had been a great open row-boat, longer than the later Gokstad ship (79 feet, 24 metres) the Oseberg ship (68 feet, 21 metres) and the Ladby ship (68 feet, 21 metres). These Scandinavian ships had been built with proper keels, allowing for propulsion by sail as well as by oar.

How had the Sutton Hoo vessel been carried for a third of a mile (.5 kilometre) overland from the river, and up the 100 foot (30 metres) escarpment? It is assumed that it was hauled or pushed on rollers, and placed above the trench cut in the soil. It was then held by ropes and lowered as the rollers were removed. The mound had been built above the ship after the burial chamber had been made amidships. The labour must have been enormous.

No vestige of this wooden burial chamber remained. It had been crushed by the weight of the soil. Phillips estimated that it had been $17\frac{1}{2}$ feet (5.3 metres) long and had looked a 'bit like Noah's Ark'. Within that area probably lay the chieftain's grave goods. The difficulty was to remove the earth without allowing the sides of the excavations to cave in. The archaeologists felt they had little time, for war was imminent. They worked slowly, using paint brushes and needles to turn each speck of earth. The first piece of treasure to come to light was a golden pyramid which may have hung from a sword belt. It was in perfect condition and nothing like it had been found in England before.

'Each day of that exciting week,' wrote O. G. S. Crawford, the editor of *Antiquity* and one of the specialists drawn to the excavation, 'yielded some rich find often of a type hitherto unknown.' He anticipated the hidden things to come and was not disappointed. There were objects the archaeologists did not expect to find. Many of the treasures were corroded or too delicate to touch. They were wrapped and removed for cleaning and restoration at the British Museum laboratory. Several years elapsed before they could be assessed and described.

Two early discoveries suggested a royal burial. An iron spike, 6 feet 4 inches (1.9 metres) long, and capped by a bronze stag, turned out to be a standard, a symbol of sovereignty usually carried before the king in ceremonial processions. The whetstone was another such symbol. This great four-sided stone weighed 6 lbs $4\frac{1}{2}$ ozs (2.85 kilos). A sombre human face had been carved on each side of the stone. It was beautifully shaped and almost in mint condition. Nothing comparable to it is known. Bruce Mitford, keeper of the British and Medieval antiquities at the British Museum, calls it 'this fantastic piece'.

The burial yielded the remains of a large circular shield, fragments of a helmet, an iron-bound bucket, two heavy bronze bowls, a six-stringed musical instrument, silver bowls and platters, drinking horns, a great silver dish, an iron lamp, golden harness, epaulets, a huge golden buckle, leatherwork, a sword 3 feet (.9 metre) long, encased in its scabbard, a purse containing thirty-seven golden coins, and two spoons marked with the names of 'Saulos' and 'Paulos'. There was also considerable jewellery which Bruce Mitford called 'the most gorgeous of the finds'. One great gold buckle weighed $14\frac{5}{8}$ ounces (414 grams).

Everything had been supplied for the needs of the individual in his after-life. The richness of the grave goods indicated his place in society. The emblems of royalty suggested a royal person, almost certainly a king. But there was no skeleton at Sutton Hoo, and complete absence of the personal ornaments usually found in a pagan grave. The contents of the mound conformed to the description of a ship-burial given by the Anglo-Saxon poet, Beowulf, who is believed to have lived early in the eighth century, possibly within a hundred years of the burial at Sutton Hoo. Describing the burial of a mythical Danish king, Beowulf wrote:

> Then Scyld departed at the destined hour,
> that powerful man sought the Lord's protection.
> His own close companions carried him
> down to the sea, as he, Lord of the Danes,
> had asked while he could still speak.
> That well-loved man had ruled his land for many years.
> There in the harbour stood the ring-prowed ship,
> the prince's vessel, shrouded in ice and eager to sail;
> and then they laid their dear lord,
> and giver of rings, deep within the ship

by the mast in majesty; many treasures
and adornments from far and wide were gathered there.
I have never heard of a ship equipped
more handsomely with weapons and war-gear,
swords and corselets; on his breast
lay countless treasures that were to travel far
with him into the waves' domain.
They gave him great ornaments, gifts
no less magnificent than those men had given him
long before, when they sent him alone,
child as he was, across the stretch of the seas.
Then high above his head they placed
a golden banner and let the waves bear him
bequeathed him to the sea; their hearts were grieving,
their minds mourning. Mighty men
beneath the heavens, rulers in the hall,
cannot say who received that cargo.

The mound at Sutton Hoo had yielded the richest treasure ever found on British soil. To whom did it belong? If the objects had been buried with no intention of being reclaimed, they reverted to the owner of the land, Mrs Pretty. Her right of possession was confirmed by a coroner's inquest. If the nation wanted the treasure it would have to buy it, at some fantastic cost. Mrs Pretty solved the problem by generously presenting the entire treasure to the nation. The British Museum took possession, concealing the wonderful finds in a bomb-proof shelter for the duration of the war.

The argument, first mooted in 1939 and not yet finally settled, recommenced after the war. Who had the king been, and why had he not been buried in his ship, according to pagan practice? One thing only seemed certain. He had been a member of the royal house of East Anglia, the first kingdom established by the Anglo-Saxons who had invaded England following the withdrawal of the Roman legions in about A.D. 450. They came from Northern Europe and Scandinavia, bringing with them their ancient customs and traditions.

The possibility that the body had been cremated and the ashes had disintegrated is discounted on the ground that there is no known example of a body cremation without the burning of both grave goods and ship. Otherwise the burial had been in accordance with heathen tradition, the inhumation of a chieftain surrounded by his goods of outstanding richness. The absence of the body posed both a puzzle, and a possible pointer to the man's identity.

The thirty-seven gold coins provide the strongest clue. They had been minted all over Western Europe, in France, Belgium, the Rhineland and Switzerland, but no two coins had been derived from a single mint. Several bore the names of identifiable kings. They were found together in the purse. How long had they been hoarded? The collection suggested a royal treasure, comprising, possibly, gifts from other kings.

All the coins belonged to the Merovingian period in Europe when more than 2,000 mints were in operation. Knowledge of this coinage is still imprecise. Several numismatic experts have given their opinions. Early on their consensus indicated that the coins had come together between A.D. 650 and 660. But in 1960 the French authority on Merovingian coinage, M. Lafaurie, placed the assembly of the Sutton Hoo hoard at about 625. His opinion has been supported by Dr J. P. C. Kent, keeper of the British Museum's department of coins and medals. His provisional verdict is 'not later than 630 for any coin; and 625 as the likely date for the assembly'. Another leading authority, Mr Philip Grierson, adheres to the old chronology (*Antiquity*, 1952).

Thus the coins provide only a rough and controversial guide to the date of the burial. To identify the king whose ship and goods, but not his body, were buried at Sutton Hoo, we need to consult the Venerable Bede, who wrote his *Ecclesiastical History* in about A.D. 700. Bede describes the conversion of East Anglia to Christianity, beginning with the baptism of Redwald who ruled as 'Bretwald', or supreme king. He died in 624 or 625. According to Bede, Redwald had been 'admitted to the sacrament of the Christian faith in Kent, but in vain; for, on his return home, he was seduced by his wife and certain perverse teachers and turned back from the sincerity of his faith'. Redwald erected in the same temple both an altar to Christ and a smaller one to the devil.

Redwald may have hoped to gain from both possible worlds,

or he may have remained a pagan at heart. There is another possibility. Did he die a Christian and receive burial in consecrated ground? Did his pagan subjects accord him a traditional funeral, a cenotaph lacking only his body? The presence in the grave of the two spoons bearing the names of Saul and Paul is interesting. They may have been Redwald's christening spoons.

This apparently convenient identification of Redwald does not satisfy everyone. One of the coins is claimed to have been minted by the Gothic King Dagobert I, who died in A.D. 638, twenty-five years after Redwald's death. According to this estimate, the hoard of coins could not have been assembled much before 650.

Redwald was succeeded by Sigeberht and Ecgric (or Aelthelric) who acted as joint rulers. Sigeberht was exiled to France in 630, where he was converted to Christianity. He entered a monastery, leaving Ecgric to rule alone until 640 when he joined Ecgric to fight the Mercian King Penda. Both were killed soon after. Ecgric was succeeded by King Anna, a devout Christian. He died in 654 and was given a Christian burial at Blythburgh.

Sandra Glass ('The Sutton Hoo Ship Burial', *Antiquity*, 1962) has suggested that Anna erected the Sutton Hoo memorial for the heroic Ecgric, supplying his cenotaph with the symbol of royalty. She points out that a burial of such magnitude, using so much of the royal treasury, could only have been carried out by a king for a king. Did the Christian Anna allow the pagan warriors who had survived the battle with the Mercians to erect a memorial to their hero? C. W. Phillips, however, conceives the possibility that Anna was the king for whom the memorial was erected, possibly for political reasons, by his pagan subjects. He too was slain by Penda. According to yet another theory, the memorial was erected to Anna's brother and successor, the Christian Aethelhere. His body was lost in flood waters following the battle of Winwaed. That may have accounted for the absence of a body at Sutton Hoo.

Despite these intriguing suggestions, the general choice identifies Redwald as the Anglo-Saxon king who was honoured. He was an early king of the dynasty which built its palaces at Rendlesham, 4 miles (6 kilometres) up the river Deben from Sutton Hoo. A crown weighing 60 ounces (1.86 kilos) was dug up there in 1690. That it was melted down suggests that it was made of gold or silver. The kings established their cemetery at Sutton Hoo. No clump of trees then obscured the heath from the river from where the mounds could have been clearly seen, silhouetted against the skyline, 'high and broad and visible from afar to all seafarers', as Beowulf described his own future grave.

WHERE WAS CAMELOT?

Out of the blue, and for no apparent reason, twelfth-century England and France suddenly became flooded with legends about a mythical King Arthur, the founder of a knightly order. His knights quest for the Holy Grail. Arthur marries his lady-love and builds his palace at Camelot. Betrayed and mortally wounded in battle he is buried at Glastonbury. This legendary Arthur was the creation of the age of chivalry, designed to express its ideals of bravery, virtue and courtly love.

The real Arthur appears to have been a British general who fought the Saxon invaders about A.D. 500. He won great battles, culminating in his victory at Badon. His great feat was to delay the conquest, thus giving the uncouth Saxons time to become more civilized and enabling his Celtic countrymen to retire to their Welsh and Cornish fastnesses and survive as a racial entity. Arthur himself was probably a Romanized Briton, possibly of mixed ancestry, educated, sophisticated and versed in Roman military techniques.

Britain had been a Roman province for 400 years, defended by the legions. They were withdrawn from the frontiers after the sack of Rome by the Goths in A.D. 410. The Dark Ages had begun. Britain fell under the rule of a number of petty kings. They were too weak to resist the waves of Saxons, Angles and Jutes who poured across the North Sea. By 465 they had over-run Kent and established themselves east of the line from the river Humber in the north to the town of Southampton on the English Channel. They encroached westwards, raiding and pillaging. The Celtic kings, we think, placed Arthur in command of their combined forces. He may have raised a body of mailed horsemen, some of them possibly the sons or grandsons of legionaries who had married and settled in Britain.

The earliest reference to Arthur is by the chronicler Nennius who died in 811. Referring to the Saxon conquest, he said: 'Then Arthur fought against them in those days with the kings of the Britons.' Nennius lists Arthur's battles, the twelfth being at Mount Badon, 'where fell nine hundred and sixty men in one day'. None of these battle sites has been definitely located. Badon has been identified as at Badbury Rings in Dorset, Badbury Camp in Berkshire and Badbury by Liddington Castle in Wiltshire, and is variously dated in 499 and 518.

Tentative identification of these battle sites suggests that Arthur ranged Britain, and may have campaigned in Scotland, employing his mobility to throw back the Saxons. His soldiers may have been mounted on black horses, a cross between the native fell ponies and the larger black Fresians left behind by the Romans. This possibility led in 1971 to the suggestion that the inn sign 'The Black Horse', widespread in certain areas, recalls the scenes of Arthur's great victories.* His black horsemen became enshrined in legend and their memory was perpetuated by pub signs. Mr Wildman presents his case with persuasive logic. Nonetheless, it may be one of the dottier theories of history.

There is nothing to link Arthur definitely with a place named Camelot. The name is thought to have been invented by the twelfth-century poets to provide Arthur with a palace fit for a king. Or did they derive it from local tradition as chronicler John Leland claimed he did in 1542? Visiting the county of Somerset he was told that 'Camalat' was the name borne by the hill by the village of South Cadbury and that Arthur 'much resided there'. Corroboration for this local identification appeared to be supplied by the ancient fortifica-

* Wildman, S. G., *The Black Horsemen: English Inns and King Arthur*, Garnstone Press, 1971.

tions girding the hill's summit, 1,200 yards (1,100 metres) in circumference, and by its name 'Camelle' or 'Camel', recorded in the Domesday Book. The local people called the hill 'Arthur's Palace', as the antiquarian John Camden learned in the sixteenth century. Arthur was still associated with the site in 1723 when William Stukeley visited 'Camelet Castle'.

Encouraged by these ancient traditions several local antiquarians dug on the hill, unearthing pottery and coins. Several items were donated to the Somerset County Museum at Taunton.

A chance discovery revived interest in the 1950s. Pieces of pottery from the site were recognized by Dr Ralegh Radford as belonging to the fifth and sixth centuries, Arthur's period. Radford was a recognized authority on Dark Age Britain. His report in the *Proceedings* of the Somerset Archaeological Society caught the attention of other archaeologists.

Could the local folklore embody an ancient memory of the time when Arthur had made 'Camelot' his stronghold? Such a possibility was not as remote as it may seem. Tradition lingers long in rural England. For example, at Bosham in Sussex, the story was passed from generation to generation that King Canute's teenage daughter had been accidentally drowned in the harbour. This verbal tradition was startlingly confirmed in the early 1900s by the discovery, during repairs to the church, of a coffin containing the bones of a young girl.

These ancient clues, and Dr Radford's discoveries, led to the formation in 1965 of the Camelot Research Committee. Sir Mortimer Wheeler became its president, and his one-time pupil, Leslie Alcock, was appointed its archaeological director.

Alcock and his many helpers faced a huge task, the excavation of the hill's plateau, 18 acres (7 hectares) in extent. South Cadbury Hill rises 250 feet (76 metres) above the surrounding countryside, commanding a wide view from its ancient earthen ramparts. Trial digs showed that it had been occupied as a hill fort, one of the many which dot southern England, since Neolithic times. In their early reconnaissance the archaeologists were guided by the crop marks, the green patches disclosed by aerial photography. These indicated the places where pits and trenches had been dug. Smaller excavations in three zones disclosed ancient storage pits and the post-holes which had provided the frames of houses. Some of these were 15 inches (38 centimetres) in diameter, indicating large buildings.

These discoveries suggested that a major operation would be worthwhile. That would require considerable money and a band of devoted workers. The committee's appeal raised £15,000 and offers of help from the students of University College, Cardiff, interested parties as descendants of Arthur's Celtic retainers. Enthusiasm for the search for Arthur's Camelot reached national proportions. The B.B.C. sent its cameramen to record the work, and the site was visited by so many eager tourists that the committee found it necessary to appoint guides and issue leaflets explaining its work.

At the start of the 1967 season, the archaeologists were offered by a Mr Mark Howell the use of an instrument he had devised to locate metal objects and rock fractures under the surface. This 'banjo', as it became called from its shape, comprised a boom with a radio transmitter at one end and a receiver at the other. Tests showed that it was sensitive to metal and required no expert qualifications to operate. It enabled the archaeologists to set up a grid system of recordings, which greatly assisted their work. The Oxford Laboratory for Archaeology also provided a formidable range of electronic instruments including the well-proven proton magnetometer which is highly sensitive to geophysical anomalies.

The early test digs and the readings obtained by these instruments encouraged the archaeologists to excavate at two places, at the ramparts on the southern side of the hill and at the plateau's highest point, where the post-holes indicated traces of large buildings.

Exploration at the south-western gateway in the ancient ramparts disclosed successive chronological layers, at the highest level the wall face of a massive mortared stone rampart and gateway. Coins and pottery, and the building style, identified this as the 12–20 foot (3.6 to 6 metres) thick rampart built by the Saxons during the reign of King Ethelred the Unready, who had used the hill as a mint. They dated the structure about A.D. 800–900.

The lower, more ancient layer disclosed a pit containing the bones of thirty men, women and children jumbled together. Nearby were found hoards of sling shot, Roman coins and the hinge of a Roman cuirass. Lower still ran an ancient cobbled roadway, worn by feet and rutted by cart tracks. Weapons and burnt pottery dated the massacre in the first century A.D., in the decade of the Roman conquest when General Vespasian had captured more than twenty British hill forts. The ancient Britons had defended Cadbury, dying in its defence. The Romans, to prevent refortification, destroyed the ancient Celtic ramparts, the earthen bank and ditch which dated from Neolithic times.

These discoveries showed that the hill's ramparts had been destroyed in about A.D. 50 and had been rebuilt by the Saxons after their conquest of the region in about A.D. 550. Between these layers, the pre-Roman and the early Saxon, the archaeologists found a chaotic mass of earth and piled stones, separated by a thick layer of soil from the pre-Roman, and a thinner layer from the Saxon periods of occupation. This 'stony bank', as it became termed, comprised four courses of stone, one above another, on which had been piled an earthen rampart topped by a timber breastwork. This fortification had been built in the Celtic manner, but no Celts had lived on the hill for 400 years. Someone had refortified Cadbury Hill between 450 and 550, in the period of the Saxon westward advance.

Evidence derived from other parts of the hill suggested that Cadbury Hill had been rebuilt as the fortress of a great military leader, and had been a wealthy and important settlement.

Excavations of post-holes revealed the outline of a rectangular building, 63 feet long and 34 feet wide (19 by 10 metres). It had occupied the dominant position at the top of the hill. Could it have been the chieftain's feasting hall and home? Sherds of pottery dated the building in the Arthurian period. With nothing more than its foundations to work upon, the archaeologists reconstructed the building as a wattle and daub structure held together by a timbered framework with a thatched roof. There had been doors in each long wall. An open centre hearth was likely, but the evidence had been ploughed away by modern farmers. The foundations fitted the size range of contemporary halls, for example at Castle Dore in Cornwall and Yeavering in Northumberland.

The excavations at the gate and on the hill exhausted the information gathered about the A.D. 500 period. By the end of 1970 the archaeologists had investigated only one-fifth of the plateau's surface. They had found nothing to prove conclusively that Cadbury Hill had been Arthur's Camelot. But the circumstantial evidence seemed convincing. Arthur would have needed a fortified base. Why not Cadbury Hill? It was an ancient hill fort, in a commanding position, close to the Fosse Way leading north and the Hard Way coming from the east. Nearby runs the river Cam, possibly the site of Camlann, the battle where Arthur received his mortal wound from his British opponent Medrant. 12 miles (19 kilometres) to the north west rises Glastonbury Tor, beside it the abbey, Arthur's traditional resting place.

Arthur's reputed relics and those of his wife were discovered in 1190 enclosed in a hollow tree trunk in a grave of great depth. The bones were exhumed and transferred to a tomb within the church. The tomb was opened in 1278 in the presence of Edward I. The contemporary account, the *Annals of Waverley*, states that the bones of King Arthur were of great size, in keeping with his traditional height and girth. They were dispersed when the tomb was destroyed during the Reformation.

People at Cadbury believe that Arthur sleeps in a huge cavern within the hill. Somewhere on the plateau is a stone slab giving access to the cave. The Reverend James Bennett, a keen antiquarian, stated in 1890 that on opening up a hut there he found a flagstone, the manhole leading to the cave. Unfortunately he did not record the hut's position.

But Arthur does not always sleep. Twice a year on Midsummer Eve and Christmas Eve, you can hear the hoof beats of the horses, as the king and his men ride down from Camelot to drink at the spring which bears his name.

American Mysteries

THE WHITE GODS OF TIAHUANACO

Tiahuanaco has engendered more speculation, erudite, fantastic and even absurd, than any other ruined city. It has been called the world's most ancient city, the cradle of American or even of world civilization, built by an antediluvian race which survived a worldwide catastrophe in the high plateaux of the Andes. It is also claimed to have been built by bearded white men, culture-bearers who crossed the Atlantic to found a new civilization.

Perched 12,500 feet (3,800 metres) up in the clouds, Tiahuanaco poses more questions than can be answered.

The region of Lake Titicaca, near to which Tiahuanaco stands, is one of the most desolate spots on earth, and unlikely to have supported a large population. 'It is the last place in the world,' says its principal excavator, Wendell C. Bennett, 'to expect a great stupendous archaeological site.' Yet its builders 'created the most elaborate and purest manifestation of culture' in all South America. They have been called the most expert workers in stone the world has ever seen.

Tiahuanaco was already a ruin when the Incas ruled Peru between A.D. 1200 and 1532, when Pizarro conquered their land. To the Spaniard's inquiries the local Aymará Indians made no claim for their ancestors. Asked who had built the city, they said they were white, bearded men of another race.

That so little of Tiahuanaco remains today is due to the vandalism of the Spaniards, who wished to exterminate ancient memories of pagan gods, and to the depredations of the modern railway contractors, who quarried its stones to provide ballast for their tracks. Nineteenth-century travellers remarked structures which no longer exist. Many of the houses in the local village and its church have been built of stones taken from the ancient city.

Two chief and two smaller buildings remain.

The Akapana, or so-called fortress, is a pyramid structure in which a natural mound has been shaped and faced with stone. It is 700 feet (210 metres) long and 500 feet (150 metres) wide, rising to 50 feet (15 metres) above the plain. Its summit, which covers 300,000 square feet, (27,000 square metres), was reached by a stone stairway and a stone conduit leads from a depression on its top to the ground below.

The temple, or the Calasasaya, is approximately 440 feet (135 metres) from east to west. The upright stones may once have supported a stone roof. Some of these uprights are 14 feet high, 4 feet wide and 2½ feet thick (4.2 by 1.2 by .7 metres). Access to the temple was obtained by six stone steps each of which is 10 feet in width, 3 feet thick and 20 feet long (3 by .9 by 6 metres). At either side stand sculptured monoliths.

The Gateway of the Sun is the most remarkable feature of the temple. It is formed of one block of stone 10 feet long, 11 feet high, and 2 feet thick (3 by 3.3 by .6 metres), and weighing almost ten tons. On its front, above the doorway, is a carved façade which centres around the figure of the supreme god of the universe, Viracocha. In his hands, each of which has only four fingers, he holds a spear thrower and a quiver containing two spears. His tunic is bound by a girdle covered with puma heads. On either side of him are twenty-four attendants portrayed running towards him, and beneath his throne are sixteen carved figures. No similar sculptures have been found elsewhere in Peru. Because of the marks on his cheeks, Viracocha has been called the 'weeping god of Tiahuanaco'.

The reverse side of the gateway is no less interesting. On each side of the doorway are rectangular niches so accurately cut and mathematically perfect that it is not possible to find a deviation of more than 1/50 inch (.5 millimetre) in their angles and surfaces. These niches are cut to a depth of 1 foot (30 centimetres) in a series of concentric steps, and all this was done with stone tools.

By the temple is one remaining statue. It stands twice the height of a man and is known as the 'friar' or 'bishop'. It appears to be holding a book. One of the early Spanish visitors, Cieza de Leon, has described two other statues which no longer exist, both 18 feet (5.5 metres) high. There was also once an immense stone lizard. Two smaller heads, taken from the ruins, now stand outside the village church.

Cieza says that beyond the buildings:

are two stone idols, of the human shape and figure, and the features very skilfully carved, so that they appear to have been done by the hand of some great master. They are so large that they seem like small giants, and it is clear that they have a sort of clothing different from that now worn by the natives of these parts. They seem to have some ornament on their heads. Near these stone statues there is another building. Their antiquity and the want of letters are the causes why it is not known who built such vast foundations, and how much time has since elapsed; for at present there is only a wall very well built, and which must have been standing for many ages. Some of the stones are much worn. At this part there are stones of such enormous size that it causes wonder to think of them, and to reflect how human force could have sufficed to move them to the place where we now see them, being so large. Many of these stones are carved in different ways, some of them having the shape of the human body, which must have been their idols. Near the wall there are many holes and hollow places in the ground. In another place, more to the westward, there are other ancient remains, among them many doorways with their jambs, lintels, and thresholds, all of one stone. But what I noted most particularly, when I wandered over these ruins writing down what I saw, was that from these great doorways there came out other still larger stones upon which the doorways were formed, some of them thirty feet broad, fifteen or more long, and six inches in thickness. The whole of this, with the doorway and its jambs and lintels, was all one single stone. The work is one of grandeur and magnificence when well considered. For myself I fail to understand with what instruments or tools it can have been done; for it is very certain that before these great stones could have been brought to perfection and left as we see them, the tools must have been much better than those now used by the Indians.

The two smaller structures that remain are called Palacio, 196 feet (60 metres) from east to west, and the Puma Puncu, meaning the gateway of the puma. Both contain huge dressed stone slabs, some of which weigh more than a hundred tons. These blocks are bound together by notches with T-shaped tenons, and by copper clamps. Wendell Bennett found in 1932 a second statue, a tall, forbidding figure, 24 feet (7.3 metres) high and 42 to 50 inches (1.05 to 1.27 metres) wide.

George E. Squire who visited Tiahuanaco in 1878, before the worst depredations of the railway contractors had taken place, says: 'In no other part of the world have I seen stones cut with such mathematical precision and such admirable skill as in Peru, nor in all Peru have I encountered any compared with those which are scattered about the plains of Tiahuanaco.' He noted two structures which have since disappeared: a building known as the Hall of Justice, the stones of which measured 25½ feet by 14 feet by 6½ feet (7.5 by 4 by 1.9 metres), and what appeared to be a miniature representation of a sacred building.

That the ruins were even more extensive at the time of the Spanish visits in the sixteenth century can be seen from the account by Garcilasso de la Vega who quotes a priest named Diego de Alcobasco. He says:

Here there are some very grand edifices, and amongst them there is a square court, fifteen *brazas* (about ninety feet) each way, with walls two stories high. On one side of this court there is a hall, forty-five feet long by twenty-two broad, apparently once covered in the same way as those buildings you have seen in the house of the sun at Cusco, with a roof of straw. The walls, roofs, floor and doorways are all of one single piece, carved out of a rock, and the walls of the court and of the hall are three quarters of a yard in breadth. The roof of the hall, though it appears to be thatch, is really of stone. For as the Indians cover their homes with thatch, in order that this might appear like the rest, they have combed and carved the stone so that it resembles a roof of thatch. The waters of the lake wash the walls of the court. The natives say that this and the other buildings were dedicated to the Creator of the universe. There are also many other stones carved into the shape of men and women so naturally that they appear to be alive, some drinking with cups in their hands, others sitting, others standing, and others walking in the stream which flows by the walls. There are also statues of women with their infants in their laps, others with them on their backs, and a thousand other postures.

Another account relates the story of a Spaniard who dug up a huge human head of gold whose face was similar to those of the statues above ground. The Spaniard also found an image carved from a single block of stone 60 feet long and 14 feet in diameter (18 by 4 metres). It took thirty men three days to destroy it.

Another visitor, a Jesuit named Father Cobo, noticed the remarkable size of the stones and their great antiquity.

Who will not wonder how, they being so large, they could have been carried by human strength from the quarries where they were cut to the place where we now see them? And the matter becomes all the more puzzling when it is remembered that no such stones as these exist for leagues about, and that it is well known that all the folk of this New World were lacking in such inventions as machines, wheels and windlasses, not to mention draught animals.

Modern archaeologists estimate that the city was built and that its civilization flourished between A.D. 200 and 600. Some place it later, between 800 and 900. These dates are deduced from the pottery, painted in rich blending colours, found at the site. The buildings replaced or evolved from an earlier primitive culture which may date back to 1000 B.C. Even so, Tiahuanaco seems to have sprung up suddenly, without the long formulative period usual in a growth culture. The sudden emergence of this unique civilization, high in the Andes, has been taken to support the belief that it was due to the arrival of white and bearded men.

There appears to have been a great influx in about A.D. 450 of new people who landed on the coast from balsa rafts and canoes. This theory, looked upon askance by orthodox scholars, seems to be supported by the legends collected by the many Spaniards who endeavoured to learn the ancient traditions relating to Tiahuanaco. These forty chroniclers seem to have told much the same story.

Cieza de Leon visited Tiahuanaco in about 1551, probably the first European to do so. He included a chapter in his book *Chronicle of Peru*, 'On the Tiahuanaco Village and Great and

Ancient Buildings seen there'. He asked the natives about what was there before the Incas ruled. They said that, long before the establishment of the Inca dynasty, there were bearded and white-skinned people, like the Spaniards, living on the largest island in Lake Titicaca. They had been massacred by the Indians. This statement seems to be inconsistent with other information given to Cieza. While their ancestors were praying for the return of light (possibly after an eclipse of the sun), the sun rose in great splendour from behind the island.

And immediately after this event, they tell that from the south there came and stayed a white man of tall stature, who in his appearance and person showed great authority and veneration, and that as they saw he had great power, turning hills into plains and plains into hills, making fountains in the solid rocks, they recognised such power in him that they called him Creator of all made things, Beginning thereof, Father of the Sun, beside this, they say that he made greater things, as he is said to have given men and animals their existence, and finally that wonderful benefits came from his hands. And the Indians who told me this had heard from their forbears, who had also heard it from the songs which these had had since very ancient times, that he went off northwards along the Sierras while accomplishing these wonders, and that they never saw him again. In many places they tell how he gave rules to men how they should live, and that he spoke lovingly to them with much kindness, admonishing them they should be good to each other and not do any harm or injury, but that instead they should love each other and show charity. In most places they generally call him Ticciviracocha, but in the province of Collao they call him Tuapaca, and in other places around there Arunaua. In many parts temples are built to him, in which they placed stone statues in his likeness, in front of which they made sacrifices. The large stone statues which are at the site of Tiahuanaco must be from those times. And although they relate of his former fame this which I tell of Ticciviracocha, they cannot tell more of him, neither that he returned to any part of his kingdom.

Juan de Betanzos, who recorded traditions about the same time as Cieza, had a unique opportunity to collect aboriginal stories, for he had married an Indian girl and spent his life with her people. Betanzos wrote:

In ancient times, they say, the country and province of Peru was in darkness, having never light or day. There were, at the time, certain people in it, which people had a certain chief who commanded them and to whom they were subjected. Of the name of the people and the chief who commanded them they have no recollection. And in those times, when all was night in this land, they say, that from a lake in this country of Peru, in the province of Collasuyo, there came a chief called Con Ticci Viracocha who, they say, had with him a certain number of people, which number they do not recollect. And after he had sailed from this lake he went from there to a site that is close to this lake, where today is a village called Tiahuanaco, in the aforesaid province of the Collao. And as he went thither, he and his own, forthwith there improvisedly, they say, that he made the sun and day, and ordered the sun to move in the course it now moves and afterwards, they say, he made the stars and the moon.

When I asked the Indians what shape this Viracocha had when their ancestors had thus seen him, they said that according to the information they possessed, he was a tall man with a white vestment that reached to his feet, and that this vestment had a girdle; and that he carried his hair short with a tonsure on the head in the manner of a priest; and that he walked solemnly, and that he carried in his hands a certain thing which today seems to remind them of the breviary that the priests carry in their hands. And this is the account I received on this subject, according to what the Indians told me. And when I asked them what this person called himself . . . they told me that his name was Con Ticci Viracocha Pachayachachic, which in their language means, God, Maker of the World.

Viracocha is reputed to have travelled north and departed from the coast of Ecuador, where, in 1958, pottery of an unusual type, unknown elsewhere, was dug up. Radio-carbon tests indicate an age of 3000–2500 B.C., 1,000 years earlier than the earliest known Peruvian pottery. This discovery has been taken to indicate a trans-Pacific contact about that time. Thor Heyerdahl believes that the bearded white men who created the civilization of Tiahuanaco left the coast by raft and reached Easter Island where they built statues resembling those found at Tiahuanaco.*

* *American Indians in the Pacific*, Allen and Unwin, 1952.

Similar stories of visits by bearded white men were told by the ancient Aztecs and Mayas, the peoples of Mexico and the Yucatan who achieved civilizations equalling or surpassing that of Tiahuanaco.

Cortez, who reached Mexico in 1519 and Pizarro who conquered Peru in 1532 were welcomed as returning gods, the sons and brothers of the bearded white men who had brought the arts of civilization to these trans-Atlantic lands. The chief of these culture-bearers was called Quetzalcoatl by the Aztecs, and Kukulcan by the Mayas.

According to Cortez, the Aztec Emperor Montezuma told him:

We have known for a long time, by the writings handed down by our forefathers, that neither I nor any who inhabit this land are natives of it, but foreigners who came here from remote parts. We also know that we were led here by a ruler, whose subjects we all were, who returned to his country, and after a long time came here again and wished to take his people away. But they had married wives and built homes, and they would neither go with him nor recognize him as their king; therefore he went back. We have ever believed that those who were of his lineage would some time come and claim this land as his, and us as his vassals. From the direction whence you came, which is where the sun rises, and from what you tell me of this great lord who sent you, we believe and think it certain that he is our natural ruler, especially since you say that for a long time he has known about us. Therefore you may feel certain we shall obey you, and shall respect you as holding the place of that great lord, and in all the land I rule, you may give what orders you wish, and they shall be obeyed and everything we have shall be put at your service. And since you are thus in your own heritage and your own house, take your ease and rest from the fatigue of the journey and the wars you have had on the way.

The Spaniards learned that Quetzalcoatl had been a supreme god or high priest, a teacher, a wise law-giver and merciful judge. He forbade human sacrifice, teaching that flowers, bread and incense were all that God demanded. He prohibited wars and forebade fighting, violence and robbery. Although the Aztec religion required human sacrifice, he was held in affectionate veneration. He was tall of stature, white or reddish in complexion, clothed 'in a long white robe strewn with red crosses, and carrying a staff in his hand'. He brought with him builders, painters, astronomers and draughtsmen. He passed from place to place and disappeared. According to some traditions, he died on the east coast of Mexico, and was buried on the sea shore by his followers after they had burned his body and his treasures. Another tradition related that Quetzalcoatl and his companions embarked on a raft and sailed towards the rising sun, the direction from which they had come.

The Mayas, the highly civilized people of Yucatan, had two culture heroes, Itzamna and Kukulcan, who had arrived at different times and had come from opposite directions. Itzamna had been their guide, instructor and civilizer. He was their first ruler and priest, teaching them how to please the gods and heal the sick. He taught the use of letters and devised the calendar. He was an historical personage, referred to in their traditions and inscriptions. Kukulcan came later, accompanied by twenty men, who wore flowing robes and sandals, had long beards and bare heads. He was a great architect and pyramid builder. He discouraged fighting and under his benevolent rule the people prospered. He did not die but disappeared under the earth, according to one tradition, because of the people's ingratitude.

It is possible that these Indian traditions may have been coloured by the views of the Spaniards who recorded them. They may have described these culture heroes in their own terms, misunderstanding or misinterpreting the stories they were told. Some modern investigators believe that Quetzalcoatl, Kukulcan and Viracocha were gods who had been accorded human form, part of the great pantheon of Indian religious belief. Quetzalcoatl, whose name denoted the 'feathered serpent', for example, was the lord of the winds. The civilizations of the Mayas, Peruvians and Aztecs, they claim, were indigenous and owed nothing to outside influences.

The diffusionists, those who believe that all culture stemmed from a common source, assert that these pre-Columbian American civilizations sprang up suddenly without any long evolutionary period, and point to their resemblances with the civilizations of Egypt, Mesopotamia and the Aegean Sea. Like the Egyptians, the Mayas built pyramid structures. They possessed an embryonic, hieroglyphic form of picture writing. The diffusionists stress the remarkable paradox of traditions of visits by white-skinned, long-robed, bearded men held by the brown-skinned, loin-cloth-wearing, beardless Indians of tropical America.

A Caucasoid element in the population has been observed by the anthropologists who have examined the mummified bodies found in the Peruvian desert and in rock-tombs. Many of these bodies have cranial shapes and silky, soft, brown, red and wavy hair, features alien to the aborigines of America. The American Indian is of Mongoloid extraction, with coarse black hair and yellow skin.

Early pottery vessels found in Peru and in the lands to the north depict people wearing full-length robes, with long beards reaching to the waist. Thor Heyerdahl, the principal exponent of the diffusion theory, considers that these pictures represent people of the Arabo-Semitic type, as does the art of the Olmecs, the people of eastern Mexico who may have been the precursors of the Mayas and Aztecs. Certain Olmec pictures depict two contrasting ethnic types, one remarkably negroid, with thick lips, flat broad nose and round face, the other strikingly different and almost Semitic in type, with narrow face, sharp profile, strongly hooked nose, thin lips and beard. Neither type bears the slightest resemblance to any ethnic group known to have existed in aboriginal America.

Frescoes discovered in the Temple of the Warriors at Chichén Itzá in Yucatan in 1931 depict a sea battle between two contrasting racial types, one with white skins, long flowing yellow hair, men who are shown nude and circumcized, the other dark-skinned and wearing the typical Indian feathered head-dress and loin cloth. Several of the white-skinned sailors are being led away as bound captives. A white prisoner with long yellow hair reaching to his waist is being sacrificed by two dark-skinned men. Another tries to escape by swimming, his long golden hair floating on the waves.

The Mayas enjoyed their golden age between A.D. 300 and

850. They built great temples which they abandoned to build elsewhere. Palenque ceased to erect hieroglyphic monuments in 784, Copán in 800, Tilsa in 830, Oxtintok in 850 and Uaxactún in 889. Yet for 500 years the priestly astronomers had never neglected to set up a *stele* every twenty years to mark the passage of time. The builders of Tiahuanaco reached their highest activities between A.D. 450 and 900. Their cultural hero, Viracocha, came and went in the fifth century. By the Mayan calendar Quetzalcoatl arrived and departed in the eighth century.

These dates rule out the possibility that Quetzalcoatl, Kukulcan and Viracocha were Egyptians, Cretans, Greeks or Phoenicians whose great civilizations had by then long since passed away. Their successors, the Romans, were not venturesome seamen.

Even less certain is the belief, advocated by the diffusionists, that the ancient Greeks knew of the existence of a great continent across the Atlantic, between Europe and Asia. They seem to have imagined the habitable world as girdled by the river Oceanus beyond which lay a realm of dust and darkness. References by certain Greek authors to a trans-Atlantic continent may have been no more than inspired guesses, derived from their understanding of the earth's spherical shape. Greek mythology can be interpreted to transfer the voyages of Odysseus and the travels of Hercules to the far West, in some trans-Atlantic land.

Plato, in his account of Atlantis, is thought to be describing America when he refers to a number of lesser islands beyond the lost continent which provided a route to the 'opposite continent surrounding the ocean'. His near contemporary, the fourth-century B.C. historian, Theopompus of Chios, described a continent of infinite extent lying in the ocean between Europe and Asia. Its warlike people had once fitted out an expedition to invade the Mediterranean world, and had reached the land of the Hyperboreans, probably the Greek name for the Britons.

The first-century A.D. Roman historian Plutarch relates a story which he claimed to have heard in Carthage. Every thirty years parties of pilgrims from Britain sailed westward to another island where the midsummer nights were short.

They sail on for a further 600 miles (965 kilometres) through a sea full of drifting ice and debris to 'the great continent by which the ocean is fringed'. They enter a large bay, the coast of which is inhabited by Greeks. This Carthaginian story may reflect a tradition, which they may have learned in Britain, referring to the island-hopping route to North America which the Norsemen used more than 1,000 years later.

The Greeks and the Phoenicians, and the latter's Carthaginian colonists, certainly sailed to Britain and possibly beyond. The fourth-century B.C. Greek navigator Pytheas, who went in search of tin and amber, sailed to the mysterious Thule, possibly Iceland.

The Phoenicians were the great explorers of antiquity. They circumnavigated Africa in about 600 B.C. The fifth-century B.C. Carthaginian Hanno explored the west coast of Africa and Himilco sailed northwards to Britain. They, or other Carthaginans, discovered the Canary Islands and possibly the Cape Verde Islands and Madeira. They may have reached the Azores and entered the Sargasso Sea. They appear to have told tales of shoals, shallows and mud-banks, possibly to deter their commercial rivals from venturing into the Atlantic, an ocean full of peril.

Diodorus of Sicily, writing in about 21 B.C., attributes to the Phoenicians the discovery of a large island, with great navigable rivers and delightful climate, many days' sail west from Africa. He would surely have used a stronger term than 'many' had they voyaged for months to discover a trans-Atlantic continent.

Whether Phoenicians or Greeks could or would have crossed the Atlantic by design is doubtful. They could, no doubt, have sailed in hope, via the Azores or Canary Islands, to the West Indies. A vessel may have been driven across by chance from Spain, or from Lixtus on the Morrocan coast where the Carthaginians had established colonies by 500 B.C. The Phoenician ships would have been capable of such voyages, utilizing the same easterly trade wind as Columbus in 1492. As well as war galleys, the Phoenicians built the larger and sturdier *gaulos*, a tubby merchant vessel. Xenophon describes it as having spars, rigging and considerable storage space. It may have equalled in size the Portuguese caravels of the fourteenth and fifteenth centuries which were between 50 and 500 tons' burden. The Phoenicians gained a high reputation for seamanship. They may have been able roughly to assess latitude, by measuring the sun's inclination with a pointer, but they (like all seafarers before 1770) did not have any reliable method of determining longtitude, the distance they might be sailing westwards.

Phoenician or Greek seamen would have found it harder to return to Europe, for it required knowledge that the only possible route in sailing-ship days lay up the American coast as far as Bermuda, before turning eastwards to Spain. That was the route taken by the Spanish flotas bringing the riches of the New World to Europe.

Ancient knowledge of the New World may have been no more than an inspired guess. Eratosphanes, the third-century A.D. Greek librarian of Alexandria, thought that were it not for the extent of the Atlantic as an obstacle, it would be possible to sail from Spain to India on the same parallel. The Roman geographer, Strabo, writing two centuries earlier, accepted that India lay only a few days' sail from Spain with a following wind. Neither scholar imagined the existence of a continent in between. Isodore of Seville wrote in the seventh century, 'The philosophers say that beyond the ocean there is not any land.'

Medieval European knowledge of the Atlantic seems to have been confined to belief in the existence of several islands, the 'Isles of the Hesperides', 'Fortunate Islands' and the 'Isles of the Blessed', fabled utopias identifying probably the Azores, the Canaries and Madeira. Another fabulous island called Antilla may have been one of the Azores. It is reputed to have been reached and settled in A.D. 714 by an archbishop and seven bishops fleeing from Spain following the Moorish conquest. Could they have been the white bearded men who seem to have reached Mexico about that date? Antilla was rediscovered in 1447 by the crew of a Portuguese ship. They reported it was still inhabited by Spaniards. The island of Brazil is named in several old well-authenticated maps, none of which hints at the existence of a trans-Atlantic continent. The Norsemen who reached Newfoundland in about A.D. 1000 had no idea that they had stepped upon the outskirts of a great new continent. Other trans-Atlantic voyages are reputed to have been made by Irish monks, Welsh princes and Basque seamen. Prince Madoc's voyage in 1170 to a fertile island to the west of Ireland is thought to be legendary.

The famed exploits of St Brendan are accorded slightly higher standing. The Irish monk sailed out into the Atlantic in about A.D. 565. He seems to have reached Iceland and possibly Greenland. He, or other Irishmen, may have sailed to Labrador before the Norsemen. *The Saga of Eric the Red* acknowledges the presence of men wearing white garments. Another version of the *Saga* relates the story of a Norse ship which had been blown off course. It comes to a land inhabited by people who appear to be speaking Erse. Brendan's voyage is a wondrous story cloaked with myth. The only evidence that he may have reached America comes from the statement that he landed on a group of flat islands, their surrounding seas filled with shoals of monster fish which could easily be seen because of the clarity of the water. It is difficult to fit this description with islands other than the Bahamas or West Indies. Other Irishmen are reported to have founded a colony in Florida.

No building, fully authenticated inscribed stone or European object has been found in America, other than at Anse aux Meadows in Newfoundland, the Norsemen's colony, to substantiate belief that Europeans may have crossed the Atlantic. A supposed Phoenician inscription is described on p. 206 and the origin of the caves on Mystery Hill, in New Hampshire, are discussed on p. 184. No likely voyagers fit the descriptions of Quetzalcoatl, Kukulcan or Viracocha. Thor Heyerdahl's voyage in the reed boat Ra in 1970 showed only that an Egyptian voyage across the Atlantic would have been possible.

There remains one other possible contender for the title of first Atlantic voyager. Following the Moslem conquest of the West in the seventh century, the Arabs became the inheritors and exploiters of the ancient knowledge of mathematics and astronomy. The Caliph Mamun broke into the Great Pyramid of Egypt in search of the lost knowledge in 840. Writing in the twelfth century, relative to the discovery of 'What it is that encloses the ocean, and what its limits are', the Arab geographer Idrisi, mentions the voyage from Lisbon of a party of

eight men. Following eleven days' sail from the coast they come
to a sea 'of which the thick waves had a fetid odour, concealed
with many shoals and were dimly lit'. By this description it
seems they may have reached the Sargasso Sea of seaweed,
between the Azores and the West Indies, before turning for
home. The contemporary author Honorius calls it 'the curdled
sea'. Idrisi also refers to the Atlantic voyage of the brothers
Magrurin between 712 and 1100.

Evidence for an Arab discovery of America is as precarious
as it is for Phoenicians, Greeks or Irish. But one point is
interesting. By the time Idrisi wrote, the Arab mathematicians
had adopted the numeral zero. Did they acquire it from the
Hindus or from the Mayas who were familiar with its use in the
fifth century?

Quetzalcoatl's, Kukulcan's and Viracocha's reputed morality
suggests that they were Christians, but strange Christians
indeed who failed to preach the glorious return of their dead
Messiah, the doctrine of original sin and the practical uses of
the wheel.

THE MAYAS BUILD, ABANDON AND REBUILD

The Mayas of Central America built great cities, occupied them
for hundreds of years and abandoned them, moving elsewhere
and building again. Why they did so is one of the mysteries of
history, a puzzle which several theories have attempted to
explain. To understand the solutions offered we need to know
something of the Mayas.

Although glimpsed by the Spanish conquistadores, the existence of a number of ruined cities in the jungles of Yucatan,
Guatemala and Honduras did not become known to the outside world until early in the nineteenth century. A Spanish
commission visited several. Its report, a translation of which
was published in London in 1822, aroused great interest at the
time when the great cities of Nineveh and Babylon were giving
up their secrets.

A famous English eccentric, Lord Kinsborough, became convinced these cities had been built by the Lost Tribes of Israel. He spent eighteen years proving his theory by the publication of a vast work in nine volumes which sold at £175 a set and brought him to a debtors' prison. Another no less enthusiastic theorist, La Plongeon, declared they had been built by the survivors of lost Atlantis.

Meanwhile the Maya cities had been visited in 1839 by an American traveller, John L. Stephens, a graduate of Columbia University, who published two books on the subject in 1841. This heightened interest in the Mayas led to the rediscovery of the Spanish Bishop Diego de Landa's *History*, first published in 1560, which preserved some of the ancient traditions of the Mayas and which printed three of their codices. Research into Mayan history was carried a stage further by the English archaeologist, Alfred Maudslay who between 1881 and 1884 published a book in five volumes. Since then on-the-spot research has been undertaken by several American universities and museums, and by the Mexican National Museum.

Despite the intensive efforts of these investigators we still know less about the Mayas than we do about the ancient civilizations of the Middle East. Although they were the only pre-Columbian American people with a system of writing, very few Mayan inscriptions survived the Spanish conquest, and only one-third of their hieroglyphs have been deciphered. This lack of historical information is partly offset by the preservation of traditions by their descendants, a million of whom still inhabit the same area, a race linked to the great days of their glorious past by a few hundred years, and who live much the same lives as their ancestors.

Much has been learned from the study of the Mayas' ruined cities. As far as they knew they were the only people on earth. They lived completely isolated from other peoples making similar progress, the factor which so greatly influenced the growth of cultures in Mesopotamia and Egypt. The Mayas achieved standards in many ways equal to, and in one respect far surpassing, these great cultures. They came on the scene far later than the Sumerians, the Egyptians and the Greeks, and their civilization lasted for barely a thousand years. They discovered so much so very quickly that it is amazing they did not learn more. They showed flashes of amazing genius, yet they failed to put it to practical purpose. They visualized eternity, but were incapable of understanding the principle of the true arch or of the wheel. They learned to count in millions but they did not know how to weigh a sack of corn. They were obsessed by the mystery of time. Its eternity and its passing enchanted them. They evolved a system of mathematics capable of counting backwards and forwards for 400 million years.

They calculated exactly the movements of the heavenly bodies. They were able to predict to the second the rising and setting of the sun on any particular day, the transits of Venus and eclipses of sun and moon. They estimated that the year numbered 365.2420 days, whereas its true length is 365.2422 days. Their calendar was more accurate than both the Roman Julian (365.2500) calculation and the calendar introduced to Europe by Pope Gregory in 1782 (365.2425).

They took their observations with crossed sticks levelled at a fixed point on the horizon, and they assessed the results over hundreds of years. They worked out a mathematical system of position, whereby the value of the cyphers changed according to their juxtaposition, with the result that hundreds, thousands and millions of years could be shown by symbols, greatly simplifying mathematics at a time when the Romans had to write MDCCCXLVIII to signify the year 1848. Expressed in our terms the Mayas could have written four million pounds as £4m. They employed dots and bars for numbers up to 20, their vigesimal system, adding symbols and changing their positions to attain any number required. That this simple method was not an obvious one is shown by the failure of the Western world to adopt it. No great European mathematician found such a simple way of lightening his labours. The Mayas made an even greater advance in mathematics. They conceived the quantity of zero, a thousand years before the Hindus discovered it and the Arabs put it to use.

Yet the Maya genius failed to understand that the earth goes round the sun, and they imagined the universe as a watery firmament in which the earth rested on the back of two giant alligators. Their paradoxes were astonishing. They were concerned more with mysticism than with the art of living. The Mayas possessed but never fully exploited the germ of progress. They never progressed beyond the Stone Age, yet with their stone tools and implements they built cities equalling the grandeur of Karnak and the durability of Nineveh. The Mayas, in the words of Eric Thompson, one of their two modern investigators, 'came from seeming nowhere, blazed like a meteor, grew dim and became extinct'.

Their civilization sprang into being, fully armed and in complete flower, during the first centuries of the Christian era. The Mayas suddenly became great builders, mathematicians and expert astronomers, a state of progress without evolution which has been taken by some theorists to suggest they received an initial impetus from outside, from lonely European voyagers who managed to cross the Atlantic a thousand years before Columbus. This is only a guess. It seems more probable that the sudden emergence of Mayan culture was due to one genius, a man with an abnormal mind, a philosopher who in the jungles of Central America equalled the genius of the Old World.

The Mayas did many wonderful things. They made balls of rubber for their intricate wall game – in which a goal was so rare that upon one being scored the players were accorded the right to seize the spectators' clothes, which resulted in a mass flight from the arena. They made waterproof clothing of rubber, and they discovered dyes and pigments. They found and cultivated many wild plants, including cocoa which they called 'hot swizzled drink'. They domesticated the turkey. It is believed that they even invented a mechanical stone-thrower. They experimented in what we would call chemical warfare, by hurling hornets' nests at their enemies. They built roads across swamps and they employed the local limestone in their gigantic structures. They never got further than the primitive corbelled arch, in which stones are laid together, converging at the top, although the true arch stared them in the face when their buildings collapsed.

Their hieroglyphic system of writing was embryonic; picture writing only, which they failed to evolve into a phonetic alphabet. Their symbol for water was a piece of jade, because water, like jade, was precious. They used their writing to express their spiritual needs rather than to record history or to eulogize the deeds of individuals. Decipherment is slow because there is no Rosetta Stone to supply a key. As a result we know next to nothing of their literature, but one deciphered example suggests the Mayas had a poet as noble as the author of the first chapter of Genesis. Describing the Creation he wrote:

The world was not light. There was no day, there was no night; there was no moon. Then they perceived that the dawn was coming; then the dawn came. Sky, earth, trees and rocks were set in order; all things were created by God. Thus he was there in his divinity, in the clouds, alone and by his own effort, when he created the entire world, when he moved in the heavens in his divinity. Thus he ruled in his great power. Every day is set in order according to the count, beginning in the east, as it is arranged.

Mayan sculpture is one of the great glories of pre-Columbian America. To our modern eyes it may seem over-elaborate and distorted. This is because of the symbolism the Mayas set out to convey. Rigid adherence to the style and convention resulted in hideous forms. The Mayas were capable of giving their pictures vitality and movement, and they concentrated chiefly on low reliefs, frequently achieving a three-dimensional quality. Their art symbolism was intended to please the gods, not humans. They also carved wood and painted pottery.

Mayan history is divided into two periods, the Old and the New Empires. These categories can be misleading for the culture stages overlapped. Like all American Indians, the Mayas were of Asiatic origin, part of the wave of immigration which came from Siberia, via Alaska, during the past 20,000 years. Their origin is attested by their physical characteristics, slanting eyes, beardless faces and the 'Mongolian spot' at the base of the spine. Attempts have been made to link them with the cultures of Mesopotamia and Egypt. That is a tribute to their amazing genius.

Why the Mayas progressed whereas their neighbours stagnated is one of the many problems of their history. They evolved a great culture in a humid, swampy jungle. They were forced to fight continually against the primordial forest, and in the end it engulfed them. For hundreds of years the Mayas of the Old Empire responded to the challenge of their environment; finally they gave up in despair and moved away to the arid uplands of Yucatan. That is one of the theories presented to account for their sudden abandonment of the great cities they had built in the Peten area.

Yucatan thrusts into the Gulf of Mexico like a giant thumb. At its base the hand spreads out into a mountainous, forested area comprising what is now Guatemala and Honduras, the hinterland in which the Old Empire flowered, an area of 125,500 square miles. A land flowing with milk and honey, if it could be cultivated. Therein lay the snag. Laboriously the Mayas cleared patches in the jungle to grow their maize; working with stone tools, they were forced to burn and uproot. Lacking proper equipment they were swamped by weeds. After a few years they had to abandon their fields and start again. That, according to one theory, is why they deserted their original cities. They were driven forth to find an easier land.

The great cities of the Old Empire were in existence by A.D. 300. The next five centuries saw its golden age. In the Peten area vast temple complexes were built at Uaxactún, Tikál, Palenque, Copán, and many other sites. By then the Mayan picture-writing and their numerical system were fully developed. The great temples were built, oriented to the points of the compass and constructed for the observation of the heavenly bodies by fixed points. That necessitated the raising of platforms 160 feet (49 metres) high, above the level of the surrounding jungle.

Despite their work of burning and clearing, the Mayas had time and inclination for these great public works. Only forty-eight to seventy-six days a year were required, it has been estimated by the scientists of the U.S. Department of Agriculture, for the peasant to raise sufficient food for his family. As long as they were persuaded that the temple building was to their advantage, the Mayan common man was prepared to devote his leisure to erecting great structures of stone. The impetus came from the Mayas' obsession with time. As an agricultural people they required to know the exact dates on which their cultivation needed to be based. The astronomical data collected supplied this vital information. It served their spiritual needs also, for the Mayas were a deeply religious people, a race who believed that the forces of nature, the gods, required frequent propitiation, a service which the sacerdotal aristocracy set out to perform on the people's behalf by ceremonies and incantations. Like all primitive peoples, the Mayas, with all their knowledge, were slaves to superstition. They hoped to achieve the gods' cooperation by magical rituals.

They believed that the god Hunab Ku had created the world. He took no further part in human affairs. He was the head of a pantheon of lesser deities, forces of both good and evil, their patrons and enemies, the principal of whom was called Itzamna, the lord of the heavens, the friend of man. There had been several worlds, each destroyed by a deluge, due to the peoples' sins. They lived in constant fear that their world too would come to an end. Man possessed an immortal soul, and human life was an eternal struggle between the forces of good and evil. The future world contained a good and a bad place, a heaven and a hell. The Maya religion incorporated a philosophy which brought its adherents to final disaster and destruction by another more powerful faith. The Maya believed that the end always justifies the means. They never understood the great truth, appreciated by Western thought, that absolute power always corrupts, and that good ends never justify immoral means.

The Mayan creation myths were most ingenious. The creator God cried 'earth', and land appeared. He planted it with trees, made rivers run, filled it with animals, assigning to each its own habitat. There was one thing missing, God found: the animals could not speak so there was no one to praise him. He set out to make a superior being from mud, but the mud dissolved in water. He then created beings of wood; they spoke and reproduced themselves, but they were dry and bloodless so he destroyed them by rain. A few puppets survived and from them the monkeys descended. Finally God made man from maize. But the first men were too clever. God, not wishing man to be his equal (surely an echo of the idea contained in the story of the Garden of Eden), dulled his eyes. He created women to be the wives of men. Having done all this, the creator caused dawn to break and the sun rose. The men worshipped their creator.

The existence of these general ideas, so similar to those of Western man's heritage, in an isolated part of the world, suggests that man had begun to question his origin long before the American Indians trekked away from Asia.

A few intelligent men ruled the Mayas, each a priest-king in his own city, each city a state. They and their followers controlled the common people, the mass of the population who may have numbered as many as three million. They set them building while they themselves sought to enlarge the frontiers of human knowledge. While the priests plotted the courses of the stars and decreed the day on which sowing should start, the peasants laboured to build the giant temples and spacious courts which shaped a dozen cities. Each stone was carried by hand and worked with stone tools. Each building was erected without any mechanical aid. No words can do justice to the architectural genius and the labours of the Mayas. When the now famous ruins were discovered they were strangled by giant trees, the roots of which had torn stone from stone. Many of them have been reconstructed.

There is no such thing as a typical Maya city, observes Eric Thompson, who has examined all the known sites. But they all have certain features in common, of which the most important is the ceremonial court flanked on all sides by terraces, platforms, pyramids and temples. The great court at Tikál, he suggests, gives a general idea of all such centres. It measures 400 feet east to west and 250 feet north to south (120 by 75 metres). It is bounded by two huge temple-crowned pyramids, reached by wide staircases, the whole mass of masonry having a volume of half a million cubic feet. On the court's north side lies a large platform capped by four pyramids. Continuing his description, Thompson says:

A fantastic sight it must have been to an observer standing in the centre of the great court and facing north. On each side of him was a huge pyramid with its temple and soaring roof crest rising like a volcano; before him stood rows of stelae and then that sort of Kremlin with its nine smaller temple-crowned pyramids. Everywhere his gaze would have fallen upon acre upon acre of stuccoed surface, like creamy icing over writhing masks of gods on façades and roof crests and smoothly spread on geometric equilibrium of stair and terrace – dynamic, and static in silent conflict. His eyes would have been caught by doorways of temples, black in shadow or with a gay textile drawn across the gaping mouth.

Behind him the observer finds another acropolis, and beyond it a ravine topped by a further great pyramid and another platform 12 feet (3.6 metres) high. Palenque possesses many underground passages, leading from one pyramid to the other, their purpose religious hocus-pocus. By employing these secret passages the Maya priests, impersonating their gods, could appear miraculously and startle their flock.

No early Mayan city was walled or fortified: amongst the loose confederation of city-states there was no warfare, no militarism, no waste of valuable strength. For 500 years the Mayas fought the engulfing forest, scratching out areas to cultivate, building, sculpturing, propitiating the gods and adding to their astronomical knowledge. Throughout the Peten area there was tremendous activity. A dozen great cities raised their buildings in patches of cleared jungle. Then, suddenly, in the ninth century of our era, the whole edifice of civilization collapsed. The ancient Mayas abandoned their cities to the trees and monkeys and migrated northwards to the uplands of Yucatan, where the Lesser Descent, as it is known in Maya tradition, has preceded the Greater Descent.

Mayan colonies had been established in Yucatan hundreds of years before. Now the Mayas left their primitive home and migrated to the far-flung outposts of their empire. It was as if the Romans had abandoned the Eternal City and decamped to Britain. Why the Mayas abandoned their great cities has been discussed by two authors, men who both spent their lives studying the Mayas and excavating their ruined cities.

Dr Sylvanus Morley dismisses such easy explanations as earthquakes, climatic changes, recurring epidemics, foreign conquest, civil war and intellectual exhaustion.* There is no

* *The Ancient Maya*, Stanford University Press, 1956 (third edition).

175

evidence that the Old Empire was struck by any of these disasters. The Mayan migration was caused, he believes, by the complete failure of their agricultural economy. The system of clearing forest patches was followed too long, he thinks. It ceased finally to yield enough food to supply the growing population, for the clearing of patches resulted in the formation of artificial grassland, to fight which the Maya had no tools. Each man-made clearing became swamped by weeds; the old clearings were abandoned and new clearings made. Gradually, the Mayas ran out of land. Their economic plight led to discontent and their leaders, like Moses of old, led them away to seek a better land. By the tenth century of our era the great cities of Peten were silent and empty.

Eric Thompson (*The Rise and Fall of the Mayas*, 1956) does not accept Dr Morley's theory. He agrees that the building activities in the Peten area ceased abruptly and the people moved away. In some cases he finds the work ceased so suddenly that buildings were left unfinished. Copán ceased to erect hieroglyphic monuments in A.D. 800, three other cities in Campeche in 810. Tila in 830. Oxtintok in 830. Uaxactún in 889. Yet for 500 years the priests of each city had set up a *stele* every twenty years to mark the passage of time. The last recorded date at Palenque was even earlier, in 784.

Thompson believes the growth of grass would have been too slow to have suddenly overwhelmed cultivated areas. A heavy population remained in the area long after the cities were abandoned. The priestly kings and their followers were driven away. Thompson visualizes a series of peasant revolts against the theocratic minority and nobles, caused perhaps by their ever-growing demands for service in the construction work and in the growing of food for an increasing number of unproductive mouths. He finds signs of a divorce between the minority who were lost in the problems of time and the majority who had to sustain them. Exotic religious cults, he suggests, may have driven a wedge between the priests and the peasants who accepted the theocracy's preoccupation with the study of time only as long as it yielded results beneficial to the whole community, information important to agriculturists.

Revolutionary ideas spread across the Peten lowlands. In

city after city the ruling class was driven out or massacred: the 'Bastille was stormed'. Rude, uncultured leaders took command. The great ceremonial centres were allowed to decay, the ancient walls collapsed, the giant pyramids became clad in foliage, and whole cities were submerged by the jungle reaching back to claim its own. Deprived of its guiding hand, the Old Empire died.

The Peten leaders, driven out by economic collapse or by the revolt of their serfs, the masses whose interests they had ignored in their pursuit of pure knowledge, in their obsession with the mystery of time, led their followers in a great exodus to the colonial cities of Uxmal, Mayapan and Chichén Itzá, in northern Yucatan, where the Mayan civilization reached fresh heights. They entered a new golden age, achieved a new culture, one now sharpened by outside influences. It lasted for 500 years.

The Mayan renaissance was marked by the influx of new leaders, a new religion, different customs and new ideas and by the introduction of mass human sacrifice. Within a few years of the Great Descent, the wind of change blew down the Yucatan peninsula. The preoccupation of the priestly nobles in the passing of time, in astronomy and its prophetic implications, was rudely shaken by the arrival of alien Maya-speaking peoples from Mexico. They introduced a new impetus. Militarism replaced science. The new cult of human sacrifice demanded the capture of prisoners.

Towards the close of the tenth century a new leader appeared from the north. In Mexico he was named Quetzalcoatl, meaning the 'plumed serpent'; the Mayas called him Kukulcan. He conquered Chichén Itzá. The Mayas clustered together in self-protection, forming the League of Mayapan, their principal city.

The full story of the wars between the Yucatan city-states, which raged on and off for three centuries, is lost in confused tradition. Only a few isolated episodes are related by the later Mayas. One passage in their ancient chronicles tells a story reminiscent of the Helen of Troy episode, in which Chichén Itzá was besieged because the bride of Ah Ulil, the ruler of Itzamal, had been kidnapped by a man named Chac Xib Chac.

Chichén Itzá was taken between 1194 and 1234 and Mayapan was itself sacked in 1441, at the end of a period of civil disorder which reduced the whole country to chaos. A terrible epidemic of smallpox which fell on Yucatan in the year 1480 completed the disruption of the New Empire. The Mayas fell easy victims to the Spanish conquerors between 1527 and 1535.

A few ruined cities, three written codices saved from destruction by the Spaniards, several hundred stone dating *stelae* and our scanty knowledge of their great intellectual achievements are all that remain of this remarkable people. Availing themselves of a fertile soil, though difficult to work, the Mayas raised themselves from the status of a primitive tribe, having no advantage over the other aboriginal inhabitants of the Americas, to a cultured people, building and erecting great stone cities, peacefully engaged for centuries in sustaining life and increasing their knowledge. Their greatest achievement was a numerical system far in advance of the rest of humanity. They made calculations to an accuracy which Europeans failed to attain until modern times.

They did all this starting from scratch culturally, living in complete isolation. They showed great ingenuity, but they failed to conceive the principle of the wheel, known to the rest of the world for over 10,000 years, one of the chief marks of a civilized people. Yet they made pottery toys with dogs set on wheels. Their genius was turned to impractical things, to the pursuit of pure knowledge. They failed to respond fully to the challenge of life.

Why the Mayas declined and fell is an intriguing mystery, as impenetrable as is the true reason why they abandoned their early cities. 'We may safely acclaim the ancient Mayas as the most brilliant aboriginal people of this planet,' declared Dr Morley. But they never progressed out of the Stone Age. Why they failed to reach further heights has excited many imaginations. The Mayas, it seems, lacked the will to progress. Their environment was not too hard to stifle development, but it was too soft to force them out of their physical lethargy and intellectual fatalism.

Maybe their civilization contained the seeds of its own decay. Fundamentally, Dr Morley finds, the Maya suffered from an imbalance of protein in their diet and from lack of sexual impulse. The nervous tension which has forced white men to excel was lacking from their lives. The average pulse rate of the modern Maya, Dr Morley observed, is only 52, 20 points less than that of the European. The Mayas remained static because they lacked the white man's dynamism. They were too content, too easily led, too inclined to live and let live to become a great power in the Western sense of the term.

Yet in a way they surpassed others. We think of the brevity of time; they thought of its enormity. They visualized eternity, which no other people had succeeded in imagining. Time for the Mayas swept forward in an endless crescendo, in calculations by which they could have forecast the falling of Easter Day 400 million years hence. History repeated itself, they believed, and they sought to foretell the future by understanding the past. They saw time as an unending march from the far distant unknown past to the equally distant and unknown future, a world without beginning or end, an endless progression of days, with form but without meaning, a philosophy of history absent from European thought until the twentieth century.

The Mayas' decline, if it was economic in cause, proves the adage that all national disasters are agrarian in origin. If it was caused by the revolt of the masses, it warns of the danger of intellectualism divorced from reality. Their final destruction may have been due to their lack of centralized authority. Only an organized people, willing to sacrifice some of its personal freedom, can survive against powerful foes, we believe today. That theory may be proven by the Mayan collapse. Above all, the Mayas became over-obsessed with the mystery of time. Their over-preoccupation with mystical ideas may serve to remind us of the danger that in their search for the stars the scientists may forget their peoples' more urgent needs for earthly survival.

THE PRINCE OF PALENQUE

Dr Alberto Ruz was convinced that many unknown archaeological treasures still lay hidden in the rubble of palaces, temples and pyramids. He had been appointed director of research at Palenque in Yucatan in 1949. It was the most important step in his professional career since he had started excavating in Mexico in 1938. His predecessors had revealed many of the lost Mayan cities, huge buildings cloaked and hidden in the dense and mysterious jungle. Hacking down the trees, some 120 feet (37 metres) high, they had exposed city after city, the forgotten world of America's most advanced native civilization.

Ruz devised his own plan; to seek for architectural structures beneath the still visible buildings. The Mayas had been in the habit of erecting temples upon solid pyramids, reached by a steep flight of steps. They seemed to have done that with the Temple of Inscriptions at Palenque. It had been an important religious centre for it contained three stone panels carrying the longest known Mayan hieroglyphic inscription. The temple's floor, made of great stone slabs, had not been explored.

One slab caught Ruz's eye. Its edges were perforated with holes, each sealed by a stone plug. What could have been their purpose? The answer might lie beneath the slab. Clearing away the rubble, Ruz observed that the temple's walls continued under the floor instead of stopping at that level, a sure sign that something might be found beneath. Withdrawing the plugs, Ruz levered up the slab. A steep flight of steps disappeared in the darkness below. On the top step lay a box-shaped construction containing two jade ear-plugs and a stone coloured red.

Ruz had no idea that he stood on the brink of an archaeological discovery which would rival Howard Carter's opening of Tutankhamen's tomb in the Valley of the Kings. Nor had he any conception of the difficulties that lay ahead. The stairs leading into the pyramid's interior had been blocked with stones mixed with clay. They had coagulated into a solid hard mass. The excavators would need to gouge them out from above, working within a confined space. Four periods of two and a half months each were required to clear the obstruction. Forty-five steps down the mysterious staircase took a U-turn and continued downwards for another twenty-one steps. That brought the excavators to the pyramid's base at ground level, 73 feet (22 metres) below the temple platform. Two narrow galleries cut through the stones brought in fresh air from outside.

At the bottom of the steps lay a corridor, on its floor yet another box of offerings, richer than the first. It contained three pottery dishes, two shells, seven jade beads, a pair of circular ear-plugs shaped like a flower, and a beautifully shaped tear-drop pearl, its lustre still well preserved. Ruz felt he was approaching the object of his search, now in its second year.

The corridor ended in a blank wall completely blocking the passage. It was a solid obstruction several metres thick made of stone and lime. A triangular stone, 7 feet (2 metres) high, had been let into the wall, blocking the entrance. At the foot of the slab lay a heap of bones, the skeletons of six young people, one female. Had they been sacrificed to the Mayan gods? Or had their presence in the doorway a deeper meaning?

The workmen displaced the triangular slab, enabling Ruz to squeeze through the entrance. It was for him a moment of indescribable emotion. He found himself in an enormous crypt, a fairy palace, for from its roof hung a curtain of stalactites developed by centuries of dripping water. Around the walls strode a great procession of priests modelled in stucco and larger than life size.

Almost the whole of the crypt was occupied by a colossal monument, seemingly a ceremonial altar, 27 feet (8 metres) square and weighing 20 tons. It rested on an enormous monolith 6 cubic feet (.17 cubic metres) in size supported on six great blocks of chiselled stone. Its sides were carved in beautiful reliefs. But finest of all for its unsurpassed execution and perfect state of preservation was the great stone covering the whole. It

was richly carved in heavy hieroglyphic inscriptions, symboliz-
ing the Mayas' hope for eternity and their expectation of
triumph over death. There were also thirteen date signs corresponding to the beginning of the seventh century A.D., the height
of Mayan achievement.

Up to now, Ruz had believed he had found a ceremonial
crypt, the place of some secret religious rite. But the crypt's
entrance had been blocked and sealed.

Ruz bored a hole in the apparently solid base of the monolith. The bore penetrated into a hollow space. A piece of wire
thrust in emerged flecked with particles of red paint, the colour
always associated with the Mayan dead, the living blood which
promised resurrection and gave hope of immortality. The paint,
with the offering found on the stairs and in the corridor, were
unmistakable evidence of a burial – in an extraordinary
sepulchre. To prove that, it was necessary to raise the stone. It
measured 13 by 7 feet (3.80 by 2.20 metres) and weighed five
tons. Lifting it would be an exacting, risky job.

Ruz took his team of workmen into the forest. They felled
a hardwood tree and cut it into sections of different lengths.
They lowered them down the staircase and brought them into
the crypt. Four large sections of the tree's trunk were inserted
beneath the corners of the stone slab. Four motor-car jacks
were placed in position, on their tops. Every possible pre-
caution was taken to prevent the stone from slipping.

The lifting operation began at midday on 7 November 1952.
Twelve hours' working lifted the stone inch by inch. By mid-
night it had been raised 2 feet (.6 metres), by next morning to
4 feet (1.12 metres), high enough for Ruz to peer inside. The
cavity within was covered by a highly polished slab shaped like
an oblong, narrow O with two branches like ears. It formed the
lid of the cavity which had been carved in the shape of the
human form from the solid block of stone. Four perforations
in the slab were plugged with stones. Withdrawing them, Ruz
raised the slab. It was the most impressive moment of his
career.

The floor and base of the cavity were painted red. On its
floor lay a human skeleton, covered over with fine jewels, suggesting the form and contour of the flesh which had clothed

the bones in life. Only a person of very high rank could have aspired to a sumptuous mausoleum of such impressive richness. His teeth had not been filed or encrusted with jade, and his cranium had not been deformed, the practices usual for individuals of the highest social Mayan rank. He had been a man of above average Mayan height. He did not appear to have been of Mayan origin. Yet he must have been a king or prince of Palenque.

He had been buried wearing a diadem made from tiny discs of jade and each hair of his head had been divided into separate strands encased in tiny jade tubes. Beneath the diadem lay a small jade plate cut in the shape of a vampire, representing Zotz the god of the underworld. His neck had been girdled by a collar composed of jade beans, shaped as spheres, cylinders, floral buds, open flowers, pumpkins, melons and a snake's head. The two ear-plugs were shaped as flowers. A square jade plate, covered with hieroglyphic inscriptions, ended in a flower-shaped bead. Behind one ear reposed a marvellous artificial pearl formed by uniting two pieces of mother-of-pearl, polished to give the appearance of a pearl of fabulous size. His breast had been covered by nine concentric rings with twenty-one tubular beads in each. His wrists had borne bracelets, containing 200 jade beads, and each finger of both hands bore great rings of jade. One ring was carved in the form of a crouching man. The right hand held a great jade bead, the left hand another, the one cubical and the other spherical in form. Two great jade beads lay at his feet. By the left foot stood a jade idol carved in the form of the sun god. A beautiful head carved in jade had been inserted within the mouth space, the dead man's means of sustenance for life beyond the tomb.

Even more magnificent was the face mask, made of jade mosaic with eyes of shell, each iris marked and the pupils darkened. The mask had slipped during burial and lay beside the face. The flesh had decomposed, the rich clothes in which he had been dressed had disintegrated. Beneath the body had been placed vessels of clay, containing food and drink, and two human heads modelled in stucco.

At the end of the burial and on the closing of the crypt, six young relatives or retainers of the dead man had been sacrificed to act as his companions and servants on his journey to the world beyond. Their heads and teeth had been deformed, the practice customary amongst the nobility alone.

Ruz noticed a curious feature of the burial. From the sarcophagus a carved serpent seemed to rise and ascend the steps leading to the crypt's threshold. There it became transformed into a tube running through the corridor, up the staircase and into the temple. This, he thought, represented a magical union between the deified being and the priests who needed to explain his mandates.

Ruz's discovery of the pyramid tomb **is** unprecedented in Mayan archaeology. Thousands of men toiled to construct the pyramid above and around the tomb and staircase. They built it to challenge the centuries, to fulfil the Mayas' obsession with eternity. Yet the prince may not have been a Mayan. There is no clue to his identity other than the conclusion that he must have been a unique figure.

MYSTERY HILL

'A mystery, a baffling and somewhat annoying mystery.' That was the comment of one of the many tourists who each summer visit Mystery Hill, North Salem, in the American state of New Hampshire. 'I try not to think about it,' the man told the official guide. He doubted 'if we shall ever learn the truth'. Other equally exasperated sightseers and investigators have echoed his words.

Mystery Hill lies 40 miles (64 kilometres) north of Boston and 25 miles (40 kilometres) from the Atlantic coast. Sprawling over an acre of woodland are twenty-two grotesque, cell-like structures built of unmortared granite rocks, some huge and heavy. Another site visitor, Vincent Fagan, assistant professor of Architecture at Notre Dame University, was perplexed at what he found. He thought, 'The big things are too little, the small things so big.' There was at one and the same time 'gigantic confusion and childish disorder, deep cunning and rude naivety'.

Despite half a century of investigation, no one has advanced an acceptable solution to the puzzle posed by these beehive buildings and passages which seem to ramble over the hillside in chaotic incoherence. No one knows who built them or why. The theories range from a Bronze Age structure, a Viking settlement, a nomadic Indian shelter, a colonial homestead and a robbers' hide-out. They are attributed to Phoenicians, Norsemen, Irish monks, colonial farmers and Jonathan Pattee.

Pattee lived on the hill from 1826 to 1848. His farmhouse burned down in 1855. The stone structures became called Pattee's Caves and the legend developed that he had built them with the aid of his five lusty sons. Pattee was reputed to have been a mail-robber, a fugitive from justice, the operator of an illicit whiskey still, a link in the 'underground rail road' which smuggled fugitive slaves to Canada, and a harmless Yankee eccentric who created the structures. 'Just for the hell of it'.

Sober investigation has disclosed that Pattee had one son, and was a prominent, wealthy and highly respected member of the community. He had been trustee of the village funds and had donated a house to serve as a school. None of his descendants, who still live locally, have been able to explain the caves, other than to express their total disbelief that Pattee could have built such useless structures. He may have used them as a sheep pen. One piece of evidence to be mentioned later indicates that they were in existence long before Jonathan Pattee came to live at North Salem. Following his death, the hill was ransacked by builders. They are believed to have quarried and carted away several tons of stone. The site became a children's playground.

William B. Goodwin came to North Salem in 1936. He had been told by a friend that the structures seemed to resemble the megalithic ruins of Europe and the Mediterranean. Goodwin was an insurance executive and a keen amateur antiquarian. He was obsessed by the belief that Irish monks had crossed the Atlantic long before Columbus. He bought Mystery Hill, determined to prove that its stone structures had been a monastery. Hearty and voluble, Godwin became belligerent and angry when his theory was laughed at by eminent archaeologists. He went blindly on, destroying in his excessive enthusiasm every clue which might have proved his theory or any other. He cast aside any object which failed to tally with his pet theories. He spent the rest of his life in a futile effort to prove he was right, and in acrimonious argument with people who offered advice.

The structures descend in steps on the eastern side of the hill, and are intermixed with low stone walls, lacking shape or direction. Some of the 'caves' are dwarfish in size, measuring 2 to 3 feet (.6 to .9 metres) high. All are built by the most primitive method known to man, by the piling and fitting of stones which are held together by their own weight and skilful arrangement. Where they are roofed, the primitive corbelled method of vaulting was adopted, whereby slabs are laid horizontally, not radially as in the true arch, each progressing a little further beyond the one below. That results in two converging walls.

Looking from the top of the hill, the visitor sees an artificial ramp, banked and walled, facing east. Below is a pit, in its centre a huge flat stone, having the profile of a bell, and weighing four tons. It stands on four squat legs and around its edge runs a clearly defined gutter leading to a spout. This Sacrificial Stone, as it is called, is the greatest enigma of all. Even Goodwin admitted that it denied his Irish monks theory. He shovelled away the debris which filled the space beneath, destroying every possible clue to the shrine's origin.

Below the Sacrificial Stone lies the main structure, a covered passage leading to a chamber. Both contain enigmatic features. 6 feet (1.8 metres) within the entrance is a stone ledge, just wide enough to hold a person lying with knees drawn up. At the farther end the passage widens into a chamber 22 feet long and 6½ feet in height (6.7 by 2 metres), and shaped like a Y. It also contains a seat and, even stranger, a shaft leading horizontally through 8 feet (2.4 metres) of stones to the open air, beneath the Sacrificial Stone. Voice tests show that it is highly resonant. Was it the speaking tube of an oracle? Did it enable the priest, concealed within the chamber, to speak in an eerie voice to the devotees grouped around the altar? One of the arms of the Y appears to have been constructed to act as a chimney. A louvred stone is believed to have acted as a damper.

Further down the slope is another crudely constructed artificial cave, less than 3 feet (.9 metre) high. It is reached by a passage roofed with heavy slabs of stone, from which open several other low chambers. Some investigators believe that they have detected rude carvings on these stones which appear to depict a bull and a horned gazelle, a species unknown in North America. Elsewhere 'inscriptions' resembling the Phoenician alphabet have been observed. These discoveries are thought to be fanciful.

The stones, some of which weigh twenty tons, used to form these structures have all been dressed with crude tools. One slab has been pierced through leaving a very rough hole. Some investigators believe that these buildings were erected to a measure close to the ancient cubit.

Two other features have excited interest. From the chambers two stone drains, one 60 feet (18 metres) and the other 40 feet (12 metres) long, descend the hillside. They were constructed presumably to prevent the buildings from becoming flooded. Two wells have also been found. One is 18 feet (5.5 metres) deep and was constructed with three curved sides and one straight – to accommodate a ladder, it has been suggested. Both are filled with water and debris. One is thought to lead to a subterranean chamber.

A stone locked in the decayed stump of a tree dates the structure prior to 1769, the earliest date by when the tree could have taken root. It belongs to a species of pine which grows at the rate of 1 inch (2.5 centimetres) every six years, and was in existence long before Jonathan Pattee built his farmhouse above one of the structures, which served him as a cellar.

Apart from the tree stump, which was too decayed for its rings to be counted, little has been found to date the site precisely. Gary Vescelius, who investigated the ruins in 1955 under the supervision of Dr Julius Bird of the American Museum of Natural History, sank ten test holes. He found 7,000 artifacts, the majority of which belonged to the Point Peninsula or Owasco Indian cultures which are dated about 1000 B.C. A stone hoe seemed to have derived also from this archaic period. Old turf levels, excavated in 1969, yielded a similar date by Carbon-14 chronology. Frank Glynn, president of the Connecticut Archaeological Society in 1958, unearthed some ancient-looking pottery of sun-baked clay. He believed it to be unknown in North America but common in the eastern Mediterranean. Other artifacts seem to date from the early European settlement period, thus implying two levels of occupation, one Indian and the other colonial.

Similar stone structures, containing small corbelled chambers dug into hillsides, have been found in New Hampshire, Vermont and Connecticut. Some of these are known to have been built by early colonial settlers. These structures may have served as rude shelters, while the farmers found time to build regular houses. Others may have been storage or sheep shelters, or even slave quarters. The colonial farmers reached the valley beneath Mystery Hill soon after 1730.

Andrew E. Rothovius, an experienced American archaeologist, familiar with eastern Mediterranean cultures (who has sent me reports and articles about Mystery Hill) describes the site as one 'to drive an archaeologist frantic with frustration to think how much precious evidence may have been carelessly destroyed'. Goodwin, he says, 'restored' many of the structures which in 1936 were partly submerged underground. Mystery Hill is now owned by the Early Site Foundation. It has been largely avoided by archaeologists who fear, it is thought, being taken for cranks.

These massive stones were not assembled for fun. What could have been their purpose? The Sacrificial Stone suggests a pagan cult centre, the oracle a shrine. No early colonial farmer, it is claimed, could have anticipated future discoveries of oracles in ancient lands. The speaking tube suggests parallels with the temples of Malta and Greece. Phoenicians are another choice. But why would Irish monks, Maltese temple builders, or Phoenician traders have marched inland for 25 miles (40 kilometres) to construct such a building? The local Woodland Indians would hardly have allowed foreigners to establish themselves in their midst. It would be strange indeed had they constructed these structures. The Indians north of Mexico were not builders in stone.

Hugh O'Neil Hencken, curator of European Archaeology at the Peabody Museum, Harvard University, calls Mystery Hill 'one of the enigmas of archaeology'. In one sense it is unique, it is one of the few places in the world with a do-it-yourself mystery open to the public.

WHERE WAS VINLAND?

Until 1837 the voyages of the Norsemen to North America were dismissed as myths, the poetic fancies of generations of bards and story-tellers. Then the Danish historian, Carl Rafyn, proved conclusively that the famous *Sagas* were based on solid fact. They were family histories transmitted partly by word of mouth and also in manuscript before they were finally collected and written down in the thirteenth and fourteenth centuries. They reflect first hand information, a description of events which led Professor Frdtjof Nansen (*Northern Mists*, 1911) to see the whole thing before his eyes, and which he found it difficult to believe had not occurred.

The Norsemen's voyages are one of the most romantic episodes of history. While all Christendom prepared for the end of the world in the year one thousand, the men of Scandinavia pushed out across the Atlantic, colonised Iceland and Greenland and discovered America, five hundred years before Columbus reached the West Indies.

But where did the Norsemen land? Where was the Vinland of the *Sagas*? They provide clues relating to the climate of that country, its cosmographical features, its natural products, its natives and the lengths of the explorers' voyages.

There are two principal collections of *Sagas*, the Book of the Icelanders or the *Hauks Book* as it is sometimes called, containing the earliest accounts of the voyages written by the scholar Ari Thorgilsson, who was known as 'the Learned'. He died in 1067. He thus lived close to the events he describes. The *Flatey Book* incorporates the Greenland *Sagas*, which tell the stories of Leif Eriksson and his brothers and sister.

The *Sagas* are not the earliest extant source of information about Vinland. Writing in 1070, the German chronicler, Adam of Bremen, who gathered his information in Denmark, stated that an island had been found 'which is called Vinland, since there grew wild grapes and they give the best wines. There is also an abundance of self-sown wheat there.' His words show that knowledge of Vinland was widespread in northern Europe at that early date.

The *Sagas* relate that the New World was accidentally glimpsed by Barni Herjolfsson who had been driven off course on his voyage from Iceland to Greenland. He sailed from south to north and sighted three different lands. He did not land and he was chided for his lack of curiosity on his arrival in Greenland. His descriptions excited the colonists' hopes that they might find the things they lacked in Greenland, timber for their houses and grazing for their cattle.

Leif Eriksson set off from Greenland on his exploratory voyages to the West about AD 1003. He hired Barni's boat and took with him 25 men. From the combined information contained in the *Sagas*, we learn that he landed first at a place he called Helluland, meaning flat rock land. It was a barren land, rocky, lacking grass and its mountains were covered with huge glaciers. He sailed on finding a second land, flat, covered with forests and flanked by wide, sandy beaches. He named it Markland, or Forest Land. Sailing on for two days before the north-east wind, he sighted a third land where an island lay north of the mainland. The ship entered the sound which lay between the island and the cape projecting northward from the mainland. Leif and his men went ashore at a place where a river flowed out of a lake. He decided to winter there and his men built large houses and constructed 'time marks' or erections from which they could take bearings.

The description continues:

There was no lack of salmon in the river or in the lake, and they were bigger salmon than they had ever seen before. The land was so bountiful that it seemed to them that the cattle would not need fodder during the winter. There was no frost in winter, and the grass hardly withered. Day and night were of more equal length than in Greenland and Iceland. On the shortest day of the year the sun was visible in the afternoon as well as at breakfast time.

There were also fields of wheat growing wild.

Leif divided his men, sending one party each day to explore the country. A man named Tykir, who is described as a 'southerner', meaning probably a German, returned to report that he had found grapes and vines. The Greenland *Saga* confirms the significance of his discovery by adding Tykir's statement: 'It is certainly true for I was born where there is no lack of vines and grapes.' Tykir is thereby turned into a credible witness. However, the name 'Vinland' by which the third land became known, may not have owed its origin to this alleged discovery of grapes.

Leif and his men returned to Greenland in the spring. He did not apparently revisit the new land, but left further exploration to his brothers and sister. Sailing from the settlement on the southern tip of Greenland, Thorvald reached Helluland in two days, and the 'Wonder Beaches' of Markland in another two days. He continued on to Vinland with his 135 crew men. He was killed in a battle with the natives, people the Norsemen called 'Skraelings', and who used skin-covered boats. Thorvald's men stayed for two years before returning to Greenland.

Another brother, Karlsefini, took men, women and cattle, intending to settle in Vinland. During his two years stay two of his men came running to report that they had discovered grapes and wild wheat and an abundance of grass. They are described as 'Scots', in other words people who might recognise grapes. The Norsemen nearly starved during their first winter which was very severe, being rescued from famine by their discovery of a stranded whale. They adopted an ingenious method to catch fish. They dug trenches where the land and sea met at high-tide. When it receded it left fish caught in the trenches. Karlsefini's men were also attacked by natives. Two Norsemen were killed. Their deaths made Karlsefini realise that, even though it was a good land, because of the natives, fear and strife must always be part of life there. He returned to Greenland carrying valuable pelts, vines and grapes.

Leif's sister Freydis took a mixed party to Vinland, intending to settle there. The expedition ended in disaster because the unmarried men ran after the married women. Fighting broke out and Freydis slew five women with her own hand. She returned to Greenland after an absence of one year.

Other voyages may have been made. Some Norsemen may have sailed farther to the south. No mention is made of landfalls. A piece of anthracite coal found in Greenland suggests that one voyage reached Rhode Island, the only place on the Atlantic seaboard where that type of coal is found in outcrop.

The Norsemen do not seem to have succeeded in making a permanent settlement in Vinland, due probably to the determined opposition of the more numerous and equally well-armed Skraelings. Some Norse settlements may have existed in 1121 when Erik, the Bishop of Greenland, set out 'in search of Vinland'. We are not told if he reached that land. The Norse colonists stayed in Greenland until about 1400, by which time they had abandoned their settlements. Why they left has been the subject of considerable discussion. Skeletons show that the colonists remained robust and healthy. They were on friendly terms with the Eskimos. They may have been decimated by plague. More probably, the climate changed. Around the year 1000 the Northern Hemisphere enjoyed a warm spell. That gave way in the thirteenth century to increasing cold which led to what has been termed the 'Little Ice-Age'.

The reawakened interest in the *Sagas* led to enquiry to ascertain the location of Vinland.

The references in the *Sagas* to grapes seemed to point to Massachusetts, on the northerly line for their growth at 42° N. Cape Cod seemed to fit the required conditions for Vinland. On the eastern American seaboard salmon are not found to its south, or grapes to its north. The shallow sounds, now named Nantuchet and Vineyard Sounds, seemed to fit the *Sagas* descriptions, as did the statement that, on the shortest day of the year, the sun was still visible at the time of the Norse evening meal, which was taken about 4.30 pm. On that day the sun sets at Boston, forty miles to the north, at that time. But another statement seemed at variance with what was known of the early history of the area. The English colonists who reached there in 1639 encountered the local Indians. They did not use skin boats.

Some corroboration for the selection of this region is claimed for the existence at Newport, Rhode Island, of a 'Norse' tower.

The building is a 17th century grist-mill, which is referred to in Colonial Records in 1677. Unfortunately the so-called 'Vinland Map' has nothing to do with Vinland. The discovery was announced in 1965 by Yale University of a hitherto unknown Map of the World, dated about 1440. It portrays in the Western Atlantic an island named 'Vinland'. Its publication led to some remarkable detective work which resulted in it being dubbed a modern forgery.

Its ingenious and unidentified faker created a map so fiendishly plausible that it deceived even the most eminent scholars, including the late R. A. Skelton, Superintendent of the Map Room at the British Museum (Skelton, R. A., Marston, T. E. and Painter, G. D. *The Vinland Map and the Tartar Relation*, 1965). The Map, drawn on thin parchment, had been bound with an authentic copy of the *Tartar Relation*, an account of the Asiatic travels of the Franciscan Friar, Johannes de Plano Carpini, who led a mission to the Mongols in 1445–47.

Other than its representation of Vinland and Greenland, the Map conformed to conventional 15th century geographical knowledge, with certain strange variations. It portrayed Vinland as an island with deep inlets and prominent capes, and attributed its discovery to the 'companions' Bjarni and Leif Eriksson, an unusual conjunction for the *Sagas* relate that Bjarni only sighted the new lands which were discovered four years later by Leif. The Latin legend also recorded the actual journey to Vinland in 1117 of the Apostolic Legate Erik Gnupsson, whereas the Icelandic Annals, composed in 1319, stated only that he set out.

The map-maker had elongated Vinland latitudinally north and south for 1500 miles, reaching approximately the position of the West Indies. Greenland was shown as an 'island', a fact unknown until 1690. All three lands, Iceland, Greenland and Vinland conformed, it was claimed by the doubters, far too closely with their relative positions on the modern map.

Cape Cod was not Vinland. The 'grape' clue upon which that identification was largely based is now recognised as being fallacious. Nor could Vinland have lain that far south.

This is the appropriate moment to introduce the man who

solved the riddle of Vinland. A Norwegian lawyer who became an explorer, Helge Ingstad lived with an Eskimo tribe in the Arctic and served as Norwegian Governor of Greenland. His interest in the ancient Norse settlements there led him to search for Vinland (*Westward to Vinland*, 1969). First he studied the *Sagas*.

Ingstad noticed that the men who recognised 'grapes' were not Norsemen. One was a 'Southerner', probably a German, the other two were described as 'Scots'. It seemed that the later story-teller had chosen these 'foreigners' to prove the discovery of grapes, because Norsemen would not have been credible witnesses. Another oddity struck Ingstad. On one voyage grapes were found in the land north of Vinland, and were picked in winter. This episode had all the characteristics of a fairy tale. Had the original oral tradition said no more than that the explorers had made wine? Had the later story tellers assumed that meant they had found grapes?

Ingstad noticed that in ancient literature from the Pentateuch onwards, grapes were frequently connected with distant lands. Wild grapes and fields of grain were abundant in the fabulous Fortunate Islands. Dense forests of 'wine trees' grew in the lands described in the 6th century Irish legends of St Brendan. In the popular view, explorers were expected to find grapes, just as today they might be asked if they had found oil.

Ingstad reasoned that the Norsemen had found wild berries from which they had made wine. These 'grapes' were probably similar to the 'red wine berries' which the traveller William Alexander found in Nova Scotia in 1624. These 'squash-berries' as they are now called, grow throughout Maritime Canada, are red and tasty, and are similar to European red-currants. Wine is still made from them in Newfoundland.

Further confusion may have arisen from the use of the Scandinavian word *vinboer* to describe these wine berries. It did not follow that 'Vinland' meant the 'land of grapes'. Had the word *vinboer* been written with a long 'i', it would have meant 'grassland'. The Norsemen found timber and good grazing in Vinland. It would therefore have been natural for them to have named the place 'Grass Land'.

Another factor seemed to locate Vinland far to the north of Cape Cod. The Norsemen were experienced seamen. Whatever else in the *Sagas* might be obscure, their sailing directions would have been accurate.

The Norse explorers used ships similar to the Knarr, the broadly built merchant ship used by the Greenlanders, and to the Gokstad ship which was excavated in south eastern Norway in 1880. It was built in the middle of the 9th century and was $77\frac{1}{2}$ ft long and 17 ft broad at the widest point. It carried a mast and a square-rigged sail and was rowed by 16 oarsmen on each side. The Norwegian Magnus Andersen sailed its replica across the Atlantic in 1893. It maintained an amazing speed, making five and six knots on the average, even eleven at times. By maintaining such an average speed, the Norsemen, who were adept at using currents, would have travelled about 150 miles every twenty-four hours. They used the word *dogr* to describe a day's sail. According to the *Sagas* few *dogrs* were needed to reach Vinland.

For example, Barni, the accidental discoverer of the New World, having missed Greenland, sighted one land and sailed for two days before sighting another. Three more days brought him to a land covered with glaciers. He sailed from south to north, and four further days sailing brought him to the southern tip of Greenland. He had sailed nine days from the land he had first sighted. This appears to have been the later Vinland. Leif sailed in the opposite direction to Barni. The first land he found was covered with huge glaciers, a description which fits Baffin land. That island would have been his natural first land fall for the current would have carried his ship northwards into the Davis Strait, and across that Strait at its narrowest point.

From Helluland, Leif sailed to Markland, where he observed its extensive white beaches and forests, a description which accords with the coast of Labrador. He reached the third land, after having been at sea for two days. Thus, Vinland lay not far to the south of the second land.

Other factors seem to indicate that Vinland could be identified with Newfoundland, particularly with the northern shores of that island. The coastal route from Greenland comprises 1300 nautical miles, nine or ten days sailing time by Norse standards. This was, however, conjecture. Ingstad looked for proof. The Norsemen had built 'large houses' in Vinland. Only their discovery would convince the sceptics.

Ingstad set out to look for his 'needle in a haystack' in 1960. His travels occupied eight summers. He started from Rhode Island and worked his way northwards, travelling by bus, on foot, and occasionally by air-plane. He searched for a place having grasslands, forests in their rear, with a shore flanked by a cape and opposite an island. A stream ran from a lake into the sea. On mid-winter day, the sun set about 4.30 pm.

Reaching the most northerly point of his journey, Ingstad found no difficulty in identifying Helluland with Baffin land, and Markland with Labrador, a rocky land having wide sandy beaches. He returned to Newfoundland, a land of comparatively mild climate abundant in forests, grasslands, and rich in fish and game. Its native Indians had adopted the Eskimo skin-boat, according to the earliest European voyagers.

Everywhere he went, Ingstad enquired for traces of 'old houses'. At one fishing village his inquiry brought the suspicious question, 'What do you want with old things like that?' 'To dig them up', he replied. 'That's what you say, but you don't fool me', he was told. Ingstad got the drift of what the fellow meant when he continued in a sharp tone of voice: 'Any treasure that is supposed to have been buried around here we'll be able to find by ourselves.'

Ingstad travelled from one fishing village to another asking the same question. At last came the hoped-for answer. 'Yes, I seem to have heard about something like that over at L'Anse aux Meadows.' The 'Big Chief' of that village was more helpful. 'Yes, there is something like that over by Black Duck Brook,' George Decker told Ingstad. He took him to the bay. A river wound its way from a small lake through level country, amongst grasslands, emptying into the bay. Off shore lay a large island, Great Sacred Island. A cape jutted to the northward. In the distance Ingstad recognised the coast of Labrador. L'Anse aux Meadows was a good and beautiful place. The name meant 'Cove to the Meadows'. Salmon were abundant.

Red-currants, gooseberries, and raspberry bushes grew there. On mid-winter day, the sun set about 4.30 pm. Everything fitted. But conjecture was not proof.

Ingstad found that proof. A short distance inland from the beach rose a terrace, containing a number of indistinct overgrown erections. Only digging would reveal their secrets. Several summers were required to excavate these sites.

Ingstad and his helpers uncovered the foundations of eight buildings, including a 'long-house', 70 ft long and 55 ft wide, which had been divided into six small rooms. The largest was 26 ft by 14 ft. These rooms contained hearths, and cooking-holes. Another small building proved to have been a smithy. The ashes taken from the hearth were subjected to the Carbon 14 Dating Test. It dated them in AD 1080 plus or minus seventy years, about the time of the Norse voyages. The foundations of these houses conformed to those in the ancient Norse settlements in Greenland. Ingstad found no graves, tools or weapons. A norse spindle-whorl proved their occupation by Norwegian women. Three hundred yards behind the houses and silhouetted against the sky rose a ridge on which were four collapsed cairns. Were these the time-marks which the Norsemen had erected on the horizon to tell the time for their evening meal? Ingstad carried out an experiment. He cut trenches on the beach between high and low tidemarks. When the high tide receded it left fish within, just as the Norsemen had found.

Seldom has a theorist been more completely vindicated. Ingstad's identification of Vinland at L'Anse aux Meadows is now unquestioned. He had found the early Norse settlement in the New World. What, he wondered, had been the fate of these intrepid explorers, the men and women who had sought a better land in which to live? Several European voyagers, he recalled, had remarked the white skins and fair hair of many of the local Indians. Some of the Norse colonists may have been absorbed within an Indian tribe. The survivors abandoned their settlement and returned to Greenland, where they lived on amicable terms with their Eskimo neighbours. In their turn they may have been driven back to Scandinavia by climatic change. Leif and his successors may have discovered America fortuitously, at a time when the northern climate was more benevolent. That does not detract from their great adventure. It makes it easier to understand.

Fables and Hoaxes

THE KENSINGTON RUNE STONE

At the height of the controversy raised by the publication of its inscription, the Kensington Rune Stone was hailed by the chief of the United States Bureau of Ethnology as 'probably the most important archaeological object ever found in North America'. The stone was accorded the place of honour in the Smithsonian Institute's National Museum at Washington. A huge replica, weighing 2½ tons, was solemnly unveiled in 1951 at the Rune Memorial Park at Alexander, Minnesota.

The controversy surrounding the inscription, which purported to describe the fate of a Norse expedition which had perished in the heart of the North American continent, developed late, half a century after the stone's discovery in 1898.

Its discovery, as is too often the case with ancient objects, is shrouded in mystery due to the failure of its finder to authenticate the alleged facts. Olof Ohman stated subsequently that he had unearthed it from the roots of an aspen tree while he was clearing a knoll on his farm near Kensington, Douglas County, Minnesota. The flat stone lay face downwards firmly held by the tree's roots. His small son drew attention to its strange markings. The stone, which is 31 inches long, 16 inches broad and 6 inches thick (78 by 40 by 15 centimetres), was exhibited in a shop window. It's markings were immediately recognized as runes, the ancient Scandinavian lettering. This speedy recognition was not surprising in a predominantly Scandinavian community. It gave rise to suspicion later.

The runologists to whom the stone was submitted for examination had no hesitation in dismissing its inscription as a clumsy forgery. Its language was too modern. It contained an impossible mixture of Swedish, Norwegian and English words, pointed out Professor Breda who held the chair of Scandinavian Languages at the University of Minnesota. It was unthinkable, he said, that the inscription related to a Norse voyage in the eleventh century. Breda was unable to decipher the inscription's numerical symbols. His chief reason for rejecting the inscription, its presumed date, later become one of the strongest points for its support.

The stone was returned to Ohman who used it as a door-step to his barn. It lay unnoticed for nine years until it was spotted by Hjalmar Holland. He was collecting material for a book about the Norwegian settlers in Minnesota, and had made a study of runes. An explanation of runic numerical symbols by a Norwegian philologist in 1909, enabled Holland to supply the missing date.

In old runic symbols, to each upright stave one transverse line was added for each unit up to five, thus

$$\Gamma = 1 \text{ and } \mathsf{F} = 2.$$

As there was not enough room to add transverse lines up to ten, the first five were collectively represented by a circle, cross lines then being added for each additional unit up to ten.

The group of symbols at the end of the inscription were preceded by the word 'ahr' (year) thus presuming a date. The symbols were:

ΓFΡF

Holland translated these symbols to denote the year 1362. The chief reason for the stone's rejection, that its language was incompatible with the eleventh century, had apparently been overcome. The inscription related to an expedition in the fourteenth century by when, according to Holland, the old Norse language had been superseded by a period of linguistic transition, following the union of Norway and Sweden in 1319. The mixture of old words and new forms was characteristic of this development.

Holland translated the inscription to read:

1. (We are) 8 Goths (Swedes) and 22 Norwegians on
2. (an) exploration journey from
3. Vinland through (or across) the West [i.e. round about the West] We

4. had a camp by (a lake with) 2 skerries one
5. days journey north from this stone
6. We were (out) and fished one day After
7. we came home (we) found 10 (of our) men red
8. with blood and dead Av(e) M(aria)
9. Save (us) from evil
   Edge
10. (We) have 10 of (our party) by the sea to look
11. after our ships (or ship) 14 days journey
12. from this island (in the) year (of our Lord) 1362.

The message stated five main facts. 1. The party was composed of eight Goths and twenty-two Norwegians. 2. They were on an exploration journey from Vinland to the west. 3. Ten of their number had been killed at a camp by a lake in which were two skerries or small islands, one day's journey north. 4. The place where the inscription was made was an island. 5. It was fourteen days' journey from the sea where they had left their ship.

Holland attributed the mixture of Norwegians and Swedes in one party, which would have been impossible in the eleventh century, the period of the Norse voyages to Vinland, to the union of the two kingdoms in 1319. He claimed that the inscription had been condemned in 1899 on erroneous premises, and he became its enthusiastic advocate.

He pointed out that the place where the stone was found, on the southern slope of a wooded knoll standing 44 feet (13 metres) above grassy marshlands could by no stretch of the imagination be called an island, nor could it conceivably have been thought an island at the time when the first settlers reached Kensington. But a survey of the area had shown that some 500 years before the marsh was part of a string of lakes, many of which still exist, which stretched across central Minnesota. This fact was of recent knowledge and it could not have been known to a forger in the last century who would thus hardly have named the spot an island.

The fourteenth century, when the two languages were undergoing amalgamation and the Latin alphabet was beginning to supersede Runic, would, Holland claimed, have been a difficult period in which to place a literary forgery. Only a scholar versed in medieval religious practice would have seen the need to represent the first syllables of the holy name as 'A.V.M.'

Dealing with the technical aspects of the inscription, Holland wrote:

All thing considered, the Kensington inscription seems linguistically to be a logical fourteenth century product of such personnel as the inscription mentions. Dialectically, the inscription seems to be predominantly Gothic, which probably means that the artisan who inscribed the stone was a Goth ... mixed with his Gothic dialect there are a number of words of probably Norwegian usage which may be the echoes of the dictation of the commander of the expedition or some other Norwegian member.

The stone was described by Professor Winchell, the state archaeologist of Minnesota, as greywacke, a very hard stone which weathers slowly.

To convince the sceptics and to substantiate the inscription, Holland needed to show that such an expedition had reached North America about the year 1360 and that it could have penetrated deep into that continent. The early Norse voyages had been of brief duration and had not continued, as far as was known, after the end of the eleventh century. It was inconceivable that Norsemen could have made an overland journey from Newfoundland, their Atlantic landfall, into Minnesota. Seafaring Norsemen would have adopted a water route.

Dismissing the possibility of the St Lawrence river–Great Lakes route because of the Niagara Falls, Holland chose the mouth of the Nelson river in Hudson Bay as the expedition's landfall. Ten men had been left there to guard the ship. The remaining twenty had taken the after-boat and had progressed inland for 1,000 miles (1,600 kilometres), approximately fourteen days' journey, by following rivers and by making portages. Ten members of the party had been scalped by Indians. The survivors had inscribed their obituary on the stone while resting on an island amidst a string of lakes. They, too, had been massacred by Indians or perhaps became absorbed within a tribe. The ten men left to guard the ship may have returned to Norway.

Holland inspected this hypothetical route from Hudson Bay to central Minnesota, finding the mooring stones to which the Norsemen had tied their boat. Each stone bore a drilled hole, one inch (2.5 centimetres) in diameter, which exactly conforms to the bits used by the 1860 settlers. They drilled holes in stones to insert explosives by which to blast them, in order to clear the land and provide building material.

Holland traced a record of an expedition which had probably sailed from Norway in 1355, some of whose members may have returned in 1364. As exploratory expeditions were then infrequent, it seemed possible that this was the one which had reached Kensington.

In a letter that has survived, Magnus Erikson, the first joint King of Norway and Sweden, instructed Paul Knutson in the autumn of 1354 to lead an expedition in search of the lost colonists of Greenland, the news of whose disappearance had been brought to Norway in 1348. It was significant, thought Holland, that Magnus had instructed Knutson to take men 'from my retinue', as well as his own. Magnus's Swedish origin implied that his men were Swedes, which accounted for the mixture of Swedes and Norwegians in the same party. Finding Greenland deserted, according to Holland's interpretation, Knutson spent nine years in search of the lost colonists, reaching Minnesota where most of his men, and possibly he himself, were killed. Knutson disappeared from Norwegian records after 1355.

While Knutson's expedition may have been planned, there is no evidence that it ever set out, far less that any of its members returned.

Holland died in 1963, aware that his beautifully woven theory had been torn to shreds, but unrepentant. The Danish runologist Erik Moltke had pointed out in 1950 that the language of the inscription belonged not to the fourteenth but to the nineteenth century. At least half its letters could have been copied from a Swedish runic calendar which had been published in the eighteenth century. The forger had invented several symbols, some of which had not been taken over from other languages until the sixteenth century. 'Even the non-specialist,' remarked Moltke, 'will observe that the text, when it is transcribed into Latin, is easy to read.'

Final proof of the forgery came from the discovery, in the archives of the Minnesota Historical Society, of a copy of the inscription which differed in fifteen places from the wording on the stone. This had been the draft from which the forger had worked.

The stone's faker had probably been its discoverer, the farmer Olof Ohman. He may have been helped by two friends, also of Scandinavian origin, Andrew Andersen, another farmer, and Sven Fogelblad, a one-time clergyman who had obtained a degree from the University of Uppsala.

Ohman had been born and raised in a remote district of Northern Sweden where runes were still used by the peasants. He had been educated at a school where the two chief subjects taught were religion and Swedish history, with particular emphasis on the romantic period of the reign of King Magnus. After his death a book was found amongst his possessions, in which he had written his name in 1891, entitled (in English) *The Well-Informed Schoolmaster or the Foundation of Popular Knowledge*, which had been published in 1883. It contained a chapter on 'The Swedish Language and its Development', which quoted a prayer from 1300 ending with the same words as in the inscription 'Deliver us from evil'. That page in the book seemed to have been particularly well-thumbed.

Ohman may have been spurred to concoct his forgery by the publicity accorded in 1893 to the voyage across the Atlantic of the replica of the Gokstad ship, which had been excavated from a Viking burial mound in Norway in 1880, and by the bitter argument raging at that time as to whether Norsemen or Columbus had first discovered America. The vessel was exhibited in Lincoln Park, Chicago, where Ohman may have seen it. Fired by patriotic zeal, Ohman set out to prove not only that the Norsemen had reached the North American continent, but that they had penetrated into its heart. By a masterstroke of invention he described the place where the inscription had been written as an island. The knoll rose from a swamp which frequently became flooded. On the other hand, he cut the inscription using a chisel with the regular one-inch bit, the gauge common in America in 1898.

THE PARAHYBA INSCRIPTION AND THE METCALF STONE

The Parahyba inscription is claimed to provide proof that the Phoenicians discovered South America 2,000 years before Columbus reached the West Indies. The stone on which the message is alleged to have been inscribed has not been seen by any scholar.

The story starts on 11 September 1872 when a person who signed himself Joaquim Alves da Costa, wrote to the president of the Instituto Historico in Rio de Janeiro. He said that his slaves had found an inscribed stone on his plantation at Pouso Alto near Parahyba. His son had made a copy of the inscription, which the writer enclosed. It was given to a member of the Instituto, Ladislau Netto, to study. Recognizing the characters as Phoenician script he commenced a study of ancient Semitic languages in the hope of deciphering the inscription. Fearing that he might prove unequal to the task he sent copies of sections to Ernest Renan, the French authority on these languages. He sent him sections only to prevent the savant from scooping him with the story. Not surprisingly Renan pronounced the inscription a fake.

Netto failed either to locate the stone or to identify its owner. There were several places called Pouso Alto in Brazil and two called Paraíbas, one in the province of that name in the north, and the other in the south, nearer to Rio de Janeiro in a district famed for its iron mines. Netto pursued his investigation, corresponding with Wilberforce Eames, the librarian of the New York public library. Had not this correspondence come to light, it is probable that the inscription would have remained condemned as a clumsy forgery.

It was unknown or forgotten in 1967 when Dr Piccus, professor of Hispanic Studies at the University of Massachusetts at Amherst, bought in a rummage sale at Providence, Rhode Island, a scrap book which had once belonged to Wilberforce Eames. It contained his correspondence with Netto and a copy of the inscription. Piccus gave a xerox copy to Cyrus B. Gordon, professor of Mediterranean Studies at Brandeis University, Massachusetts. His advocacy of its genuine character has revived interest in the inscription. The English translation made in 1874 reads:

We are sons of Canaan from Sidon, the city of the king. Commerce has cast us on this distant shore, a land of mountains. We set [sacrificed] a youth for the exalted gods and goddesses in the eighteenth year of Hiram, our mighty king. We embarked from Ezlon-Geber into the Red Sea and voyaged with ten ships. We were at sea together for two years around the land belonging to Ham [Africa] but were separated by a storm [literal translation: 'from the hand of Baal'] and we were no longer with our companions. So we have come here, twelve men and three women, on a new shore which I, the Admiral control. But auspiciously may the exalted gods and goddesses favor us!

Professor Gordon favours his own translation* which varies slightly from this text. He prefers the date the nineteenth rather than the eighteenth year of King Hiram, and names the 'here', the new shore reached by the seafarers as the 'Island of Iron'.

Gordon believes that the inscription was made by Phoenician seamen who had set out on their voyage from the port of Ezlon-Geber, an island in the Gulf of Aqaba, at the head of the Red Sea. He identifies King Hiram as the third king of that name who ruled the cities of Tyre and Sidon, the Phoenician capitals, from 555 to 533 B.C. He dates the voyage in 534 B.C. It circumnavigated Africa (as the Phoenicians certainly did do in that century, according to Herodotus) in order to avoid traversing the Mediterranean. Rounding the Cape of Good Hope, the Phoenician seafarers sailed up the Atlantic to Brazil, which, according to Gordon's interpretation, was their intended landfall, a place already known to the Phoenicians as a source

* *Before Columbus: Links between the Old World and Ancient America,* Turnstone Press, 1972.

of iron. That, in his opinion, is the meaning of the name Brazil. He bases his belief on the derivation of the Semitic word, which was written as HDT. The term 'Hadd' came in later Arabic to denote iron. Such an Arabism, he thinks, is not strange in a text emanating from the Gulf of Aqaba, on the coast of Arabia.

Gordon cites textual evidence to prove the inscription's authenticity. The inscription as a whole follows a tripartite format – the identification of subjects, the commemoration of events and the appeal to the gods – which, although now confirmed by other Semitic texts, was unknown in 1872. This, and certain other ancient grammatical usages now established, could not have been known to a nineteenth-century forger. Netto himself was unaware in 1874 that by the addition of a suffix the numeral digit was turned into nineteen, rather than eighteen, as he read it. Examples proving the significance of this suffix were unknown until 1957. The expression 'hand of Baal' to indicate 'divine will', was unrecognized until 1939 when it was noticed on a Phoenician inscription.

Commenting on the rediscovery of this long-forgotten inscription, Professor Gordon remarked, 'After all, these ancient people, could with any luck, have made any trip that we can make today.'

Professor Gordon also accepts as genuine certain discoveries which have been made within the United States and which seem to suggest that Jews (not the Lost Tribes) may have crossed the Atlantic. The characters inscribed on the Metcalf Stone, found by a man of that name near Fort Benning, Georgia, suggest Mediterranean affinities. Hebrew coins of Roman date (around A.D. 135), he says, have been found near Hopkinsville, Tennessee, and Roman coins at Clay City, Kentucky. The former have been identified as coins struck by Simon Kokhba, who led the second great Jewish Revolt against the Romans. They bear his name on one face and on the other the statement that they were struck in 'Year 2 of the Freedom of Israel', i.e. A.D. 133. An inscription found at Bat Creek in the Appalachian Mountains appears to have been written in Hebrew. It was found in 1894 in a burial mound containing nine badly decayed skeletons. The text of the inscription is still in process of decipherment. It appears, like the coins, to date from the period of the Second Jewish Revolt.

Professor Gordon conceives the possibility that these Jewish migrants were refugees who travelled from the Old World to the New in hope of a better life. One hopes they found it after their lengthy voyage across both the Mediterranean (2,000 miles) and the Atlantic (3,000 miles). Such a voyage would have been particularly arduous for Jews who were not sea-farers.

Opium for the People: Twentieth-Century Formula

God died in Mexico City some time after the end of World War II. His passing caused little stir. He had been largely forgotten. Following his spectacular creation of the earth and of all living things, he had done nothing. Unimportant as he had become, his death nonetheless left a vacuum, a void awaiting the genius of a new Moses, of other myth makers. They detected the formula for the modern religion, the new opium to drug the masses. They found it in Space, man's new horizon, and belief in extra-terrestrial life, the new mysticism.

MYTHS VERSUS MATHEMATICS

The plagues of Egypt and the dividing of the Sea of Passage at the time of the Exodus of the Children of Israel can be explained as natural phenomena. But that easy solution is not accepted by Dr Immanuel Velikovsky. He sees these happenings as the first manifestation of the early stages of a cosmic catastrophe which struck the whole earth and which reached its zenith fifty-two years later when, as Joshua was pursuing the Canaanite kings at Beth-horon, 'the sun stood still in the midst of heaven and did not go down about a whole day'.

Most people who have read this passage in the tenth chapter of the Book of Joshua dismiss it as a wild exaggeration of a later writer anxious to show that for Israel on its onward march even time stood still. Dr Velikovsky accepts its literal truth. On a day some time in the middle of the second millennium B.C., the earth either ceased to rotate or tilted over on its axis.

By the advancement of this theory, and by his explanation

of the cause of these phenomena,* he launched a formidable assault on the entrenched dogmas of astronomy, geology and historical biology. He challenged Newton's belief in the general orthodoxy of the universe, his doctrine of celestial harmony. He propounded a heresy as abhorrent to modern scientists as were the opinions of Galileo and Copernicus to medieval ecclestiastics. Heretics are no longer burnt at the stake; they are ignored.

Velikovsky's theories were boycotted by the scientific establishment. An influential group of American astronomers tried to block the publication of his first book. They exercised pressure on the publisher, threatening to withdraw their own textbooks. The high priests of astronomy claimed to be the sole arbiters of scientific truth. 'If Dr Velikovsky is right, the rest of us are crazy,' asserted Professor Howard Shapley, the director of the Harvard College Observatory. He and his colleagues castigated the heretic's book without having read it.

Why are Dr Velikovsky's views so outrageous? If the sun stood still for a whole day, the most fundamental beliefs of astronomy are denied, for, whatever else is uncertain, it is assumed that the earth has *always* rotated from west to east and it has *always* taken 365 days, 5 hours and 49 minutes to go round the sun. Velikovsky claims that the earth's movements have been erratic, that it once ceased to revolve and that, previously, it took only 360 days to complete its orbit.

Dr Velikovsky believes that some 3,500 years ago, and again 700 years later, the earth was affected by the appearance in the sky of a giant comet which eventually became the planet Venus. The close proximity to the earth of this comet caused, at its first appearance, certain phenomena and, at its second and closer appearance, the effect of prolonged day and night in different parts of the world. Dr Velikovsky, who is a scholar not an astronomer, claims to have found world-wide traditions of these unusual catastrophes and an Egyptian eye-witness description of the occurrences recorded in Exodus.

The first clue found by Dr Velikovsky to suggest that the standing still of the sun, recorded in the Hebrew Book of

* *Worlds in Collision*, Gollancz, 1950. *Ages in Chaos*, Sidgwick and Jackson, 1953. *Earth in Upheaval*, Gollancz, 1956.

Joshua, was something more than an old wives' tale came from the preceding verses which state that great stones were cast down from heaven. Taken in combination these statements implied an unusual state of affairs which, if they were true, must presumably have been witnessed by peoples other than the Israelites. If a day was prolonged in one part of the world, a long period of darkness must have been prevailed elsewhere. Dr Velikovsky found that there were many traditions of prolonged darkness in the western hemisphere, and in the eastern half of the world of a day of unusual length, both accompanied by stories of a cosmic cataclysm.

These widespread traditions suggested that the earth, at an undisclosed date, had been struck by some appalling catastrophe, the confused memory of which had been preserved in the form of myths. They seemed to recall a battle in the sky from which Venus, hitherto unknown, emerged as a planet. It is a question of myths versus mathematics. The one appears to suggest that his theory may be true, the other to prove its falsity.

Many of the ancient traditions of the Peruvians, Mayas and Mexicans of America were recorded soon after the Spanish conquests. Amongst them Dr Velikovsky found the following: Mexican annals related that the sun did not appear for a fourfold night and that fifty-two years before another catastrophe had occurred. The Mayas believed that some time in the past there had been a period of cataclysm in which the sun's motion had been interrupted and the waters had turned red. The sacred book of the Mayas, the *Popol-Vuh*, says: 'It was ruin and destruction . . . the sea was piled up . . . it was a great inundation . . . people were drowned in a sticky substance raining from the sky . . . the face of the earth grew dark and the gloomy rain endured days and nights . . . and then there was a great din of fire above their heads.' The entire population was annihilated. Other Central American myths contain stories of a deluge of sticky rain of bitumen from heaven; men were seized by madness and tried to escape it by sheltering in caverns but the caverns were suddenly closed. The cataclysm was preceded by a collision of stars and was followed by an inundation of the sea. The Peruvians had similar traditions. A pattern of legends suggested that a cosmic catastrophe, resulting in a long period of darkness accompanied by tidal waves, hurricanes and by the fall of giant stones and bloody rain from the sky, preceded the appearance of a new planet.

Outside the western hemisphere there were similar traditions which told that the day was prolonged. Chinese chronologies reported that in the time of the Emperor Yaltou: 'The sun did not set for a number of days; the forests were set on fire, a high wave reaching the sky poured over the land.' The Altai Tatars spoke of a catastrophe in which 'blood turned the whole world red', and the Voguls of Siberia said that 'God sent a sea of fire upon the earth'.

Many ancient cosmological myths referred to a battle in the sky in which the planet god slays a sky monster, usually a dragon or a serpent. According to the Mayas: 'The sun refused to show itself and during four days the world was deprived of light. Then a great star appeared and it was given the name of Quetzacoatl.' That means 'feathered serpent', a term which may indicate a comet with a tail. In other myths, the battle was between Bel and the Dragon, Marduk and Tiamat, Isis and Seth, Vishnu and the Serpent, and Zeus and Typhon. In the Greek myth the final act of the sky battle takes place at lake Serbon on the borders of Palestine and Egypt.

Other traditions and myths suggested that the new star, which disrupted the movement of the earth and caused a world conflagration, was a comet which became Venus. The Greek Pythagoreans claimed that one of the planets had been a comet, and it is variously described as having had feathers, a beard, horns, a crown of awful splendour, or as scattering its flame in fire.

Dr Velikovsky claims that Venus was hitherto unknown and that these traditions record its birth. The astronomical charts of the Hindus, Babylonians and Mayas, all of whom were particularly interested in astronomy, show only four planets. In the Hindus table of planets, dated 3100 B.C. Venus alone is absent and the Babylonians named Venus, 'the great star that joins the other great stars'. Even more significant are the astronomical tablets of the Assyrians, found at Nineveh. They comprised the year-formula of an early king named Ammizaduza, and appear to show either obvious errors or that the orbit of Venus was previously different. Sky charts found in an Egyptian tomb dating from the period of Queen Hatshepsut show the stars in reversed orientation.

In Velikovsky's interpretation Venus came into conjunction with the earth and, 700 years later, with Mars. These near collisions caused the stoppage or tilting of the earth and the change in the length of the year. They also reversed the direction of the earth's rotation. He finds proof of this in certain traditions.

In the *Statesman*, Plato speaks of the 'changing in the rising and setting of the sun and other heavenly bodies, how in these times they used to set in the quarter where they now rise' and 'at certain periods the Universe has its present circular motion, and at other periods it revolves in the reverse direction. Of all the changes which take place in the heavens this reversal is the greatest and most complete.' Herodotus was told by priests in Egypt that four times since Egypt became a kingdom 'the sun rose contrary to his wont: twice he rose where he now sets and twice he sets where he now rises.' The Chinese recall that 'only since a new order of things has it come about that the stars move from east to west'. The Eskimos of Greenland believed that the world had turned over. The Aztecs of Mexico, during the long period of darkness, wondered where the sun would reappear from and were surprised when it rose in the east.

That the length of the year altered is indicated, Dr Velikovsky believes, in the sudden change by nearly all Middle East peoples, for no apparent reason, from a year of 360 days to one of $365\frac{1}{4}$ days, in or about 747 B.C., when he believes that the near collision between Venus and Mars occurred. It is usually assumed that this change was made from the old method of reckoning by a lunar calendar to that of the solar year, to rectify the obvious inaccuracy of the old system.

The sun had stood still previously fifty-two years after the start of the catastrophe which caused the unusual events which accompanied the Exodus.

Dr Velikovsky believes that the plagues of Egypt, the pillar of cloud by day and of fire by night and the division of the waters of the Sea of Passage were early manifestations of the contact as the earth brushed through the comet's tail. Red dust and hot stones descended upon the earth and gave rise to hurricanes and tidal waves.

If this was the cause of the phenomena which accompanied the Exodus, then the Egyptians could hardly have failed to notice them. Dr. Velikovsky claims to have found in the Papyrus Ipuwer an Egyptian record which seems to parallel with remarkable exactness the story related by Exodus.

To bring the events related in the Papyrus Ipuwer into chronological relationship with those of Exodus it is necessary to drop 500 years from Egyptian history. Dr Velikovsky thinks that the Exodus, and the accompanying cosmic catastrophe, took place in about 1500 B.C. He believes that the flight of the Isrealites from Egypt preceded the invasion of the Hyksos for, according to the Papyrus Ipuwer, the disasters that struck Egypt, which appear to be the same disasters that are described in Exodus, were followed by the invasion of Asiatic conquerors. This brings forward the date of the expulsion of the Hyksos (if these invaders were they) to about 1000 B.C., and consequently a complete revaluation of the dates of the pharaohs who are usually associated with the period of the Exodus. According to Sir Arthur Weigall (*Flights into Antiquity*) Ipuwer describes a proletarian revolution that took place in Egypt in about 2200 B.C.: 'Men have dared to rebel against the Crown, and a few lawless men have attempted to rid the land of its monarchy. The old order has perished. The Palace is overthrown in a minute.'

Thus a prodigious reversal of the accepted dates of Egyptian chronology is required to bring the Papyrus Ipuwer into line with the events described in Exodus.

The papyrus commences by saying: 'The land turns round like a potter's wheel. The towns are destroyed. All is ruin. The residence is overturned in a minute. Years of noise. There is no end to noise. Oh, that the earth cease from noise, and the tumult be no more.' Then comes the description of happenings that appear to parallel those related by Exodus. Papyrus: Plague is throughout the land. Blood is everywhere. Exodus: There was blood throughout the land of Egypt. Papyrus: The river is blood. Exodus: All the waters that were in the river

214

were turned to blood. Both accounts refer to the undrinkability of the waters and state that people thirsted.

Next, according to Exodus: 'The hail smote every herb of the field and brake every tree.' The papyrus says that, 'Trees are destroyed. No fruit nor herbs are found.' Exodus states that there was a very grievous hail and fire. The papyrus says that gates, columns and walls were consumed by fire. Both sources appear to indicate the destruction of crops. The murrain of beasts described by Exodus is paralleled in the papyrus which says, like Exodus, that the cattle moan and were left to stray.

According to Exodus the ninth plague was thick darkness. The papyrus relates that, 'The land is not light', which may have been the Egyptian way of saying the same thing.

Both Exodus and the Papyrus Ipuwer describe the tenth plague in terms which suggest an earthquake. The papyrus says that, 'the residence is overturned in a minute'. According to Exodus: 'And Pharaoh rose up in the night, he and his servants, and the Egyptians; and there was a great cry in Egypt; for there was not a house where there was not one dead.'

Both documents describe the death of children. Exodus says that they were the 'first born', or eldest children. Velikovsky overcomes this improbable selectivity by suggesting that the Hebrew word for 'first born' could also have meant 'chosen'. Only the children of the wealthier Egyptians who lived in brick houses were killed. The houses of the Israelites, built of mud, may have escaped demolition.

Exodus and Papyrus Ipuwer appear to refer to the same series of events as are related in the tradition of other peoples. As the earth passes through the tail of the comet, red dust turns the waters red and makes them undrinkable. The heat engendered by its close proximity causes vermin, frogs, flies and locusts to propagate at a feverish rate, the crops are destroyed by a hail of fire, darkness covers the earth, and, finally, an earthquake kills many of those who live in houses.

Next, according to the papyrus, the slaves revolt (the Israelites?) the dwellers in the marshes flee, and the king of Egypt perishes under unusual circumstances. The description of the pillar of cloud and fire of Exodus appear to be paralleled in the papyrus: 'Behold the fire has mounted up on high. Its burning goes forth against the enemies of the land.' These pillars of cloud and fire may have been either substances pouring from the comet or the eruption of a volcano in the peninsula of Sinai.

Dr Velikovsky thinks that the scene in the sky impressed human imagination so profoundly that it became recorded in the traditions of many peoples. The heavens were a battleground, a scene of unparalleled terror and splendour. The head of the comet, a mass of fire and smoke, seemed to the Israelites like a pillar of fire and cloud sent to guide them on their way. To the millions who saw it all over the world it looked as though the gods were battling in the sky. The dragon was defeated by the god of light, the earth was saved. The gravitational pull exerted by the comet, together with the hurricane of wind caused by its proximity, resulted in an actual division of the waters of the Sea of Passage in which the pursuing Egyptians were engulfed as the comet's attraction lessened.

Dr Velikovsky also calls into use an Egyptian inscription found on the Palestinian frontier which may refer to the same set of disasters. It relates to the period of a King Thom and says that: 'The land was in great affliction, evil fell on the earth, there was a great upheaval in the residence, nobody left the palace during nine days, and during these nine days of upheaval there was such a tempest that neither the men nor the gods could see the faces of their next.' This seems to recall the darkness and strong winds of Exodus. The inscription says that the king fought with the evildoers in the Place of the Whirlpool, and the evildoers prevailed not. The King 'leaped into the so-called Place of the Whirlpool and was thrown up on high.'

Velikovsky found it significant that the place where the Pharaoh was overwhelmed is named Pi-Kharoti. Exodus calls the place of disaster Pi-Kharoth.

Velikovsky places the Exodus 300 years earlier than the usually accepted date. He believes that the disasters which accompanied it, the first stage of the cosmic convulsion, occurred about 1500 B.C. That was approximately the date of the great eruption of the volcano Thera, which may have destroyed the Minoan civilization of Crete, and which must have been felt throughout the Eastern Mediterranean, even in Egypt (see 'Has Fabled Atlantis Been Located?' pp. 7–14). It would seem to be a remarkable coincidence had Thera erupted at the time of a cosmic catastrophe.

Those few scientists who have bothered to discuss Velikovsky's theory reject it on the ground that the present orbits of Venus and Mars are respectively inside and outside that of the earth. If they had intersected 2,600 years ago, and if the orbits of the earth and Venus had intersected 3,400 years ago, then, according to the laws governing planetary motions, all three would continue to pass near the points at which these encounters had taken place, which is not the case.

It is objected also that nothing short of a direct hit would stop the earth from rotating. A near miss by a comet, however massive, would not have brought this about. Any appreciable slowing down of the earth's rotation would have resulted in the hurtling into space of everything movable, including the waters of the oceans.

Do these objections invalidate Velikovsky's startling claims? He asserts that there had been several global catastrophes in historical times, caused by extraterrestrial agents, and that in the most recent catastrophe Venus and Mars had played the dominant role. He claimed that his theories could be substantiated if Venus was still hot – evidence of its recent birth; enveloped in hydrocarbon clouds – remnants of its comet's tail; and had anomalous rotational motion – evidence that it had suffered unusual perturbations before settling into its orbit as a comet.

In 1963 the space-probe Mariner II confirmed that the temperature of Venus was 800°F. It possessed a 15 mile (24 kilometre) thick envelope composed, not of carbon dioxide or water as was previously supposed, but of heavy molecules of hypocarbons. Observations taken by the U.S. Naval Research Laboratory at Washington and by the Goldstone Tracking Station in California indicated that Venus has a slow retrograde motion, a characteristic unique amongst the planets.

Two more of Velikovsky's predictions have been confirmed. Radio signals from Jupiter were detected in 1964 when the planet suddenly changed its period of rotation. The truth of his revolutionary statement that the earth possesses a far-flung magnetic field has been proven. Close-up photographs have confirmed his guess that Mars is 'more moon-like than earth-like'. His assertion that the accepted dates of the Egyptian chronology are too early seems to be confirmed by the Carbon-14 tests made in 1964. Three wood samples taken from Tutankhamen's tomb yielded the dates, plus or minus fifty years, 1030 and 1120 B.C. This transfers the date of that pharaoh's burial from the fourteenth to the eleventh or twelfth century. It raises the paradox, dangerous to Velikovsky's theory, that the Exodus occurred even later than is supposed. It is usually dated about 1347 B.C.

Whether or not Velikovsky's basic theory is correct, which appears to be unprovable, he made several contributions to historical knowledge. He has shown the need to draw upon the accumulated records of human experience. He suggests that the phenomenon of the mutation of species may have been affected by catastrophism as well as by evolution. He believes that the rapid annihilation of whole species of animals may have been due to exposure to unaccustomed radiation, chemical pollution of the atmosphere and global electro-magnetic forces. He has propounded the strange doctrine that mankind lives in subconscious fear of cosmic cataclysms.

A considerable cult has developed in the United States based on Velikovsky's theories and philosophy.

STRAIGHT LINES

Riding round his native Herefordshire in the early 1920s, Alfred Watkins noticed that certain conspiculous landmarks such as hill tops, prehistoric barrows, standing stones, cairns of stones, legendary trees, holy wells and ancient churches, seemed to be connected by a web of straight lines. They ran across country, climbing hills, crossing valleys, bridging rivers and swamps and tunnelling through forests. Many followed the ancient track ways or the Roman trunk roads which had replaced them. Plotting these precise alignments on the Ordnance Survey, Watkins found that these straight lines connectly mainly the old towns and villages and even sites which had been long abandoned.

Puzzled by his discovery Watkins widened his search, finding the same network of straight tracks all over Britain. The entire country seemed to be locked in one grand design. Watkins, who was a keen amateur archaeologist, published the results of his investigations in 1925, entitling his book *The Old Straight Track.** To the day of his death in 1935 he was unable to explain the significance of these 'ley' lines as he called them. He could not decipher the 'language' of the leys. He felt they must have some deep, even religious, meaning. He had glimpsed the magic world of prehistoric Britain. These straight tracks, he believed, had been laid out by an elite class of Celtic priestly astronomers, men renowned for their supernatural powers. They had been linked by a single thread of ancient knowledge. Watkins sensed something weird yet elusive.

Watkins's discoveries were ridiculed by professional archaeologists and historians. His theories were dismissed as the wild speculations of the amateur. That was to be expected in 1925. Everyone then knew that the Ancient Briton was a barbaric savage, an ape-like creature, clothed in skins, daubed with woad and brandishing a stone axe. He performed bloody and probably indecent rites beneath mistletoed trees. Only in the 1960s was he rescued from obscurity and calumny. This pathetic and ludicrous figure has been replaced by the mathematician who devised a unit of measure which was common throughout Britain, and the astronomer who built hundreds of solar and lunar observatories. By 2000 B.C. Ancient Britons had calculated Pythagorean triangles which the Greeks are assumed to have discovered 1,500 years later.

Watkins's book gathered dust on library shelves for half a century. It was rediscovered in the late 1960s by those remarkable people who are searching for something deeper than scientific proof. They have tramped the country following Watkins's leys and finding others for themselves.

Near his home, on a ridge of the Radnorshire hills, Watkins

* Methuen, 1925.

noticed a line of seven tumuli which connected with three landmarks in the nearby village, the stone cross, the principal inn and the churchyard. Looking back from the church gate he saw the tumuli on the skyline. The church had been built on an ancient mound, probably the site of a pagan temple which had once carried the marker stone which Watkins found embedded in a bank beside the churchyard gate. In nearby Herefordshire, Watkins counted forty ancient marker stones adjoining churchyards. Transferring his search to Hampshire, he found in the Andover area eight separate instances where four churches fell into line and one in which five churches were similarly linked. An 8 mile (9 kilometre) long straight line connected Stonehenge, Salisbury Cathedral and the prehistoric rings at Old Sarum, the former site of the cathedral.

Crossing the Black Mountains, which stretch through the counties of Hereford, Monmouth and Brecon, Watkins saw his way marked by notches on the sky line where the old tracks had bitten deep into the soil. These cuttings through the hill crest were called 'bwtch' in Welsh, meaning a pass. They enabled the ancient travellers to find the tracks leading to the markets, salt-pans, and flint mines which they were seeking. Other alignments directed the travellers to Midsummer Hill or Sun Rising Hill, the sacred places of the sun worshippers. These prominent hill tops were also the beacons from which fiery warnings were flashed in times of danger.

Local folklore supplied Watkins with clues to many of the old leys. The stone by the church gate at Brilley was called the Funeral Stone. No one knew why, except that it was the custom to carry a coffin three times round it before entering the churchyard. At another village it was still the custom to stop the funeral cortège at a cross roads and say a prayer. They did that 'because it always has been done', the villagers told him.

Many of these marker stones carried names such as Hele Stone, Hurl Stone and Black Stone, and the track ways were called Mark Way, Four Marks, Markfield or Mark Lane, signifying their purpose. The leys had been marked, Watkins believed, by expert surveyors, the Cole men, meaning the wizards or diviners, and the Dod men, the men who carried sighting staffs. The name was derived from the Celtic word meaning to wave something to and fro, backwards, forwards, or up and down. The famous figure cut in the chalk on the sides of the downs at Willingdon in Sussex, with each arm extended and holding a staff, portrayed a Dod Man. Watkins also found a predominance of names, Cole Farm, Coles Trump, Coleshill, Colchester.

Talking with the villagers on his travels, Watkins discovered old folk tales which seemed to recall the days when attempts had been made to move the old ley marks. The work of building a church had frequently been frustrated by the stones being carried back by supernatural agency to the ancient site, frequently the crest of a hill. These stories reflected the struggle between the churchmen and the local people who clung to their pagan rites. He heard also the ancient lore of underground tunnels, often several miles long, connecting castles, churches, and manor houses. They were, he believed, a half-forgotten memory of the days when the secret passage was the ley, the old track in between these places.

Watkins's disciples are equally puzzled by the ley system, the 'spiritual engineering' as they call it. It seems impossible to explain these straight lines as sign posts for ancient trackways. Many of the lines run absolutely straight, through bogs and forest, over precipitous mountains. The patterns are too familiar to be coincidental.

Equally puzzling are the gigantic lines which have been spotted from the air on the Nazca desert in Peru. They cover an area 37 miles long and 1 mile wide (60 by 1·6 kilometres). They seem to have been laid out geometrically, some in parallel lines, others intersecting. They are surrounded by trapezoidal zones and by strange symbols marked in the sand. At ground level they are invisible. They can be seen only from great heights. Are they astronomical plans, or markers intended to guide space ships? They are an enigma, like Watkins's ley lines?

Watkins conceived his ley lines as a fairy chain stretching from mountain peak to mountain peak as far as the eye could reach. They may be invisible to those people who doubt the existence of phenomena which cannot be scientifically explained. There is a mystery to be revealed when someone learns to read the language of the leys.

THE ULTIMATE MYSTERY

Von Daniken may be correct in his belief that the 'gods' visited and may still be visiting the Earth. These denizens of another planet within our galaxy may be refugees from a Black Hole.

John Taylor has examined the problem posed by the gravitational collapse of great stars.* Possibly as many as 1,000 each year within our galaxy contract to a stage of such intensive density that light cannot escape from the vortex of these tunnels in space. A planet which blundered into their gravitational attraction would be sucked into the hole and crushed to pieces. The diminutive and condensed mass of matter would be ejected into another universe, different from ours both in space and time. Eventually, over a period of billions of years, the whole of our universe may disappear through these Black Holes to recreate the primordial fire-ball which exploded billions of years ago to form the expanding universe of which our Earth is a tiny part.

We do not need to worry too much, for the end of our universe may be billions of years distant, unless an unseen and invisible Black Hole is forming in our vicinity. Von Daniken's gods, beings more advanced than us, may have detected the dangerous proximity of their planet to one of these collapsing suns. They may have reached and recreated their civilization on a planet within our solar system, possibly on Saturn. They may have visited the Earth thousands of years ago, only to discard it as a place of residence.

Why, then, may they be visiting us again, watching the Earth from their flying saucers? Do they fear, and the possibility is not remote, that the Earth's scientists in their search for new sources of energy, may try to tap the vast power of gravitational collapse?

* *Black Holes: The End of the Universe*, Souvenir Press, 1973.

A little carelessness, or an accident, and the man-made Black Hole may escape and burrow its way into the Earth's interior, sucking in and destroying its matter, and us with it.

We, or what remained of us, would emerge into the future, into a new universe, to begin again the vast and unending cycle of evolution in which one universe succeeds another, starting with a Big Bang and ending in eventual gravitational collapse.

But that would not be the end, for the cycle is infinite – nothing more than the manifestation of energy, something which neither we nor Von Daniken's gods can either define or control.

WAS GOD AN ASTRONAUT?

Erich von Daniken in *Chariots of the Gods?* * believes that in the remote past, some 30,000 or 50,000 years ago, planet Earth was visited by beings from outer space who perhaps fathered humanity as we now know it. Having propagated their seed and imparted knowledge, they departed, returning to their home amidst the stars. Primitive man remembered them as the 'gods' who created life and taught the skills of civilization. The story of their visit to Earth is told in ancient myths, in the confused memories of the peoples who experienced these awesome events.

The Book of Genesis, for example, reports the creation of the Earth with absolute geological accuracy. How did the chroniclers know that minerals preceded plants and plants preceded animals? Their ancestors had been told the facts of life by the divine astronauts, the gods who spoke in the plural. They make man in 'our image, after our likeness'. And when the sons of God saw that the daughters of man were fair, they took them wives. And the daughters of man bore them children. And the children became mighty men, men of renown. Their fathers were remembered as 'the giants (who had been) in the earth in those days'. These giants crop up all over the globe, in the mythology of East and West, in the sagas of

* Souvenir Press, 1969.

Tiahuanaco and the epics of the Eskimos. Giants haunt the pages of ancient books. They must have existed.

But they did not die on earth, for no gigantic skeletons have been exhumed. Nor did their genes impart colossal size, for man has not vastly enlarged in height or breadth. These gods, or culture-bearers, chose the earth as a planet where intelligent life might take root. By their seed they created *homo sapiens*, the ancestor of modern man. They gave him knowledge which he soon forgot.

Several authors have remarked the extraordinary knowledge once possessed by certain ancient peoples. The architects of the Great Pyramid knew the secrets of mathematics and astronomy. The ancient Mayas devised an accurate calendar and correctly calculated the Venus year of 584 days. They understood that the cycles of sun, moon and of Venus coincide after 37,960 days. They believed that the gods had come down from the Pleiades. All this knowledge became lost and was not rediscovered until modern times.

Something seemed to be missing from the story of human development. Man evolved slowly over millions of years. Then suddenly he made enormous strides, a huge forward leap. He became the tool-maker, the agriculturalist, the herdsman, the city builder, the seafarer. His brain size doubled. So remarkable is this gap between *homo* and *homo sapiens* that some people have suggested that this sudden enlargement of the human brain may have been due to a burst of cosmic radiation. Von Daniken prefers to believe that man's sudden emergence as a rational animal was due to these divine visitors. He admits that his theory is speculative. He makes it hard for us to accept. He seems to shy from proof even where it may exist. For example, he implies that amongst the equipment left behind by the gods are 'electric dry batteries which work on the galvanic principle'. They are on display in the Baghdad Museum, where visitors can see them 'with electric elements with copper electrodes and an unknown electrolyte'. Surely, if such proof exists, Von Daniken could have been more explicit, stating where the object was found, and quoting the opinions of experts?

He suggests that evidence could be found to substantiate the visit of the gods' space ships, their chariots of fire, powered by atomic energy. The sand vitrifications of the Gobi desert, he says, resemble the marks impressed on the New Mexican desert following the triggering of the first atomic device. Some one should test the Dead Sea for radioactive traces of the atomic explosion which destroyed the Biblical cities of Sodom and Gomorah. He shares the opinion of certain Soviet scientists that the great Siberian disaster of 30 June 1908 was caused not by a giant meteorite as is generally supposed, but by the ejection of surplus fuel by a space craft.

The arrival and departure of these space visitors impressed the witnesses. The Hebrew prophet Ezekiel watched the landing of a weird vehicle emitting rays and raising gigantic clouds of desert sand. He heard the noise of the great rustling made by the vehicle as it left the ground. The gods even gave him a ride. The Ark of the Covenant was built by Moses to the exact instructions given by the gods. It must have been electrically charged because when Uzzah touched it he fell dead as if struck by lightning.

The American Indians saw a thunderbird in the sky. The Eskimos watched metal-birds. The Indian Ramayana hymn refers to Vimanas, or flying machines, navigating at great heights with the aid of quick silver and a great propulsive wind. At the gods' bequest, 'the magnificent chariot rose up to a mountain of cloud with a tremendous din'. It flew on an 'enormous ray which was as brilliant as the sun and made a noise like a thunderstorm'. The famous Tassili frescoes painted on rocks in the Sahara depict men wearing space suits with rods like antenna projecting from their helmets.

Von Daniken enthusiastically cites the Piri Reis map as evidence of the astronauts' visits, because the originals of the map 'must have been aerial photographs taken from a great height'. The elongation of South America, for example, is seen 'exactly' as on photographs taken from lunar probes.

The Piri Reis map has also been taken by more orthodox, if equally imaginative investigators, to prove the pre-Columban discovery of America by the Phoenicians.

A fragment of this world map was found in October 1929 in the old imperial palace at Instanbul. It is dated 1513 and signed by Piri Reis. He was a Turkish admiral, possibly of

Greek origin, and an experienced navigator and cartographer. He charted the Aegean Sea and other parts of the Mediterranean and presented his atlas of maps to the Sultan Suleiman the Magnificent. He referred to his earlier work, his map of the world, which he had given to that Sultan's predecessor, Selim II in 1507.

Piri Reis's naval career ended disastrously. As commander in chief of the fleet of Egypt he took thirty-one ships to the Persian Gulf. Returning loaded with treasure he was blockaded by a Portuguese fleet. He managed to return to Egypt, losing only one ship. The facts were misrepresented to the sultan who ordered his execution. He was beheaded in Cairo in 1554.

Piri Reis's world map, painted on thin parchment, depicts the Atlantic coasts of the Old World, the islands of the Caribbean, the isthmus of Panama, South America and the Antarctic continent free of ice. He states in his marginal notes that he had used a chart of the West Indies drawn by Christopher Columbus and charts of South America drawn by four Portuguese discoverers. He had used also twenty old charts prepared at the time of Alexander the Great, and the *Mappa Mundis* and eight maps in fragments prepared by the Arabs. He put them all together in a common scale.

No map drawn by Columbus has been found. Piri Reis says that he acquired it, or learned about it, from a Spaniard who had sailed on three of Columbus's voyages. Some of Piri Reis's information reflected current geographical knowledge. Columbus discovered the West Indies between 1492 and 1502. Amerigo Vespucci landed on the South American coast in 1499. The Portuguese Pedro Alvares Cabral was blown across the Atlantic and discovered Brazil in 1500. Piri Reis placed the West Indian islands of Cuba, Haiti and Jamaica, and the southern islands of the Bahamas, with reasonable accuracy.

In his delineation of South America he appears to have been considerably in advance of contemporary knowledge. He drew the whole continent, although 900 miles (1,450 kilometres) short of its correct length, marking two big rivers on its eastern coast, presumably the Amazon and the Plate, and positioned a mountain chain along its western seaboard. None of these features was known in 1513, the year of Balboa's crossing of the isthmus of Panama, and his sighting of the Pacific which proved that the Americas were hitherto unknown continents. Magellan rounded Cape Horn in 1520 and Pizarro entered Peru in 1530, the first European to glimpse the Andes Mountains which Piri Reis had so faithfully depicted in 1513.

Even more remarkable is Piri Reis's representation of Antarctica as a large land mass free from ice. He drew its indented coastline, stretching eastwards from below the southern tip of South America, representing the Falkland, South Shetland and other islands, including Tristan da Cunha, and correctly positioning mountain chains, bays, gulfs, rivers and plateaux.

Antarctica was not discovered until 1818 when it was revealed as an ice cap. That the ice concealed a mountainous continent was not known until 1952 when the land beneath was revealed by seismic probes. Cores taken from the bottom of the Ross Sea in 1949 by the Byrd Antarctic expedition disclosed that during the last million years Antarctica had been free from ice during four warm spells, the last of which had occurred between 4000 and 1000 B.C.

European cartographers had guessed the existence of a continent surrounding the South Pole on the theory that the northern land masses must need to be balanced; they called it Terra Australis Incognita. That theory was disposed of by Captain James Cook's discovery of Australia in 1768.

Piri Reis's source map had depicted Antarctica as it might have appeared a thousand years or so B.C.

A copy of this map was brought to Washington in 1956. It was examined by the U.S. Navy's Hydrographic Department. Its staff cartographer, M. I. Walters, called in Captain Arlington H. Mallery, and other experts. The map was subsequently examined by Professor Charles H. Hapgood, F.R.G.S., and his team of students. Hapgood published their findings in 1966 in *Maps of the Ancient Sea Kings.**

Amongst other tests, the investigators converted the map's dimensions to the modern cartographical grid. It showed that the original map makers knew how to determine longitude, an achievement not repeated until A.D. 1760. This had enabled

* Chilton Book Co. (Radnor PA), 1966.

them to align correctly the African and South American continents.

Like most ancient maps, the Piri Reis map appears to have been based on the meridian of Alexandria in Egypt, and it may have been drawn from a centre on the line of the Tropic of Cancer, near the ancient town of Cyrene. That geographical position had been used, with the city of Alexandria, by the third-century-B.C. mathematician Eratosthenes, by taking the angles of the sun at each place, to determine the circumference of the earth.

The Piri Reis map shows another peculiarity. Looked at from its centre in Egypt, the southern continents become increasingly distorted and elongated, owing to the curvature of the earth which makes those continents appear to sink away downwards. That is exactly how the earth looks, and has been photographed from lunar probes and satellites passing above Cairo. No terrestrial map maker could have so envisaged the earth.

Professor Hapgood attributes the origin of the Piri Reis map to a vanished civilization which dominated the world in a very remote period. 'We have manifold leads,' he says, 'which further research can hardly fail to develop.'

Brian J. Ford has remarked the fallacies in Von Daniken's 'fantastic' thesis in general and particularly in reference to the Piri Reis map.* The elongation of South America is not exactly the same as the view from space. Indeed, it is totally different from it. The consistency of the shape of South America in the map rules out aerial photography from a site above Cairo. Nor is the Piri Reis map 'fantastically accurate' as Von Daniken states. It is not sufficiently accurate to suggest that the draughtsman had detailed knowledge of land masses under the ice.

According to Von Daniken, having completed their act of deliberate breeding, the unknown beings returned to outer space. Von Daniken believes that they may have come from the nearest habitable planet, eleven million light years distant. They may be revisiting the earth in their flying saucers, afraid to land, and possibly aghast at the results of their interference with the development of terrestrial life.

* *The Earth Watchers*, Leslie Frewin, 1972.

Another investigator, Richard E. Mooney concludes from much the same evidence that the astronauts came and stayed.* The Earth was colonized by beings from another universe.

Von Daniken agrees that his theories lack proof. He thinks they are as valid as the beliefs of religion. Few people will deny that. The leaders of the great religions refuse to prove the existence of their God. Why should Von Daniken be expected to prove the theory which forms the basis of the new mysticism?

These theories appeal to man's craving to believe in the supernatural, his inborn desire to accept mysticism rather than face reality. They are proved by devious, spurious argument. For example, the ceremonial head-dresses, the stylized native sketches on the rocks of Tassili become space helmets, the magic lamps of fairy stories are interpreted as 'electronic communication systems', the huge blocks of stone constructed by our ancestors could only have been raised by anti-gravitational devices. Swift, the author of *Gulliver's Travels*, knew that Mars had two moons which no one in 1720 could have seen. Rather than an inspired guess, he drew on the ancient knowledge imparted by the astronauts.

Theories such as these can no more be discussed than can the existence of God. People who wish to believe in the supernatural origin of life will find them entrancing. They may even be accepted as new scientific truth. It may not triumph by convincing its opponents but becomes accepted because the opponents eventually die, and a new generation grows up which is familiar with it. This paraphrase of Max Planck's words indicates the danger. Von Daniken's books have sold millions of copies. Few scientists have bothered to point out their pseudo-logic.

* *Colony: Earth*, Stein and Day (New York), 1974.